# A Handbook on the WTO Customs Valuation Agreement

This guide to the WTO Customs Valuation Agreement is based on the authors' experiences of teaching its finer points to customs officials and policy-makers around the world. Covering the methods of valuation and the provisions on enforcement, implementation and dispute settlement, the authors give practical examples, explain interpretative decisions of national and international customs bodies, and analyze the history of its negotiation. Written as a learning tool, it helps both new and experienced policy-makers, customs officials, importers and exporters to gain a deeper understanding of the Agreement's function and aims.

Sheri Rosenow and Brian O'Shea are attorneys who have specialized in customs and international trade law for twenty years.

Sheri Rosenow is a senior counsellor for the WTO, where she specializes in customs valuation, trade facilitation and other customs-related issues. On behalf of the WTO, she has trained government officials and members of the trade community throughout the world.

Brian O'Shea is an experienced customs consultant working on the implementation of automated systems, including risk assessment and valuation applications, in South Africa and Europe.

# A Handbook on the WTO Customs Valuation Agreement

Sheri Rosenow and Brian J. O'Shea

CAMBRIDGE
UNIVERSITY PRESS

CAMBRIDGE
UNIVERSITY PRESS

University Printing House, Cambridge CB2 8BS, United Kingdom

Cambridge University Press is part of the University of Cambridge.

It furthers the University's mission by disseminating knowledge in the pursuit of education, learning and research at the highest international levels of excellence.

www.cambridge.org
Information on this title: www.cambridge.org/9781107000841



First published 2010

*A catalogue record for this publication is available from the British Library*

*Library of Congress Cataloguing in Publication data*
Rosenow, Sheri
A handbook on the WTO customs valuation agreement /
Sheri Rosenow; Brian J. O'Shea.
p. cm.
Includes index.
ISBN 978-1-107-00084-1 (hardback)
1. Customs appraisal–Law and legislation. 2. Customs administration–Law and legislation. 3. World Trade Organization. 4. General Agreement on Tariffs and Trade (Organization) I. O'Shea, Brian J. II. Title.
K4640.A66083 2010
382'.92–dc22
2010039402

ISBN 978-1-107-00084-1 Hardback

# CONTENTS

# FIGURES

# FOREWORD

This book on customs valuation is a welcome addition to the WTO Secretariat/Cambridge University Press's Handbook series. The Customs Valuation Agreement is the common system for determining the value of imports for duty assessment purposes and is therefore important to the everyday work of importers, customs officials, and others involved in international trade. However, because the Agreement is technical in nature and trade transactions can be complex, guidance and explanation of the terms of the Agreement will be useful to support its proper implementation.

Customs valuation has long been subject to GATT disciplines. As the authors note, governments recognized early on that negotiated tariff reductions could be subverted if the amount of duty collected can be manipulated through the way goods are valued. In addition, it was understood that positive trade facilitative advantages can result through adoption of a common valuation system setting out fair and transparent rules.

The WTO valuation system, which is based on the 1979 Tokyo Round GATT code, recently marked its thirtieth anniversary, an opportune time to consider whether its purposes have been realized. Experience over that time has shown that the drafters of the Agreement were successful in creating a valuation system that is comprehensive and sufficiently flexible to adapt to the changes in the way business is conducted. On the other hand this flexible structure necessarily allows for diverging interpretations of how the provisions are implemented.

The impetus for this book arose out of the authors' work with customs and other officials of WTO Member governments around the world. As a result of this work they realized that there was a need for a resource that would provide a simple, straightforward explanation on the meaning and intent of the provisions of the Agreement as well as insight on how the terms of the Agreement have been interpreted or extended by different countries, dispute settlement panels and the valuation committees.

In addition, this book, as well as the other books in the Handbook series, support the WTO Secretariat's efforts to assist Member countries in their efforts to build capacity, implement obligations and realize the benefits of WTO Membership.

I am pleased to offer this book to the trade community. I hope that the reader will find it to be a useful resource.

Pascal Lamy
*Director-General*
*World Trade Organization*

# PREFACE

The purpose of this book is to provide a detailed explanation of the history, principles, and legal terms of the WTO Customs Valuation Agreement and its associated legal texts, such as interpretative decisions of the WTO Committee on Customs Valuation. It is intended to instruct and serve as a reference for those who are new to, or have limited familiarity with, the Agreement. Expert users also may find it useful for reference purposes.

We have included test questions in this book to demonstrate the application of the Agreement to specific import scenarios. Our proposed answers to the questions, which can be found at the end of each chapter, are based on WTO and World Customs Organization (WCO) interpretative materials, as well as on rulings of various national customs administrations.

Included in the Appendices is a selection of the most important WTO valuation legal texts. Further information about the WTO Customs Valuation Agreement, as well as current and historical valuation documents issued by the WTO and GATT bodies, can be accessed via the WTO website at www.wto.org. In Appendix 8, you will find information about how to navigate the WTO website to reach customs valuation documents. This information also includes an explanation of the symbols that are used for classification of official WTO documents.

Sheri Rosenow
Brian J. O'Shea

# ACKNOWLEDGEMENTS

We would like to thank Mr. Ian Cremer, Valuation Policy Specialist, Her Majesty's Revenue and Customs, United Kingdom, as well as Mr. Eki Kim, Ms Janet Chakarian-Renouf, and Mr. Bruce Wilson from the WTO Secretariat for their review of the text and valuable suggestions.

The black and white photographs of identical and similar goods that appear in section 3.1 are by Peter Rittling (www.peter-rittling.com).


## DISCLAIMER

Whilst every effort has been made to ensure accuracy, the text and any errors that it may contain are the full responsibility of the authors. Moreover, this Handbook on the WTO Customs Valuation Agreement cannot be taken as an official legal interpretation of the Agreement, as only the WTO members, acting collectively, have the legal authority to provide authoritative legal interpretations of WTO legal instruments.

# ACRONYMS AND ABBREVIATIONS

Where used in this book, acronyms and abbreviations have the following meaning:

| | |
|---|---|
| BDV | Brussels Definition of Value |
| CCC | Customs Co-operation Council (official name of the WCO) |
| c. i. f. | Cost Insurance & Freight (Incoterm) |
| f. o. b. | Free on Board (Incoterm) |
| GATT | General Agreement on Tariffs and Trade 1994 |
| Interpretative Note | Annex I to the Agreement on Implementation of Article VII of the General Agreement on Tariffs and Trade 1994 |
| Kyoto Convention | International Convention on the Simplification and Harmonization of Customs Procedures (as amended) |
| Technical Committee | Technical Committee on Customs Valuation, established under the auspices of the Customs Co-operation Council (WCO) |
| WCO | World Customs Organization |
| WCO Compendium | World Customs Organization, Customs Valuation: WTO Agreement and Texts of the Technical Committee on Customs Valuation (2d ed. 1997) |
| WTO | World Trade Organization |
| WTO Agreement | Marrakesh Agreement Establishing the World Trade Organization |
| WTO Customs Valuation Agreement or the Agreement | Agreement on Implementation of Article VII of the General Agreement on Tariffs and Trade 1994 |

# 1

# INTRODUCTION

## 1.1 THE PURPOSES OF CUSTOMS VALUATION

### 1.1.1 What is customs valuation?

Governments have collected customs duties since the beginnings of international trade. It is recorded that Athens applied 20 percent import duties on corn and other goods, while the Romans, from well before the time of Julius Caesar, depended upon customs revenues to support the expansion and maintenance of their empire. And, where a tax must be collected, there will be disputes over rates and methods – the Roman customs collector was accused of "unfair conduct and vexatious proceedings" against the Roman merchants who, in all fairness, were said to have been commonly engaged in smuggling to avoid customs duties.[1]

Customs valuation – the subject of this book – becomes an issue where import duties are calculated on an "*ad valorem*" basis. An "*ad valorem*" duty rate is one that is expressed as a percentage of the value of the imported goods. Duties may also be assessed on "specific" basis, where a fixed amount is charged on the quantity of goods imported – such as 0.2 cents per liter of imported alcohol. Or, a duty rate on a particular import might be a combination of *ad valorem* and specific rates (a "compound rate"). Nevertheless, *ad valorem* rates are the most prominent in international trade, as they are used by WTO Members against all but a small percentage of goods in their tariff schedules.[2]

For a particular import, the amount of an *ad valorem* duty is determined by multiplying the rate (for example, 17 percent on imports of chocolate milk, in Figure 1) by the ***customs value*** of the imported goods. Thus, how customs officials determine the customs value is as important to the importer as the rate of duty specified in the tariff schedule for the goods, as both the basis – the customs value – and the rate together determine the amount of duty the importer must pay.

[1] W. Smith (ed.), *Dictionary of Greek and Roman Antiquities* (Boston: Little Brown & Co. 1859), 944–45; J. R. McCulloch, *A Treatise on the Principles and Practical Influence of Taxation and the Funding System*, third edition (Edinburgh: Adam and Charles Black 1863), 240.

[2] On average, WTO Members use *ad valorem* rates for more than 97 percent of all tariff lines in their schedules. A notable exception is Switzerland which uses specific type rates for 80 percent of its tariff. WTO, *Trade Profiles 2007*.

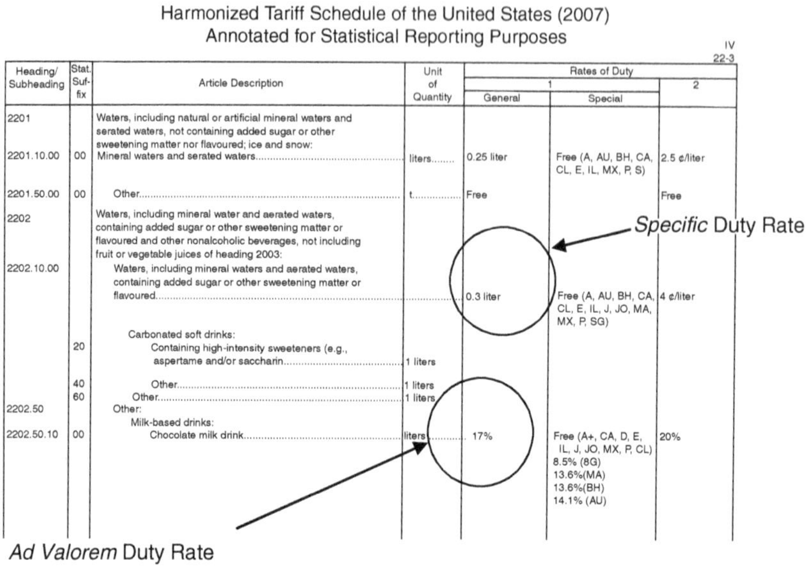

Harmonized Tariff Schedule of the United States (2007)
Annotated for Statistical Reporting Purposes

IV
22-3

| Heading/ Subheading | Stat. Suf-fix | Article Description | Unit of Quantity | Rates of Duty 1 General | Rates of Duty 1 Special | Rates of Duty 2 |
|---|---|---|---|---|---|---|
| 2201 | | Waters, including natural or artificial mineral waters and serated waters, not containing added sugar or other sweetening matter nor flavoured; ice and snow: | | | | |
| 2201.10.00 | 00 | Mineral waters and serated waters | liters | 0.25 liter | Free (A, AU, BH, CA, CL, E, IL, MX, P, S) | 2.5 ¢/liter |
| 2201.50.00 | 00 | Other | t | Free | | Free |
| 2202 | | Waters, including mineral water and aerated waters, containing added sugar or other sweetening matter or flavoured and other nonalcoholic beverages, not including fruit or vegetable juices of heading 2003: | | | | |
| 2202.10.00 | | Waters, including mineral waters and aerated waters, containing added sugar or other sweetening matter or flavoured | | 0.3 liter | Free (A, AU, BH, CA, CL, E, IL, J, JO, MA, MX, P, SG) | 4 ¢/liter |
| | | Carbonated soft drinks: | | | | |
| | 20 | Containing high-intensity sweeteners (e.g., aspertame and/or saccharin | 1 liters | | | |
| | 40 | Other | 1 liters | | | |
| | 60 | Other | 1 liters | | | |
| 2202.50 | | Other: | | | | |
| | | Milk-based drinks: | | | | |
| 2202.50.10 | 00 | Chocolate milk drink | liters | 17% | Free (A+, CA, D, E, IL, J, JO, MX, P, CL) 8.5% (8G) 13.6%(MA) 13.6%(BH) 14.1% (AU) | 20% |



Figure 1 US harmonized tariff schedule: *ad valorem* and specific rates

Today, the rules for valuing imports for purposes of assessing customs duties are well settled. They are defined in the WTO Customs Valuation Agreement (the formal name of which is the **Agreement on Implementation of Article VII of the GATT**), a system that is designed to promote fairness, neutrality and uniformity in customs duty assessment, and which is used by more than 150 WTO Member countries worldwide.

### 1.1.2 The importance of customs valuation

In 1947 – before the GATT – the average tariff rate applied by industrial countries was between 20 and 30 percent.[3] Fifty years and eight GATT rounds of tariff negotiations later, the average tariff rate applied by industrial countries on non-agricultural goods is about 5.5 percent.[4] With implementation of the 1994 Uruguay Round, for example, the US average tariff on non-agricultural goods is just 3.2 percent, and nearly half the tariff lines applicable to such goods are duty free.[5] Given these diminishing tariffs, one might ask how important is customs valuation? If import duties are reduced to trivial levels or

[3] WTO, *World Trade Report 2007*, at 207.
[4] WTO, *World Trade Profiles 2008* (simple average of applied MFN rates).
[5] *Ibid.*

Figure 2 Taxes on international trade (IMF, *Government Finance Statistics Yearbook 2007*)

disappear altogether, what use will remain for the rules that are used for their calculation?

Despite the successes of the GATT rounds, import duties stubbornly remain a factor in international trade. This is particularly true in developing countries, where the average applied rate for all goods is 16.9 percent.[6] Even in industrial countries, where average rates are low, some industrial products and sectors, and many agricultural products, remain protected by tariffs of 20 percent or higher.[7] Moreover, a number of developing countries continue to depend upon import duties for a significant portion of the national budget (see Figure 2).

Even if import duties were completely eliminated, the need for customs valuation rules likely would still exist. One important reason is the use by a number of countries of value added tax (VAT), excise, or sales taxes on imported products; these taxes, unlike customs duties are not subject to GATT/WTO tariff reductions.[8] Customs authorities commonly apply the same customs valuation rules to calculate these kinds of taxes on imports as they do for customs duties, although they are not obligated by GATT rules to do so.[9]

[6] *Ibid.*

[7] For example, the simple average duty rate applied by the European Union is just over 5%, among the lowest of WTO Members. However, the average rates applied to selected products exceeds 20% (i.e. dairy products (62.4%); sugars and confectionery (29.8%); animal products (25.4%)).

[8] VAT systems are now used in over 120 countries; they are said to have been adopted by some countries to replace the trade tax revenues lost as a consequence of GATT tariff reductions. IMF, *Dealing with the Revenue Consequences of Trade Reform* (February 15, 2005).

[9] GATT Article VII, Interpretative Note *Ad* Paragraph 1.

Apart from tax and duty assessment, customs valuation rules are used by customs authorities in their administration of non-revenue measures, such as:

- Import quotas based on customs value.
- Rules of origin. For example, a country may allow goods from a specific foreign country to enter free of duty if 50 percent of the customs value of the import is contributed by operations carried out in that foreign country.
- Collection of trade statistics.

**Customs valuation and GATT tariff bindings**

GATT Article II:3 states "no contracting party shall alter its method of determining dutiable value ... so as to impair the value of any [tariff] concessions" negotiated among GATT parties.

Under this prohibition, a country may not change its "method of determining dutiable value" to avoid tariff bindings. But this does not prevent a country from maintaining a valuation method that itself allows arbitrary assessments. In the absence of common rules, valuation could thus be (mis)used for trade protection purposes.

"It seems inequitable that while certain countries ... apply a liberal [valuation] system, others continue to apply systems which may raise the actual incidence of the duties shown in the tariff and carry many uncertainties because of elements which are arbitrary from the point of view of interested exporters in third countries. *Indeed, the global reciprocity achieved in tariff reductions might be gravely jeopardized.*"*

To illustrate the point, consider the following scenario: if the invoice value of an imported product is $100, and the bound tariff rate agreed by the country is 10%, then traders might expect a tariff barrier equivalent to $10 ($100 × 10% = $10). However, customs officials, applying a method of valuation that allows arbitrary uplifts, assign a value to the product of twice that amount. In that case, the actual tariff barrier is $20 ($200 × 10% = $20). In practical effect, the importing country has raised its tariff rate from the 10% tariff ceiling agreed in GATT tariff negotiations to 20%.

Benefits to trade that the exporting country expects from negotiated tariff binding are considerably diminished by such uncertain or arbitrary valuation methods.

* TN.64/NTB/26 (July 7, 1964) (Statement of the European Community) (emphasis added).

## 1.2 HISTORY

The WTO Customs Valuation Agreement is a result of the 1986–1994 Uruguay Round negotiations, but its terms largely repeat the 1979 GATT Valuation Code. Therefore, to understand the intent underlying the terms of the Agreement, it is useful to recall the conditions of the pre-1979 trading environment (see Figure 3). As will be apparent from the retelling, this history also demonstrates that many of the difficulties of customs valuation that are discussed

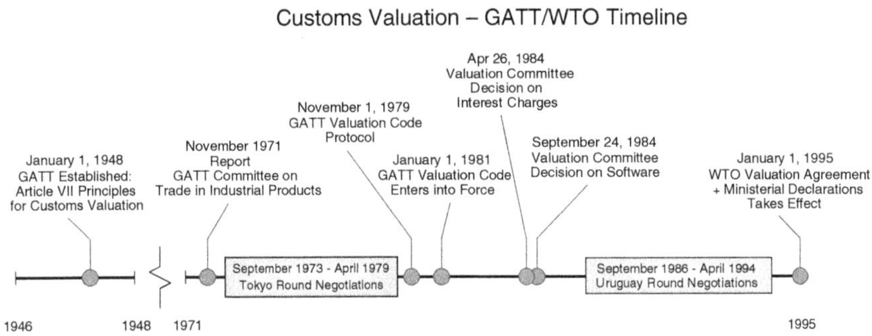


Figure 3 GATT/WTO customs valuation timeline

today – valuation of used goods, questionable invoices, (mis)use of alternative valuation methods, etc. – are by no means new or unique.

### 1.2.1 Before common valuation rules

GATT Article VII establishes general principles for national customs valuation systems. However, it does not mandate a specific valuation method, but allows countries to develop their own system, subject to these principles.

#### GATT Article VII Principles

- Customs value shall be based on "**actual value**", which is the price of the imported merchandise, or like merchandise, in sales in the ordinary course of trade under fully competitive conditions
- If "actual value" cannot be determined, Customs shall use the nearest ascertainable equivalent
- Customs value shall not be based on value of merchandise of national origin, or arbitrary or fictitious values
- Customs value shall not include internal taxes on a product that the country of origin or export refunds or exempts
- Currency conversion shall reflect effectively current value of currency in commercial transactions
- Where price of imported merchandise is determined by the quantity purchased, customs value shall be based on prices for comparable quantities or, as long as the result does not disadvantage the importer, prices involving larger quantities in sales in trade between the exporting and importing countries
- Governments shall publicize their valuation methods
- Governments shall report on steps they have taken to implement Article VII and to review the operation of their value methods, upon request of other GATT parties.

In fact, there was a large diversity and inconsistency when it came to customs valuation practices among countries before 1979. Customs valuation systems generally followed one of two conceptually different approaches: those based on a "notional" concept of value, and those based on a "positive" concept.

### *(a) Brussels Definition of Value*

The "notional" concept is represented by the 1950 Convention on the Valuation of Goods for Customs Purposes, commonly known as the Brussels Definition of Value (BDV).[10] The BDV was drafted by customs experts of the European Customs Union Study Group, and was given to the Customs Co-operation Council – now known as the World Customs Organization (WCO) – to administer.[11] The BDV had more adherents than any other valuation system. At its peak, it was applied by as many as one hundred countries, including members of the (then) European Economic Community (EEC) and most other countries in Western Europe, as well as Japan and a number of developing countries.

Under the BDV, goods are valued on the basis of their "normal price":

> that is to say, the price which [the imported goods] would fetch at the time when the duty becomes payable on a sale in the open market between buyer and seller independent of each other.[12]

Customs officials would consider the buyer's actual invoice price paid for the goods, but were free to reject it in favor of the notional "open market" price for goods of the same kind.

### *(b) Positive value systems*

A positive system of value was used by the United States and Australia, among other countries. Under these systems, customs value was generally based on the *actual* price paid for the goods, rather than an abstract or notional price that might be paid under perfect competitive conditions. Typically, these systems provided for use of secondary valuation methods, in a ranking order, where the

[10] December 15, 1950, 171 U.N.T.S. 307 (entered into force on July 28, 1953).

[11] Convention Establishing a Customs Co-operation Council, December 12, 1950, 157 U.N.T.S. 130; GATT Working Party I on the International Chamber of Commerce Resolutions, *Statement by Mr. F. Redmond-Smith, Representative of the European Customs Union Study Group*, W.7/8 (October 7, 1952). The CCC Convention was also drafted by the European Union Customs Union Study Group, a body established in 1947 to consider freer intra-European movement of goods and services in the context of European recovery from the Second World War. GATT Contracting Parties, *The Work Undertaken by the European Customs Union Study Group on Customs Nomenclature and Questions of Customs Regulations: Statement Made by the French Representative*, GATT/CP.4/45 (April 20, 1950).

[12] Annex I, Convention on the Valuation of Goods for Customs Purposes, note 10, above.

actual invoice price could not be found or used (such as where the goods were imported under a lease, and therefore a sale price did not exist).

For example, the US system, which strongly influenced the structure of the WTO Valuation Agreement, generally required customs to appraise goods first on the basis of the "export value" or price at which the goods were sold or offered for sale for export to the United States or, second, on the basis of the "United States value", which was the selling price of imported goods in the US market; and finally, if the preceding methods failed, on the basis of a "constructed value" or cost of production of the imported goods.[13]

There was also diversity in the application of both of these systems. The BDV was subject to varying interpretations in different countries. Positive systems were equally diverse: for example, the US primary valuation method was based on the export value (the price of the goods at the time of exportation to the United States), whereas Australia used the price paid by the importer *or* the price at which the same goods are sold in the export country market, whichever was higher. Moreover, as noted in the discussion below of the American Selling Price valuation method, some of the "secondary" valuation methods employed by these countries were at best complex and at worst explicitly protectionist.

### *(c) Early GATT initiatives on common valuation rules*

In the early GATT years, a few attempts were made toward creation of a common valuation system. Although ultimately inconclusive, these initiatives triggered the GATT contracting parties to begin to assess the conformity of the different valuation systems then in use with Article VII principles.[14] The results of this early work on valuation led to and informed the GATT's later valuation initiatives. There is also a direct link in the present WTO Valuation Agreement to this early history: the "prohibited methods" listed in Article 7 of the Agreement (the "fall back" method of valuation) references one or another of these older valuation systems. (More on the prohibited methods of valuation under the WTO Valuation Agreement at section 3.4.)

The earliest attempt at a harmonized valuation system within the GATT came in 1951, when the International Chamber of Commerce (ICC) proposed that the GATT contracting parties develop standard worldwide valuation rules. This ICC proposal was a reaction to the BDV which, at that time, had just been completed and opened for signature. The ICC – as the representative of business – had opposed the BDV, because it was based on the use of a "normal"

[13] See GATT Committee on Trade and Development, *Trade Barriers Arising in the Field of Customs Valuation: Note on Implications for Developing Countries of Ad Referendum Solutions*, COM. TD/W/195 (August 2, 1973).

[14] Because the GATT was a treaty and not a legally established organization (in contrast to the World Trade Organization), GATT signatories were called "contracting parties." See WTO, *Understanding the WTO* (2007), at 3.

price as determined by customs administrations. Instead, the ICC favored a simpler "rule-of-thumb method," whereby customs would be required to use the invoice price for the goods presented by the trader, absent a reason to suspect fraud.[15]

This ICC proposal was rejected as premature. With only limited information about the valuation methods used by governments, the GATT contracting parties were, apparently, unwilling to upset the *status quo*. Moreover, it was felt that the GATT should not "pass judgment" on the BDV by developing an alternative international system along the lines suggested by the ICC before the BDV had been given a reasonable time to operate.[16]

However, the ICC proposals did have one positive result. They inspired the GATT contracting parties to obtain detailed information concerning the methods governments used to determine value and the extent to which these methods conformed to Article VII principles.[17] The results of this study, published three years later, suggested that there was a significant amount of diversity in valuation practices among GATT contracting parties. In particular, it was found that governments generally used one of three different criterion to assess value:

(1) the price at which goods comparable with the exported goods are sold in the internal markets of the exporting country ("current domestic value");
(2) the price at which the imported goods are sold from the exporting country to the importing country ("transaction value");
(3) the price at which goods comparable with the imported goods are sold in the markets of the importing country ("import market value").[18]

[15] GATT Executive Secretary, *Resolutions Submitted by the International Chamber of Commerce on Valuation, Nationality of Manufactured Goods and Formalities Connected with Quantitative Restrictions (GATT/CP/123)*, G/22 (August 29, 1952). In addition to international valuation rules, the ICC proposed that the GATT contracting parties issue "general recommendations" to governments based on the following four principles: (i) "systems of valuation should not be used as a method of increasing protection"; (ii) "primary consideration should be given to the price shown on commercial invoices when determining the dutiable value of goods"; (iii) "regulations should state clearly and fully the basis of dutiable value, with adequate publicity"; and (iv) "internal duties or taxes from which exported goods were exempted should not be included in the dutiable value." GATT contracting parties did not accept this proposal, largely on grounds that these ICC principles were largely incorporated in GATT Article VII. GATT, *Report of Working Party I on the International Chamber of Commerce Resolutions*, G/28 (November 1, 1952).

[16] G/28.

[17] GATT, *Methods of Valuation for Customs Purposes: Request for Information*, L/81 (March 12, 1953); GATT, *Valuation for Customs Purposes: Questionnaire for the Ninth Session*, L/228 (September 20, 1954).

[18] GATT Contracting Parties 9th Session, *Comparative Study of Methods of Valuation for Customs Purposes* G/88 (March 2, 1955). The study also found that "apart from the nine countries which are operating a common definition of value under the Brussels Convention, there are numerous differences in practice even between countries which are using the same criterion for establishing value for customs purposes."

In late 1954 and early 1955, governments submitted a number of proposals to amend Article VII in connection with a general review of the operation of the GATT Treaty. Most of these Article VII proposals were technical in nature or narrowly targeted to overcome specific valuation problems.

One proposal did have a broader reach. The Scandinavian countries proposed that the GATT "work toward the standardization as far as practicable, of definitions of value and of procedures for determining the value of products." Under the proposal, this work would have been based upon studies and recommendations of a new "Organization for Trade Co-operation" – which was then being discussed as the permanent body to administer the GATT.[19] However, as that new trade body never came into being, neither did the Scandinavian proposal for a unified valuation system.[20]

The last major GATT initiative on valuation in these early years came in the Kennedy Round of 1964–1967. In that round, for the first time, non-tariff barriers were included in negotiations.[21] One such non-tariff barrier nominated for negotiation by a number of countries was "customs valuation including use of arbitrary or excessive values."[22] The "arbitrary" valuation practice that attracted most criticism was the use by the United States of its "American Selling Price" (ASP) method of valuation.[23] The ASP, explicitly protectionist

[19] "Members shall work toward the standardization, as far as practicable, of definitions of value and of procedures for determining the value of products subject to customs duties or other charges or restrictions based upon or regulated in any matter by value. With a view to furthering co-operation to this end, the Organization may study and recommend to Members such bases and methods for determining value for customs purposes as would appear best suited to the needs of commerce and most capable of general adoption." GATT Contracting Parties 9th Session, Review Working Party II on Tariffs, Schedules and Customs Administration, *Proposals Affecting Customs Administration*, W.9/46 (November 29, 1954).

[20] The Scandinavian proposals were referred to the working party responsible for developing the agreement on the Organization for Trade Co-operation (OTC). GATT Contracting Parties 9th Session, Review Working Party IV on Organizational and Functional Questions, *Scope of the Agreement: Proposals Referred from Working Party II to Working Party IV*, W.9/98 (December 14, 1954). The draft agreement on the OTC included a provision authorizing the OTC to undertake a "study of international trade and commercial policy and where appropriate make recommendations thereon." This provision was explicitly intended to cover the valuation studies foreseen by the Scandinavian proposal. GATT Contracting Parties 9th Session, *Report of Review Working Party IV on Organizational and Functional Questions*, L/327 Rev. 1 (April 4, 1955). However, the Agreement on the Organization for Trade Co-operation, done at Geneva on March 10, 1955, never entered into force.

[21] GATT Meeting of Ministers, May 16–21, 1963, *Agreements for the Reduction of Elimination of Tariffs or Other Barriers to Trade and Related Matters and Measures for Access to Markets for Agricultural and Other Primary Products: Resolution Adopted 21 May 1963*, MIN 63(9) May 22, 1963.

[22] GATT Sub-Committee on Non-Tariff Barriers, *Non-Tariff Measures to be Brought within the Scope of the Negotiations: Note by the Secretariat*, TN.64/NTB/8 (November 15, 1963).

[23] GATT Sub-Committee on Non-Tariff Barriers, *The Use of Arbitrary or Excessive Values in Levying Customs Duties (American Selling Price): Note by the United Kingdom Delegation*, TN.64/NTB/21 (June 19, 1964); see also GATT Sub-Committee on Non-Tariff Barriers, *Valuation for Customs Purposes: Note by the Delegation of the EEC Commission*, TN.64/NTB/26 (July 7, 1964); GATT Sub-Committee on Non-Tariff Barriers, *The Arbitrary or Excessive Valuation for Customs Purposes: Note by the Japanese Delegation*, TN.64/NTB/32 (July 15, 1964); GATT Sub-Committee on Non-Tariff

in design, required certain imports – benzenoid chemical products, rubber footwear, canned clams and knitted woolen gloves – to be valued on the basis of the price at which similar *US-origin* products were sold in the US market, rather than the actual invoice price for the goods. The use of this method was said to result in import duties well in excess of the price of the goods themselves – reportedly as much as 172 percent in the case of yellow-vat dye, for example.[24] Apart from the prohibitive effect of such rates, the ASP method was directly contrary to the GATT Article VII:2 proscription against use of customs valuation methods that are "based on the value of merchandise of national origin."[25]

The United States and European countries reached a conditional agreement in the Kennedy Round, which would have required the European countries to reduce their duties on US chemical exports if the United States ended the use of its ASP valuation method.[26] However, this agreement never entered into force. The US use of the ASP remained a major irritant in these contracting parties' trade relations until finally resolved through the Tokyo Round agreement.[27]

### (d) Precursor to an agreement

In November 1967, following the successful conclusion of the Kennedy Round earlier that year, the contracting parties met to do a stocktaking of the first twenty years of the GATT, with a view of setting a work program to enable further expansion of world trade.

Barriers, *The Use of Arbitrary or Excessive Values in Levying Customs Duties: Note by the Danish Delegation*,TN.64/NTB/34 (July 22, 1964).

[24] "Toward Agreement," *Time*, May 19, 1967, at www.time.com/time/magazine/article/0,9171,840930,00.html.

[25] If the ASP was contrary to GATT Article VII, how could it have been used by the United States? The reason is that the ASP predated the GATT. Under the terms of the 1947 Protocol of Provisional Application of the GATT, by which the United States accepted the GATT Treaty, the United States was obliged to apply provisionally Part II of the GATT (which included Article VII) only "to the fullest extent not inconsistent with existing legislation." Thus, while the ASP contradicted GATT Article VII principles, as the United States itself freely acknowledged, its use was nonetheless permitted by this "existing legislation" exception. See GATT Contracting Parties Twenty-Second Session, *Definitive Application of the GATT: Note by the Executive Secretariat*, L/2375/Add.1 (March 19, 1965).

[26] GATT, *Agreement Relating Principally to Chemicals Supplementary to the Geneva (1967) Protocol*, L/2819 (July 17, 1967).

[27] The agreement was not implemented due to the failure by the US Congress to enact necessary domestic legislation to eliminate use of the ASP. The US rubber footwear industry opposed elimination as did the powerful US chemical industry, which was said to be "almost totally opposed to losing ASP protection and question[ed] the value of it of lower duties abroad." Memorandum from Secretary of State Rogers to President Nixon (March 24, 1969) in US Department of State, Foreign Relations, 1969–1976, *Foreign Assistance, International Development, Trade Policies, 1969–1972*, Vol IV, document 188, available at http://www.state.gov/r/pa/ho/frus/nixon/index.htm.

One outcome of that review was a recognition that more focus should be given to the use of non-tariff, trade-restrictive measures, as these had the potential to offset the gains that had been made over the years by the GATT tariff reductions. The contracting parties thus ordered the GATT Secretariat to establish an "inventory" of non-tariff barriers affecting international trade, based on information supplied by governments. Once the inventory was complied and analyzed, working groups under the GATT Committee on Trade in Industrial Products were appointed to "explor[e] ... the possibilities for concrete action ... both with regard to reducing or removing such barriers and to developing possible rules of conduct." [28]

Customs valuation practices figured prominently in that inventory of non-tariff barriers: more than thirty valuation complaints were registered against over twenty countries.[29] According to the working group that analyzed the inventory, the valuation problems notified were primarily the result of the different "special valuation" or secondary valuation methods that countries applied where valuation could not be taken from the invoice price:

> the great majority of countries currently follow the practice of the Brussels Convention on Valuation (BCV), which is based on c.i.f. values [that is, costs of international transport are included in customs value] and that another smaller group of countries, including some important trading countries, use systems varying from one to another but based upon f.o.b. values of mixed in character [international transport costs not included in customs value]. Both groups use invoice values in most cases. In cases where no invoice can be produced (for example, where there is no sale) or where the invoice price appears to be unacceptable or it is not accepted, the value for custom purposes is established by the two groups according to widely differing methods.[30]

Some of the important specific valuation problems listed in the GATT inventory were the following:

1. Use of domestic prices in the country of export as a basis for valuation.
   Certain countries valued imported goods on the basis of invoice price or the price of similar goods in the export country market, whichever was higher. This system made it difficult for traders to estimate in advance their duty liability; it presented particular problems where

[28] GATT, *Review of the Work of the Contracting Parties through the Last Two Decades and Conclusions on their Future Work Programme*, L/2943 (November 28, 1967); GATT Committee on Trade in Industrial Products, *Report to the Council*, L/3298 (December 22, 1969).

[29] GATT, Multilateral Trade Negotiation, *Part 2 of the Inventory of Non-Tariff Measures, Customs and Administrative Entry Procedures: Note by the Secretariat*, MTN/3B/2 (February 12, 1974).

[30] GATT Committee on Trade in Industrial Products, *Report to Council*, L/3496, at 33 (February 10, 1971).

the goods were not sold in the exporting country market; and it was said to require exporters to divulge confidential business information in course of customs price investigations.

It also, apparently, worked to the disadvantage of exporters in developing countries where, it was claimed, prices could be higher than in international markets due to "structural imbalances and the supply scarcities" and "inflationary pressures to which their economies were often subject."[31]

2. Use of arbitrary values determined at the discretion of customs authorities.

   Under certain valuation systems which used the invoice price or price in the export country market, whichever was higher, customs or other governmental authorities were authorized to determine the value where the current price in the exporting country market could not be ascertained. The claim was made that these determinations of value were arbitrary or, at the least, not transparent.

3. Valuation based on prices for similar domestic-origin goods in the country of import.

   The US ASP valuation method, discussed previously, was identified as the main example of this problem.

4. Use of "official" or "minimum" values.

   Certain countries established, by decree or regulation, minimum prices for specified products or range of products. For example, a number of countries were said to set a minimum value for imports of used clothing, based on weight. The justification of these practices, which were more commonly found in developing countries than developed, has been explained as follows:

> The developing countries maintaining "official indicative values" for a limited number of products have stated that they have found it necessary to adopt such a system to curb "underinvoicing" of goods or similar unfair practices. It has been stated that apart from such cases, fixing official values on the basis of "average prices of imports" may be necessary for commodities which are subject to wide fluctuations in prices ... In regard to "minimum values", developing countries fixing such values have explained that they were being determined for a limited number of products, in order *inter alia*, to protect their nascent industries from competition from well-established industries in other countries.[32]

Duty is levied on the basis of the "minimum value" or invoice price, whichever is higher. The complaint of exporters, however, was that

[31] *Ibid.*

[32] GATT, *Non-Tariff Measures Affecting Trade of Developing Countries: Note by the Secretariat*, MTN/3B/23 (December 31, 1974), at 24.

the minimum values set exceeded the actual market values of the goods, to the extent that import became economically prohibitive.

5. Use of customs valuation to combat dumping.
For example, Australia applied a system of "support values" to a number of industrial chemicals. If the duty-paid price of the imported product fell below this value, an extra customs duty was collected equal to 90 percent of the difference between the two prices. Exporting countries claimed that this was, in effect, a dumping measure applied without following the dumping procedures.
6. Lack of transparency in valuation methods and procedures.
7. Inadequate facilities for appeal against decisions by customs authorities.[33]

How to resolve these barriers? A group of countries proposed harmonization of valuation systems based on the BDV, which was then applied by most of the GATT contracting parties. This proposal was, however, opposed by the non-BDV countries – *viz.* the United States, Canada, Australia, New Zealand – who believed that their valuation systems were as consistent as the BDV with GATT Article VII. These non-BDV countries also found objectionable the "extensive discretion" that the BDV allowed customs officers to reject the invoice price in favor of a notional value. Moreover, they were concerned about the "extensive distortion of existing competitive relationships among trading partners" that would result in shifting from a f.o.b.-based system to the BDV's c.i.f. system, which would mean that transportation costs would be included in customs value. On this last point, it was said that increasing the dutiable basis of imported goods by including costs of international transport would particularly impact traders in North America due to the large overland distances between ports of entry and market centers and greater distances from overseas suppliers.[34]

Accordingly, rather than unified valuation rules based on the BDV, the working group agreed to develop "draft principles" and "draft interpretative notes" for the guidance of governments. It was hoped that these would help to move existing valuation systems into closer alignment and thereby resolve the specific problems identified in the inventory.[35] These "draft principles" and "draft interpretative notes," were released to GATT contracting parties in 1971 for their consideration, and later became a starting point of negotiations in the Tokyo Round. A number of these principles thus surfaced again in the preamble to the Tokyo Round Agreement (and now the current WTO Valuation Agreement).

[33] GATT, *Part 2 of the Inventory of Non-Tariff Measures: Customs and Administrative Entry Procedures*, MTN/3B/2 (February 12, 1974).

[34] L/3496, at 37–40.

[35] GATT Committee on Trade in Industrial Products, *Group 2 On Valuation: Report by Chairman*, COM. IND/W/64 (November 5, 1971).

**Committee on Trade in Industrial Products**

*Draft Valuation Principles*

1. Valuation systems should be neutral in their effect and in no case be used as a disguised means of providing additional protection by artificially increasing the value to which the rate of duty is to be applied.
2. Valuation systems should not be used to combat dumping.
3. Valuation systems should protect trade against unfair competition arising from undervaluation.
4. Valuation systems should be of general application without distinction as between sources of supply.
5. Dutiable value should be based on equitable and simple criteria which do not conflict with commercial practice.
6. Valuation systems should keep formalities to a minimum and valuation should be based to the greatest possible degree on commercial documents.
7. Valuation systems should not prevent the quick clearance of goods.
8. The legal and administrative provisions concerning customs valuation should be accessible to the general public and be sufficiently clear and precise to enable traders to estimate in advance, with a reasonable degree of certainty, the value of their goods for customs purposes.
9. Valuation systems and practices should take into account the need to safeguard business secrets.

### 1.2.2 Tokyo Round negotiations

In the 1973–1979 Tokyo Round, the GATT contracting parties negotiated a common customs valuation system. Although harmonization on the basis of the Brussels Definition of Value was again proposed,[36] the GATT parties instead began negotiation of text on the basis of a proposal put forward by the European Community, which was said to combine the "best features" of the US, Canadian and European systems. The basic structure of the proposed agreement was a "positive" concept of value with methods of valuation placed in a hierarchy – the "good features of the United States valuation system."[37]

[36] See e.g. GATT Multilateral Trade Negotiations Group "Non-Tariff Measures" Sub-Group "Customs Matters," *Customs Matters: Communication from the Customs Co-operation Council*, MTN/NTM/W/17 (August 26, 1975); GATT Multilateral Trade Negotiations Group "Non-Tariff Measures" Sub-Group "Customs Matters," *Customs Matters: Background Note by the Secretariat*, MTN/NTM/W/7 (April 29, 1975).

[37] GATT Multilateral Trade Negotiations Group "Non-Tariff Measures" Sub-Group "Customs Matters," *Statement Made by the Commission of the European Communities at the Meeting of the Sub-Group of November 15, 1977*, MTN/NTM/W/126 (November 21, 1977). In the following chapters, we have noted some of the more obvious influences of the US value law on the text of the WTO Valuation Agreement, such as the definition of related parties and restrictions on use of transaction value (see section 2.3) and deductive value (see section 3.2).

The final result was the GATT Valuation Code, which is substantially identical in its terms to the present WTO Customs Valuation Agreement. Like other "codes" negotiated in the 1979 Tokyo Round, the GATT Valuation Code bound only those GATT Members that elected to accept its terms. As it turned out, while all developed countries signed the GATT Valuation Code, the large majority of developing countries chose not to do so.[38]

Differences between developed and developing countries were apparent during the negotiations. For example, there was reportedly "strong opposition" from developing countries to the treatment of transactions between related companies under the proposed GATT Valuation Code which, they argued, favored firms and enterprises from the developed countries. Developing countries wanted customs authorities to have greater authority to reject related-party prices where they found the prices to differ substantially from values in transactions involving like goods and for reasons that could not be justified. Also, difficulties were foreseen in the use of the deductive and computed value methods, and there was "outright opposition" to the idea that an importer, rather than the customs authorities, could choose whether to apply the deductive or computed value method.[39]

These differences could not be resolved by the end of the negotiations in April 1979. Two "competing" versions of a valuation code were thus presented to the GATT contracting parties for consideration – one favored by developed country delegations, and a modified version proposed by developing countries containing "special provisions to meet [their] trade, financial and development needs."[40]

In the end, however, the developing and developed countries compromised their differences, and in November 1979 adopted a Protocol to the Agreement on Implementation of Article VII.[41] In the Uruguay Round, the terms of this Protocol were incorporated into the WTO Valuation Agreement itself, where they now appear as Annex III.

[38] Seventeen GATT Members (the (then) EEC counting as one) had signed or accepted the Tokyo Round Agreement at the time that it entered into force, January 1, 1981. Seven of the original signatories were developing countries. GATT Consultative Group of Eighteen, *MTN Agreements: Legal Status as of 2 March 1981*, CG.18/W/46/Supp.1 (March 6, 1981). Over time, however, additional developing countries would sign onto the GATT Valuation Code.

[39] GATT, *The Tokyo Round of Multilateral Trade Negotiations: Report by the Director-General of GATT*, 72–74 (April 20, 1979).

[40] GATT Multilateral Trade Negotiations Group "Non-Tariff Measures" Sub-Group "Customs Matters," *Customs Valuation*, MTN/NTM/W/222/Rev.1 (March 27, 1979); GATT Trade Negotiations Committee, *Proceedings of the Session Held at the International Labor Office Geneva, 11 and 12 April 1979*, MTN/P/5 (July 9, 1979); GATT Multilateral Trade Negotiations Committee, *Proces-Verbal*, MTN/28 (April 11, 1979).

[41] GATT Multilateral Trade Negotiations Group "Non-Tariff Measures" Sub-Group "Customs Matters," *Customs Valuation: Agreement on the Implementation of Article VII of the General Agreement on Tariffs and Trade*, MTN/NTM/W/229/Rev.1/Add.1 (October 22, 1979).

Certain of the developing countries' proposed "special provisions" were accepted in the Protocol, at least in some form. The Protocol thus allowed developing countries the possibility to delay the application of the Code beyond five years (to ease their transition to the new valuation rules); it gave developing country customs administrations some flexibility in use of the deductive and computed value methods; and it permitted developing countries to continue use of minimum value systems on a "limited and transitional" basis.

Other "special provisions," which were *not* made part of the Protocol compromise, would have given developing countries greater leeway to reject declared transaction values in various circumstances where under-invoicing is suspected. These included, for example, provisions to put the burden of proving the validity of a related-party price on the importer; to disallow price discounts if found to be not "freely available" to other buyers under the same conditions; to treat sole agents and distributors as related parties; and to allow customs to reject declared prices, even in transactions involving unrelated parties, if found not to be consistent with prices in prior transactions of like goods.

As will be seen, these developing-country concerns about the ability of Customs under the Code to deal with under-invoicing resurface during the Uruguay Round negotiations.

### 1.2.3 Uruguay Round negotiations

The goal of the Uruguay Round negotiations, as it related to customs valuation, was to "improve, clarify, or expand, as appropriate," the Tokyo Round Code, and thereby win it wider acceptance among the GATT parties.[42] At the time that the Uruguay Round was formally launched, less than one-third of the GATT contracting parties had signed the GATT Valuation Agreement.[43]

The limited participation in the valuation and other Tokyo Round Codes, particularly by developing countries, had been a concern to GATT contracting parties and became an important focus of GATT activity in the years leading up to the Uruguay Round.[44] Both in the GATT Valuation Committee and the

[42] GATT Multilateral Trade Negotiations, The Uruguay Round, *Ministerial Declaration on the Uruguay Round*, MIN.DEC (September 20, 1986).

[43] GATT, *Report (1986) of the Committee on Customs Valuation*, L/6094 (November 20, 1986) (reporting that twenty-six countries were parties to the Valuation Agreement); GATT, *GATT Membership as at 1 June 1986*, GATT/1386 (ninety-one GATT contracting parties).

[44] The 1982 Ministerial Declaration, which defined the GATT work program and priorities for the 1980s, mandated a review of the operation of the Tokyo Round Codes, with a focus on "adequacy and effectiveness ... and the obstacles to acceptance of these [codes] ... by interested parties." GATT Contracting Parties Thirty-Eighth Session, *Ministerial Declaration Adopted on 29 November 1982*, L/5424 (November 29, 1982). Two years later, the GATT contracting parties "invited" each GATT committee responsible for administering a Tokyo Round Code to examine these issues in a special

The 35 GATT Valuation Agreement signatories (1994)

| | | |
|---|---|---|
| Argentina | Hong Kong | Poland |
| Australia | Hungary | Romania |
| Austria | India | Slovak Republic |
| Bolivia | Japan | Slovenia |
| Botswana | Korea, Republic of | South Africa |
| Brazil | Lesotho | Sweden |
| Canada | Malawi | Switzerland |
| Colombia | Mexico | Turkey |
| Cyprus | Morocco | United States |
| Czech Republic | New Zealand | Yugoslavia |
| EC | Norway | Zimbabwe |
| Finland | Peru | |

Technical Committee in the early 1980s, GATT contracting parties and observers were consulted, special meetings were held, and surveys were produced on the "obstacles" developing countries foresaw in adopting the Valuation Code.[45]

Broadly speaking, three main factors were said to influence the decision of countries not yet signatories to the Valuation Code:

1. the need to take the decision collectively or in a coordinated fashion in the framework of a regional grouping
2. concern that the Agreement might not give customs adequate possibilities to deal with false invoicing and to maintain government revenue and
3. the legal and administrative requirements to be fulfilled by signatories, for example the need to adapt national legislation and procedures and to train staff.[46]

That second point (false invoicing and government revenue) became the main focus of the discussions in the Uruguay Round negotiating group on valuation.

meeting, open to non-signatories, and to report the results to a working group specially created to carry out an overall review. GATT, *MTN Agreements and Arrangements: Fortieth Session of the Contracting Parties, Action taken on 30 November 1984*, L/5756 (December 20, 1984).

[45] See Group of Negotiations on Goods (GATT), Negotiating Group on MTN Agreements and Arrangements, *MTN Agreements and Arrangements: Special and Differential Treatment for Developing Countries, Note by the Secretariat*, MTN.GNG/NG8/W/2 (May 4, 1986).

[46] GATT Working Group on MTN Agreements, *Adequacy and Effectiveness of the MTN Agreements and Arrangements and Obstacles to their Acceptance: Consolidation of the Observations Made and Conclusions Reached in the Committees and Councils*, MDF/12 (June 11, 1985).

The negotiations on valuation were very much driven by developing-country concerns. It was made clear at the outset by some members within the negotiating group that a new customs valuation agreement or complete overhaul of the existing Tokyo Round Code was not on the table.[47] Rather, countries were asked to identify their particular difficulties with the existing agreement (taking into account the work that had been done in the preceding years in the GATT Valuation Committee), and to come forward with proposals for change to the existing text.[48]

In the end, the main subjects of negotiations on valuation were largely defined by two proposals. One, which was tabled by India, concerned the burden of proof in cases of suspected importer fraud.[49] The second, submitted by Kenya on behalf of the members of the Preferential Trade Area for Eastern and Southern African States (PTA), sought to allow the continued use by developing countries of certain valuation practices of the BDV system.[50]

### *(a) Burden of proof*

The India proposal was motivated by a concern about the efficacy of the GATT Valuation Code in dealing with valuation fraud, a concern that had been voiced before by developing country members in the early GATT Valuation Committee meetings.[51] The proposal was supported by Brazil – who had a particular difficulty with the fraudulent *over*-invoicing by importers to avoid hard currency controls – and by a number of other developing countries.[52]

[47] Group of Negotiations on Goods (GATT), Negotiating Group on MTN Agreements and Arrangements, *Meeting of 6 March 1987: Note by the Secretariat*, MTN.GNG/NG8/1 (March 23, 1987).

[48] Group of Negotiations on Goods (GATT), *Fifth Meeting of the Group of Negotiations on Goods: Record of Decisions Taken*, MTN.GNG/5 (February 9, 1987) (negotiating plan set out in annex).

[49] Group of Negotiations on Goods (GATT), Negotiating Group on MTN Agreements and Arrangements, *Communication from India*, MTN.GNG/NG8/W/9 (September 30, 1987); Group of Negotiations on Goods (GATT), Negotiating Group on MTN Agreements and Arrangements, *Customs Valuation Agreement: Justification for India's Proposal on Burden of Proof*, MTN.GNG/NG8/W/54 (October 9, 1989).

[50] Group of Negotiations on Goods (GATT), Negotiating Group on MTN Agreements and Arrangements, *Proposal Submitted by Kenya on behalf of the Member States of the Preferential Trade Area for Eastern and Southern African States (PTA)*, MTN.GNG/NG8/W/73 (March 19, 1990).

[51] See GATT Committee on Customs Valuation, *Report by the Technical Committee on Customs Valuation Concerning the Effects of False Invoicing on Customs Valuation*, VAL/W/32 (November 7, 1985).

[52] Group of Negotiations on Goods (GATT), Negotiating Group on MTN Agreements and Arrangements, *Agreement on Implementation of Article VII: Submission by Brazil*, MTN.GNG/NG8/W/57 (November 22, 1989); Group of Negotiations on Goods (GATT), Negotiating Group on MTN Agreements and Arrangements, *Minutes of Meeting 16–18 October 1989*, MTN.GNG/NG8/13 (November 15, 1989).

**EARLY PRACTICAL CONCERNS ABOUT TRANSACTION VALUE**

"[T]he price involved may be fictitious. What is known as 'double-invoicing' for Customs purposes is a common example. Such a price, if it were declared to be the actual price under [the transaction value method], would not be rejected by the Customs unless they were in a position to prove its falsity by establishing the true actual sale price. *No Customs Administration could accept the onus of such proof*."

Customs Co-operation Council, Different Systems of Valuation and their Comparative Advantages and Disadvantages 18 (1963).

The general concern was that the GATT Valuation Code placed too great a burden on customs to prove that a declared price was false before it could reject the transaction value, particularly in cases where importers and their suppliers acted in collusion to hide the fraud. This problem was particularly acute for developing countries, it was said, because they did not have access to comparative price information, the automated processes and databases, or the technical expertise needed to detect false declarations. Therefore India proposed that customs administrations be given more flexibility under the Valuation Agreement to reject suspect declared values.

The India proposal and the subsequent negotiation in the Uruguay Round are covered in greater detail in section 4.3, which deals with customs verifications under the Agreement. In short, however, while India's proposal did not result in any alteration of the terms of the Agreement itself, it did produce the important WTO Ministerial Decision clarifying the burden of proof issue, namely the **Decision Regarding Cases Where Customs Administrations Have Reasons to Doubt the Truth or Accuracy of the Declared Value**.

### *(b) Sole agents and minimum values*

The main concern of the African PTA countries was the impact that use of the Agreement would have on their government revenue, more than half of which, it was said, was derived from customs duties. The BDV concept of value – some form of which all of these countries then used – was considered more protective of this revenue than the GATT Agreement because it allowed customs officers greater flexibility to establish or "uplift" customs values when they found that the importer's declared transaction price was not consistent with open market prices.

The PTA countries thus proposed that developing countries should be permitted to include in customs value those discounts that foreign sellers allow to "sole agents, distributors and concessionaires" or other parties in special trading relationships, as they were under the BDV.

The PTA countries also proposed to extend the right of developing countries under the GATT Valuation Agreement to continue to apply "minimum values," such as official lists of minimum prices for specific goods. The GATT Valuation Code protocol allowed developing countries the possibility to continue such practices, but on a limited and transitional basis only, and subject to terms and conditions agreed by the other Code signatories in *ad hoc* negotiations. To ensure the utility of this concession to developing countries, the PTA proposed that minimum value reservations "should not be limited in scope nor subject to the imposition of restrictive terms and conditions."

The Uruguay Round response to the PTA proposal was the second of two WTO Ministerial decisions on customs valuation, the **Decision on Texts Relating to Minimum Values and Imports by Sole Agents, Sole Distributors and Sole Concessionaires**. Essentially, this decision requires the WTO Valuation Committee to give "sympathetic consideration" to developing country requests to retain officially established minimum values for a limited period, and to take into account the "development, financial and trade needs of the developing country concerned."

With regard to treatment of sole agent or distributor discounts, the WTO Ministerial decision makes no change to the text of the Agreement.[53] Rather, the decision asks the WTO Valuation Committee to recommend to the Customs Co-operation Council (now known as the World Customs Organization) that it "assist developing country members ... to formulate and conduct studies in areas identified as being of potential concern, including those relating to importations by sole agents, sole distributors and sole concessionaires."

The question of "sole agents" is discussed further in section 2.3.4 in connection with the treatment of "related parties" under the Agreement.

### *(c) A "single undertaking"*

What was given by developing countries in exchange for developed countries' agreement to these two decisions? To the extent there was a *quid pro quo* requested, it was only this: the negotiating group insisted that it should be explicitly recognized that these decisions were agreed "in the expectation that consideration of accession to the Customs Valuation Code will be facilitated and therefore participation in the Code will be increased."[54]

[53] "With respect to sole concessionaires and discounts, while understanding the revenue concerns and that the Code might provide an unfamiliar method of valuation for those who had been used to the [BDV], [one delegation] believed strongly that it was not possible to combine elements of those two fundamentally different systems. A number of delegations shared these views." Group of Negotiations on Goods (GATT), Negotiating Group on MTN Agreements and Arrangements, *Meeting of 1 June 1990*, MTN.GNG/NG8/18 (June 14, 1990).

[54] Group of Negotiations on Goods (GATT), Negotiating Group on MTN Agreements and Arrangements, *Meeting of 29–30 October 1990*, MTN.GNG/NG8/22 (November 1, 1990).

In fact, the "increased participation" in the Customs Valuation Agreement sought by the valuation negotiating group was ultimately achieved by the successful conclusion to the Uruguay Round overall. This was the implication of the "Single Undertaking" principle that was agreed at the outset of the Uruguay Round by the GATT contracting parties as the basis for their negotiations on goods.[55] Whereas the Tokyo Round allowed GATT contracting parties to pick and choose the multilateral agreements they wished to sign, the Uruguay Round's "Single Undertaking" principle required WTO Members to accept or reject the results of the negotiations as a whole, including *all* of the multilateral agreements.[56]

The Uruguay Round Customs Valuation Agreement – set out as an annex to the **Marrakesh Agreement Establishing the World Trade Organization –** was formally agreed on April 15, 1994 by the 123 governments that participated in the negotiations. The Agreement entered into force on January 1, 1995 and is, therefore, binding on each WTO Member (subject, of course, to any reservation they might have made under the terms of the Agreement; see section 4.4, below).

### *(d) Dispute settlement*

The text of the GATT Valuation Code was not changed in any substantive respect in the Uruguay Round, with the important exception of the dispute settlement provisions.

The GATT Valuation Code included a self-contained, elaborate mechanism for resolution of disputes between signatories on valuation matters. It provided the GATT Valuation Committee with authority to investigate and establish panels of experts to adjudicate parties' disputes, to obtain advice from the Technical Committee where technical issues were presented, as well as to enforce panel recommendations. The efficacy of this procedure was never tested, as the GATT valuation signatories brought no disputes to the GATT Valuation Committee during the lifetime of the code.[57]

The dispute procedures defined under the GATT Valuation Code were largely replaced by the Uruguay Round's **Understanding on Rules and Procedures Governing Settlement of Disputes**, which WTO Members have agreed shall apply to all WTO agreements, valuation included. Some additional

[55] "The launching, the conduct and the implementation of the outcome of the negotiations shall be treated as parts of a single undertaking." GATT, *Ministerial Declaration on the Uruguay Round*, Min.Dec. (September 20, 1986).

[56] "The [Customs Valuation and other Multilateral Agreements] … are integral parts of this Agreement, binding on all Members." Marrakesh Agreement Establishing the World Trade Organization, Article II:2.

[57] This is according to the GATT Secretariat's Annual Review of Implementation and Operation of the Agreement recorded from 1981 until the termination of the Tokyo Round code in 1996.

provisions that are specific to valuation dispute processing do remain part of the WTO Valuation Agreement; these mainly concern the role of the Technical Committee and its use by WTO panels in the dispute settlement process.

The WTO dispute settlement process is further discussed in section 5.3.

## 1.3 AGREEMENT OVERVIEW

### 1.3.1 The WTO standard – transaction value

The WTO Customs Valuation Agreement is based on a "positive" as opposed to a "normative" economic principle: what the value of the goods is, rather than what the value of the goods should be, is taken as the correct customs value. Thus, the Agreement's primary basis of valuation is "transaction value" which is "the price actually paid or payable" by the buyer for the imported goods. If the sale was freely negotiated (and the Agreement contains rules for valuation of sales that are not), the price the buyer pays the seller can be said to best represent the actual, market value of the product, and should be used for customs purposes. In other words, it is the buyer and seller, each acting in their own self-interest to maximize their profit, who will determine the customs value of the imported goods.

Apart from economic principle, customs valuation based on the price negotiated by the buyer and seller provides certain practical advantages for both traders and for customs authorities:

- it is transparent, predictable in application, and less open to discretion
- it conforms closely to real commercial practice
- it can be administered based on ordinary commercial records, normally available in the country of importation, without requiring importers and exporters to create and keep additional records only for customs.

### 1.3.2 Structure of the Agreement

The WTO Valuation Agreement is comprised of twenty-four articles plus three annexes.

The technical rules of customs valuation are set out in Articles 1–8 of the Agreement. The remaining articles of the Agreement mainly concern the implementation in national legislation and practice (e.g. rights of appeal and publication requirements, importer's rights to notifications and release of goods pending valuation, etc.), as well as the settlement of valuation disputes between WTO Members, and the administration and review of the Agreement by the WTO Valuation Committee and Technical Committee.

**AGREEMENT OUTLINE**

**Articles 1–8** – Valuation methods
**Article 9** – Rules for converting currency
**Article 10** – Confidentiality of valuation information
**Article 11** – Importer's rights of appeal against customs decisions
**Article 12** – Publication requirement
**Article 13** – Importer's right to release of imported goods, pending customs final decision
**Article 14** – Legal effect of Interpretative Notes (Annex I) and other annexes
**Article 15** – Definitions
**Article 16** – Importer's right to an explanation from customs
**Article 17** – Customs right to question importers on value
**Article 18** – Establishes WTO and WCO Committees
**Article 19** – Dispute settlement
**Article 20** – Special/differential treatment available to developing countries
**Article 21** – No reservations without Member's consent
**Article 22** – National legislation to conform to Agreement
**Article 23** – WTO Committee annual review
**Article 24** – Appoints WTO Secretariat
**Annex I** – Interpretative Notes
**Annex II** – Technical (WCO) Committee responsibilities and procedures
**Annex III** – Reservations and concessions allowed developing countries

**Annex I** of the Agreement contains the important **Interpretative Notes**. These, as well as the **General Introductory Commentary** elaborate the meaning of key terms of the Agreement (e.g. "price actually paid or payable," "identical goods," "similar goods," "related parties"), provide examples of how valuation methods should be applied to particular cases, and provide a general explanation of the overall purposes of the Agreement.

The commentary and interpretative notes were negotiated during the Tokyo Round at the same time as the articles of the Agreement itself[58] and thus may be said to indicate a contemporaneous view of the drafters' intentions. By virtue of **Article 14** of the Agreement, the Interpretative Notes are to be considered an "integral" part of the Agreement, and the articles of the Agreement are to be read and applied in conjunction with these notes.

**Annex II** of the Agreement defines the role, responsibility, and working procedures of the Technical Committee *vis-à-vis* the administration of the

[58] See e.g. GATT Multilateral Trade Negotiations Group "Non-Tariff Measures" Sub-Group "Customs Matters," *Customs Valuation: Revision*, MTN/NTM/W/175/Rev.1 (November 6, 1978) (draft code circulated by delegations).

Agreement. **Annex III** of the Agreement contains provisions that define rights of developing country Members to delay or make reservations against application of certain provisions of the Agreement. As noted above, this Annex III restates the Protocol to the Agreement on Implementation of Article VII that was negotiated in the Tokyo Round.

### 1.3.3 Primacy of transaction value

The **General Introductory Commentary** to the Agreement states that "the primary basis for customs value under this Agreement is 'transaction value' as defined in Article 1." The Agreement's **Preamble** further states that Members should recognize "that the basis for valuation of goods for customs purposes should, to the greatest extent possible, be the transaction value of the goods being valued."

In fact, many customs administrations apply the transaction value method to more than 90 percent of their imports.[59]

### 1.3.4 Alternative methods of value

In addition to transaction value, the Agreement defines five alternative valuation methods:

- transaction value of identical goods (Article 2)
- transaction value of similar goods (Article 3)
- deductive value (Article 5)
- computed value (Article 6)
- residual or fallback method (Article 7).

Because transaction value is "primary," these methods should be used only if it is not possible to establish a customs value under Article 1.

Unlike some valuation systems of the past, the WTO Agreement's six valuation methods are to be applied strictly in sequential order rather than concurrently. That is, customs authorities must attempt to appraise imports first using the transaction value method. If – and only if – a transaction value cannot

[59] See GATT Committee on Customs Valuation, *First Annual Review of the Implementation and Operation of the Agreement: Background Document by the Secretariat*, VAL/W/4/Rev.1 (November 17, 1981) (use of various valuation methods by seven GATT Members, including the countries of the EEC); GATT Committee on Customs Valuation, *Use of Valuation Methods by Parties: Addendum (Norway)*, VAL/W/5/Add.8 (March 25, 1982); GATT Committee on Customs Valuation, *Minutes of the Meeting Held on 10–11 November 1983*, VAL/M/8, (January 18, 1984) (paragraph 49).

be determined for reasons defined in Article 1, then appraisement must be attempted under Article 2 – transaction value of identical merchandise. If that is not possible, then valuation under the Article 3 method must be tried, and so on, through to Article 7.

There is one exception to this sequence: under Article 4 of the Agreement an importer may request customs to apply Article 6 (computed value) before Article 5 (deductive value). See section 3.2, below.

### 1.3.5 Limits of the Agreement

Although the general principles expressed in **GATT Article VII** – which the WTO Customs Valuation Agreement implements – refer to imports <u>and</u> exports, the valuation methods defined in the Agreement refer only to *imported* goods.

> **<u>GATT Article VII</u>**
>
> The CONTRACTING PARTIES recognize the validity of the general principles of valuation set forth in the following paragraphs of this Article, and they undertake to give effect to such principles, in respect of all products subject to duties or other charges or restrictions on **importation and exportation** based upon or regulated in any manner by value.
>
> **<u>WTO Customs Valuation Agreement Article 1</u>**
>
> The customs value of **imported** goods shall be the transaction value …

Incidentally, what if there is a conflict between the terms of the WTO Valuation Agreement and the terms of GATT Article VII? Which has priority? An interpretative note to the 1994 Agreement Establishing the World Trade Organization indicates that the WTO Valuation Agreement "shall prevail to the extent of the conflict."[60] This question, however, has not yet been examined in WTO panel or appellate body decisions.

Finally, as stated in the Preamble to the Agreement, Customs administrations may ***not*** use the WTO valuation rules to "combat dumping." Imports are "dumped" when a company exports at a price lower than the price it charges in its home market, and causes injury to competing industries in the importing country.

A separate WTO agreement – the Agreement on Implementation of Article VI of the GATT (otherwise known as the Agreement on Anti-Dumping) – defines the rights and obligations of WTO Members who wish to take action

[60] General Interpretative Note to Annex 1A, Marrakesh Agreement Establishing the World Trade Organization.

against dumped imports. A country should not misuse the WTO Customs Valuation Agreement (by, for example, rejecting the declared price) to deal with dumping, rather than following the detailed procedures laid out in the WTO Anti-Dumping Agreement. As strange as it may seem, for purposes of customs valuation, the price of a dumped import may be in fact an acceptable transaction value!

# 2

# TRANSACTION VALUE METHOD

## 2.1 DEFINITION

**Article 1** of the WTO Customs Valuation Agreement defines transaction value as: "the price actually paid or payable for the goods when sold for export to the country of importation adjusted in accordance with the provisions of Article 8" (see Figure 4). We will examine the elements of this important definition in some detail in the following sections.

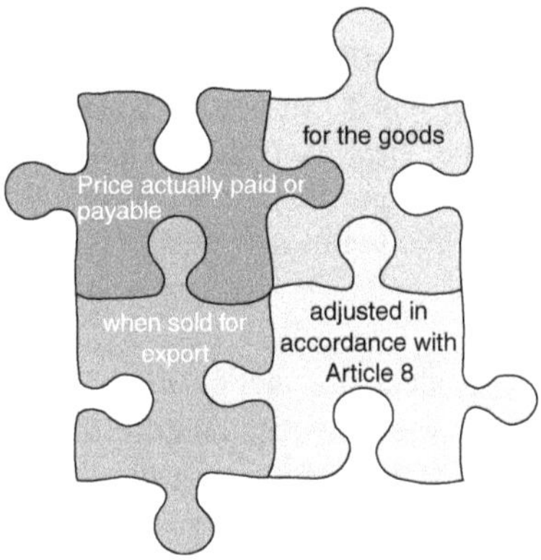


Figure 4 Transaction value definition: elements

### 2.1.1 "The price actually paid or payable ..."

Transaction value *is* whatever amount the buyer agrees to pay the seller to obtain the goods – subject to some important qualifications. In other words, *the buyer and seller themselves determine the customs value of imported goods*. Given this definition, customs <u>cannot</u> reject an importer's declared price on the grounds that:

- it is lower than prevailing market prices
- it is lower than prices for identical goods in other transactions
- it is a sale at a discount.

The customs value for exactly the same kinds of goods can vary in transactions between different buyers and sellers, or even between the same parties in different transactions over time.

> ### Common discounts
>
> **Cash discount**: the seller may sell at a lower price because the buyer agrees to pay cash for the goods instead of credit.
>
> **Volume discount**: the seller may sell at a lower price if the buyer purchases a large quantity.
>
> **Trade discount**: the buyer may be a regular or large customer whose continued business the seller wants to encourage.
>
> **Purchase discount**: the seller offers a 1 percent reduction of the price if the buyer pays earlier than the due date.
>
> Because transaction value is the price the buyer "actually paid" for the imported goods (no more, no less), the discounted price is the price used for customs value.

The treatment of discounts illustrates a fundamental difference between the WTO Valuation Agreement and a "notional" concept of value, such as the Brussels Definition of Value. New users of the Agreement (particularly those who come from former BDV countries) often expect that there should be some "acceptable discount" or a maximum discount of a price that can be allowed, or that a discount that a seller gives to just one or a limited number of buyers cannot be valid. While justified under the BDV's concept of a "normal price" for imported goods;[1] such ideas are inapposite under the WTO Agreement. Under the Agreement, the size of the discount or limitations on its availability to other buyers is not in itself a basis to reject the transaction value: the price paid or payable, net of any such discount, can be used for customs valuation purposes. (For a real-life illustration of this principle, see Case study: India customs bearing case, below.)

This statement about discounts is subject to an important qualification. As will be seen in section 2.3.4, customs can reject a transaction value between certain related buyers and sellers if the price is found to have been influenced by that relationship. In the related-party context, an "abnormal" discount given by the seller (compared to discounts the seller allows to unrelated buyers), or given exclusively to the related buyer, may be grounds for customs to question whether the parties' relationship influenced the price.

[1] The BDV required customs to adjust an invoice price if it included a discount that was not freely available to any buyer in the open market. BDV, December 15, 1970, 171 U.N.T.S. 307, Annex II, Addendum to Article I, Note 5 ("Adjustments ... may in particular be required with reference discounts or other reductions in price granted in favour of sole agents or sole concessionaires, or to any abnormal discount or any reduction from the ordinary competitive price.").

### Case study

*India customs bearings case*

*Facts:*

The importer is a company that manufactures tractors and tractor engines in India. For over thirty years, this company had imported bearings of a specific size from a supplier in Japan. However, in 1989, this relationship was "snapped" when the Indian importer discovered that it could obtain the bearings at a lower price from a local manufacturer. The Japanese company was left with a large inventory of bearings which it had already manufactured specifically for the Indian importer anticipating its continued business.

The Japanese company could not find any buyers for this particular size of bearing. Thus, in February 1993, the Japanese company contacted the Indian manufacturer and offered to sell the remaining inventory, which consisted of 3,579 bearings, for a price of Japanese Yen 826 per piece. The Indian company agreed to the offer and placed an order on the Japanese manufacturer in April 1993. The goods were subsequently exported to India in December 1993 and declared to customs.

*Valuation by India customs:*

India customs selected the declaration for review due to the large difference between the declared price and prices of similar imported bearings.

India customs called the importer's customs broker for an explanation. The broker contacted the importer who provided documents supporting his claimed price including the price list showing the normal sales price of the bearings and the letter offering the "super-discount" price.

The customs officers were still not satisfied with the value of the bearings as declared by the importer. Customs objection was based on the fact that the declared price was just 23 percent of the value shown on the price list. This is a discount of 77 percent where the normal discount offered on the price list is only 30 percent.

Customs notified the importer that it still doubted the value, and gave the importer an opportunity to respond. Customs reviewed the importer's submission but determined to reject the declared value. Customs valued the goods using the fall-back method at Japanese Yen 2,507. They arrived at the value by taking the list price and allowing a 30 percent discount.

*Administrative appeal:*

The importer appealed the case to the Customs Appellate Tribunal. The Tribunal upheld the customs decision and held that "the specially quoted price was not acceptable in preference to the ordinary price of the bearings in question as was mentioned in the vendor's price list."

*Judicial appeal:*

The issue was appealed to the Supreme Court of India. The importer argued that the merchandise should have been valued under transaction value and customs should not have used the fall-back method. The importer stated that offering discounts is a normal incidence in commerce and, given the particular circumstances of the case, a discount of 77 percent was justified. According to the importer, the reason given by the customs for not accepting the actual price paid for the bearings as the true value for the transaction was erroneous particularly when there was no allegation of fraud or false valuation.

*Judicial decision:*

The court observed that there was no allegation that the importer had misdeclared the price actually paid, or that there had been a misdescription of the goods. No reason was given by the customs for rejecting the transaction value except the price list of the vendor. In doing so, the customs not only ignored the value provisions but also acted on the basis for the vendor's list price as if a price list is proof of the transaction value. This was erroneous and can not be a reason by itself to reject the transaction value. The court observed:

"A discount is a commercially acceptable measure, which may be resorted to by a vendor for a variety of reasons including stock clearance. A price list is really no more than a general quotation. It does not preclude discounts on the listed price. In fact the offered discount was calculated with reference to the price list. Admittedly in this case a discount up to 30% was allowable in ordinary circumstances [but] there was the additional factor that the stock in question was old and it was a one time sale of 5-year old stock."

*Source*: adapted from *Eicher Tractors Ltd, Haryana* v. *Commissioner of Customs, Mumbai*, (2000) 4 Suppl. S.C.R. 597 (November 14, 2000).

### *(a) Deriving a "price"*

In most transactions, the "price actually paid or payable" for the imported goods is clear – it is the monetary amount specified in the invoice or contract between the buyer and seller.

In other transactions, however, the buyer and seller may not fix a final price for the goods prior to the importation. The price term might be left open because, for example, the goods are contracted for sale long in advance of delivery, or the seller's costs cannot be known at the time of contracting, or the market price of the commodity purchased is volatile, etc.

*Nevertheless*, the fact that a price is not established prior to importation does not necessarily preclude the use of transaction value. A transaction value can exist *if* the buyer and seller have fixed a formula or method in their agreement by which the price for the goods can be derived.

For example, the buyer might agree to pay a unit price for imported goods based on the price in effect as of the export date at an international commodity exchange (such as the London Commodity Market). Or, the buyer might agree to pay the seller's costs to manufacture the imported goods plus a specified markup. Or, in the specific case of imported iron ore, the buyer might agree to pay a price based on the amount of actual iron content found in the ore, on delivery. In such cases a "price paid or payable" can be found in the parties' agreement, and transaction value should be used.

### TEST YOUR KNOWLEDGE – CAN TRANSACTION VALUE BE USED?

• PRICING FORMULAE

Question 1: Goods are purchased under a "cost-plus" formula and the costs are not known at the time of importation. The importer declares the formula to customs when the goods arrive, but the costs will not be known until sometime after the importation. How do you assess the value of the shipment? Can transaction value be used in this case?

• PACKAGE DEALS (one price for several items)

Question 2: A shipment consists of five different types of goods. They are classifiable under different tariff categories. The goods were not sold separately but were purchased for one price. How do you assess the value of the shipment?

• BARTER DEALS

Question 3: The seller ships to the buyer a container of wheat. In exchange, the buyer ships to the seller a container of fertilizer. How do you assess the value of the imported wheat shipment?

For the answers, see p. 87.

### (b) *Direct and indirect payments*

Transaction value is the total amount the buyer actually pays for the goods. All payments the buyer makes to obtain the imported goods must be taken into account to find the total price, whether those payments are made in the past or future, or directly to the seller or to someone else for the benefit of the seller.

### LEGAL DEFINITIONS

"The price actually paid or payable is the *total payment* made or to be made by the buyer to or for the benefit of the seller" (Note to Article 1, Interpretative Notes.)

"The price actually paid or payable includes *all payments* actually made or to be made as a condition of sale of the imported goods, by the buyer to the seller, or by the buyer to a third party to satisfy an obligation of the seller." (Annex III.7, WTO Customs Valuation Agreement.)

In many cases, the full payment amount for the goods will be reflected in the invoice that the importer presents to customs with the imported goods. However, in other cases – and often for legitimate commercial purposes – the invoice price may not reflect all payments made or owed. For example, the buyer may have already paid some portion of the purchase price before the goods arrived, or will pay in installments. Other "indirect" payments might include:

- The buyer agrees to cancel the seller's debt in exchange for the goods. This might also involve a payment by the buyer: for example, the seller agrees to a lowered price for the imported goods to compensate the buyer for a prior shipment that was delivered damaged.
- The price may include payments the buyer may make to a third party to satisfy an obligation of the seller (i.e. a debt).

Any such "indirect" payments the buyer makes to the seller as a condition of sale of the goods should be taken into account when determining transaction value.

### 2.1.2 "... FOR THE GOODS ..."

As just discussed, the "price actually paid or payable" is the total payment a buyer makes for the goods to or for the benefit of the seller, whether directly or indirectly, and it includes all payments required as condition of the sale of the imported goods.

In some transactions, however, the buyer may make payments to the seller for services or other consideration that are in addition to and apart from the price "for the goods" themselves, such as payments to the seller for training the buyer's employees in use of imported machinery.

Where the buyer's payments can be shown to be *for* these kinds of separate, ancillary services or other consideration provided by the seller, rather than payments made for, or as a condition of the sale of, the imported goods, they may be excluded from transaction value.

Note, however, **Article 8** of the Agreement lists certain types of payments that must always be included in the customs value, even if not "for the goods" per se. See discussion under section 2.2, Required additions to price, below.

The Interpretative Notes and WTO Valuation Committee decisions have identified the following specific categories of payments that may be excluded from customs value:

#### *(a) Interest payments*

A buyer might purchase the goods on credit from the seller and agree to pay the seller both the purchase price of the goods plus a financing charge. Or the buyer might obtain a loan for the purchase price from a bank or third party and pay that entity the finance charge.

The financing charge the buyer pays might be considered interest *for* use of money – a loan – rather than payment *for* the goods themselves. Should such payments be included in transaction value?

In the early days of the Tokyo Round Valuation Code, there was some disparity among countries in their treatment of interest charges paid by the buyer. Some countries did not include the financing charge in customs value if the charge was separately identified from the invoice price of the goods or could be ascertained. Other countries considered the charge, if paid to the seller, to be part of the price paid or payable for the goods.[2] If interest charges were excluded from customs value, some countries worried that an opening would be created for the unscrupulous importer to reduce value for duty by overstating interest charges.[3]

To resolve these discrepancies and concerns, the GATT Valuation Committee adopted a decision, proposed by the European Economic Community, to allow financing charges paid by the buyer to be excluded from customs value under the following conditions:

1. the interest payment is distinguished from the price paid or payable for the goods (for example, the interest charge is set out separately in the invoice or is billed separately),
2. the financing arrangement in question is in writing and
3. where required, the buyer can demonstrate:
   (a) the imported goods are actually sold at the declared price, and
   (b) the interest charge does not exceed the level for such transactions prevailing in the country where, and at the time when, financing was provided.[4]

The full text of this decision, which was adopted by the WTO Valuation Committee without change in 1995, can be found in Appendix 3.

### *(b) Dividend payments*

Dividends that a buyer pays to a seller are not included in transaction value. A dividend is a return on investment in an enterprise, and is not related to a specific sale of goods. (See **Interpretative Note to Article 1** "Price actually paid or payable.")

[2] GATT Committee on Customs Valuation, *Treatment of Interest for Deferred Payment, Report by the Technical Committee on Customs Valuation on National Practices*, VAL/W/10 (October 7, 1982).

[3] GATT Committee on Customs Valuation, *Minutes of the Meeting Held on 3 March 1983*, VAL/M/6 (April 19, 1983) (paragraphs 28, 33).

[4] GATT Committee on Customs Valuation, *Decision on the Treatment of Interest Charges in the Customs Value of Imported Goods*, VAL/6/Rev.1 (October 1, 1984).

### *(c) Payments for post-importation services and costs*

A buyer might contract and pay the seller for services performed after importation of the goods, such as construction, erection, assembly, maintenance or technical assistance. For example, a seller might install imported industrial plant, machinery or equipment under a "turn-key" type contract. These are payments *for* the seller's services, rather than consideration *for* the imported goods themselves; they are therefore not properly part of transaction value.

Of course, to exclude any of these payments from transaction value, they must be distinguished from the purchase price of the goods; for example, separately billed or invoiced.

Charges for transport of the goods after importation are likewise excluded from customs value, as are import duties and other taxes imposed by the country of importation, if distinguished from the price paid or payable for the goods.[5] (See **Interpretative Note to Article 1** "Price actually paid or payable.")

### *(d) Advertizing and marketing costs*

To promote sales of the imported product in his own market, a buyer might incur costs for marketing studies, advertizing, or market testing. The buyer might even be required by the seller, under the parties' sales agreement, to undertake these kinds of activities at his own cost.

> **ADVERTIZING COSTS**
>
> An importer enters into a sales agreement with the Squeaky Shoes Company. The sales agreement requires the buyer to spend a minimum amount on advertizing in his country. Although this may benefit the seller indirectly, the advertizing costs are not part of the price actually paid or payable.

Under the Valuation Agreement, the buyer's expenses related to selling or distribution of the imported goods are excluded from customs value. When such an exclusion was first proposed by the European Communities during the GATT Tokyo Round Code negotiations, the rationale given was the following:

> [W]e have excluded the costs of advertising in the country of importation. We have done this partly because in many cases the advertising costs are

[5] Terms of sale that require the seller to pay the import duty – such as "delivered duty paid" – should be sufficient alone to "distinguish" duties and taxes from the price paid or payable for the goods. In these cases, since the import duty rate is known (and therefore customs can determine the amount of duty in the price), and the terms of sale define the price as inclusive of any duty amounts, the importer should not be required to claim the deduction or set out the amount separately on the invoice. See Technical Committee Advisory Opinion 3.1, reprinted in *WCO Compendium*.

> borne either directly or indirectly by the seller and the transaction can reasonably be viewed as an invisible export, and partly in the interests of simplification.[6]

Although the EC proposal was resisted by some countries (who, in fact, counter-proposed that the agreement specifically *include* such costs), in the end an **Interpretative Note to Article 1** was added that generally reflects the European Communities' view:[7]

> [I]f the buyer undertakes on the buyer's own account, even though by agreement with the seller, activities relating to marketing of the imported goods, the value of these activities is not part of the customs value nor shall such activities result in rejection of the transaction value.

### *(e) Software*

As a result of a 1984 decision by the GATT Valuation Committee, WTO Members can choose to apply a unique valuation treatment – different than the transaction value method – to certain computer programs or data imported on discs, tape, or other kinds of "carrier medium."

Under the BDV, the valuation system that was widely used prior to the GATT Valuation Code, valuation of imported software or data was based only on the value of the disc or tape that contained the data, plus the cost of recording the information on the disc or tape, plus profit. The value for duty purposes did *not* include the value of the software content.[8]

*However*, under the Valuation Agreement, transaction value is the price paid or payable for the imported goods. In the case of imported software on a disc, the imported goods consist of the software content – the recorded data or instructions – and the disc or other physical medium on which the software is recorded. Normally, the cost or value of the medium is trivial relative to the software content, which is what the buyer is interested in obtaining. Strictly applied, therefore, the WTO Valuation Agreement would require customs to value the imported disc inclusive of the software content, a change that might have dramatic duty impacts from the previous BDV practice.

[6] GATT Multilateral Trade Negotiations Group "Non-Tariff Measures" Sub-Group "Customs Matters," *Statement Made by the Commission of the European Communities at the Meeting of the Sub-Group of November 15, 1977*, MTN/NTM/W/126 (November 21, 1977).

[7] Under the BDV, expenses incurred by the buyer for "finding, establishing and maintaining a market for the goods in the country of importation" were included in customs value, on the theory that in an open market sale, these would be normally borne by the supplier. World Customs Organization, *The Brussels Definition of Value and the GATT Valuation Agreement: A Comparison* (1985), 10. The change from BDV practice may also be a reason an Interpretative Note was considered necessary on this point.

[8] GATT Committee on Customs Valuation, *Minutes of the Meeting Held on 4–5 May 1982*, VAL/M/4 (July 19, 1982).

Soon after the entry into force of the GATT Valuation Code, when the impact of this change in practice became apparent, proposals were made to allow the continuation of the BDV valuation treatment of imported software.[9] A number of countries, however, opposed the proposals because of the inconsistency with the transaction value definition as well as the negative impact the proposals might have on revenue from import duty.[10]

In the end, to reach a consensus on valuation of imported software, the GATT Parties agreed to allow *both* practices to continue under the Valuation Agreement – the transaction value method (valuation includes software content) and the former BDV method (valuation excludes software content).[11] The GATT **Decision on the Valuation of Carrier Media Bearing Software for Data Processing Equipment**, which was adopted by WTO Valuation Committee on May 12, 1995,[12] states that it would be consistent with the Agreement to value the imported software on the basis of *either*

1. the cost or value of the software content *and* the carrier medium, *or*
2. the cost or value of the carrier medium alone, excluding the cost or value of the software content, provided that this is distinguished from the cost or the value of the carrier medium.

The scope of this decision is limited. It applies only to data or instructions on an imported disc or other similar carrier medium. It does not apply to imports of integrated circuits, semiconductors and similar devices or articles incorporating such circuits or devices, such as imported calculators, computers or telecom equipment, which may contain some software. It does not include "sound, cinematic or video recordings." The normal "transaction value" method would apply to valuation of goods of these kinds.

The decision requires those WTO members that choose to value imported software on the basis of the cost or value of the carrier medium alone (i.e. without the value of the software content) to notify the Valuation Committee. As of April 2008, twenty-five WTO Member countries have submitted this notification.[13]

[9] GATT Committee on Customs Valuation, *Possible Amendments to the Agreement: Communication from the United States Concerning the Valuation of Computer Software*, VAL/W/7 (April 23, 1982); GATT Committee on Customs Valuation, *Valuation of Computer Software: Proposal by the United States*, VAL/W/14 (November 4, 1982).

[10] GATT Committee on Customs Valuation, *Minutes of the Meeting Held on 3 March 1983*, VAL/M/6 (April 19, 1983) (paragraphs 19–32); GATT Committee on Customs Valuation, *Minutes of the Meeting Held on 10 May 1983*, VAL/M/7 (July 7, 1983) (paragraphs 22–38).

[11] See GATT Committee on Customs Valuation, *Minutes of the Meeting Held on 10–11 November 1983*, VAL/M/8 (January 18, 1984) (paragraph 66).

[12] WTO, Committee on Customs Valuation, *Decisions Concerning the Interpretation and Administration of the Agreement on Implementation of Article VII of the GATT 1994 (Customs Valuation)*, G/VAL/5 (October 13, 1995).

[13] WTO, Committee on Customs Valuation, *Information on the Application of the Decisions on the Treatment of Interest Charges in the Customs Value of Imported Goods and on the Valuation of Carrier*

The complete text of this decision can be found in Appendix 3.

### *(f)* *Payments for damaged goods/goods not in accordance with contract*

A buyer agrees to pay the foreign manufacturer a price for goods of a specified standard or quality. On occasion, the buyer may find that the imported goods are damaged, defective, or that they otherwise do not meet the contract specifications. Is there a price "*for* the goods" as imported, or was the price agreed only for those goods that meet contract specifications?

If some or all of a consignment is discovered prior to customs clearance to have been completely destroyed – without commercial value – or lost at the time of importation, national customs rules often treat the damaged goods as if they had never arrived – a "non-importation." In that case, because the destroyed or lost goods are not imported, the question of their customs value does not arise.

**Merchandise completely worthless at time of importation national rules**

(a) *Nonperishable merchandise*. When a shipment of nonperishable merchandise, or any portion thereof which shall have been segregated from the remainder of the shipment under customs supervision at the expense of the importer, is found by the port director to be entirely without commercial value at the time of importation by reason of damage or deterioration, an allowance in duties on such merchandise on the ground of nonimportation shall be made in the liquidation of the entry.

US Customs Regulation 19 C.F.R. 158.11 (2007).

On the other hand, where the goods are partially damaged or defective, the importer may choose to take delivery. If so, is there a price paid or payable for the imported damaged or defective goods?

A note by the Technical Committee proposes one, common-sense response to this question:[14]

- If the imported goods are damaged, they cannot be considered the same goods as those the buyer agreed to purchase from the seller. Therefore transaction value – the price paid for the goods sold for export – cannot be used. The transaction value method must be

*Medium Bearing Software for Data Processing Equipment: Note by the Secretariat*, G/VAL/W/5/Rev.19 (April 25, 2008).

[14] WCO, *Explanatory Note 3.1: Goods Not in Accordance with Contract*, in *WCO Compendium*.

rejected, and the remaining methods of value must be considered in order.

- The Technical Committee notes that the fall-back valuation method under Article 7 of the Agreement likely would be used in the majority of these cases. Under that method, customs might consider as the customs value the renegotiated price between the buyer and seller, or consider the original price paid or payable paid for the goods, reduced by the cost of repair, by an insurance settlement, or the estimate of an independent surveyor.

- If the wrong goods are shipped (the buyer ordered apples; the seller sent oranges), transaction value cannot be used, for the same reason.
- If the imported goods are not the wrong goods, and are not damaged, but simply do not comply with contract specifications (such as performance or other technical specifications), transaction value can be used.

Finally, it must be noted that the question of valuation of damaged goods is often obviated by alternative customs procedures. In particular, the Kyoto Convention generally requires the repayment of duty where the goods are found to be defective or not in accordance with contract and are returned, destroyed or abandoned within a reasonable time.[15]

### Test your knowledge – should these payments be included in transaction value?

1. Under a contract for purchase of electrical equipment, the buyer agrees to pay the seller to send engineers to inspect the equipment for compliance with specifications after the equipment has been imported and installed at the buyer's factory, as well as to train the buyer's employees in handling, operation and

[15] Kyoto Convention Standard 4.19:

> Repayment shall be granted in respect of imported or exported goods which are found to have been defective or otherwise not in accordance with the agreed specifications at the time of importation or exportation and are returned either to the supplier or to another person designated by the supplier, subject to the following conditions:
>
> - the goods have not been worked, repaired or used in the country of importation, and are re-exported within a reasonable time;
> - the goods have not been worked, repaired or used in the country to which they were exported, and are re-imported within a reasonable time.
>
> Use of the goods shall, however, not hinder the repayment if such use was indispensable to discover the defects or other circumstances which caused the re-exportation or re-importation of the goods.
>
> As an alternative to re-exportation or re-importation, the goods may be abandoned to the Revenue or destroyed or rendered commercially valueless under Customs control, as the Customs may decide. Such abandonment or destruction shall not entail any cost to the Revenue.

maintenance. Should these costs be included in determining the transaction value of the imported equipment?

2. The buyer agrees to import a minimum 10,000 units of product over a one-year period, and to pay the seller a "penalty" if he fails to do so. Should this "penalty" be included in the transaction value of the goods imported by the buyer?
3. The seller submits two invoices to the buyer: one for the goods, and the other for a warranty. The warranty guarantees that the seller will repair or replace the goods if defects are found after importation. Should the invoiced warranty payments be included in the transaction value of the imported goods? Or, is the warranty payment *for* replacement goods the seller will ship in the future, if ever?

For the answers, see p. 88.

### 2.1.3 "... WHEN SOLD FOR EXPORT ..."

Transaction value requires a sale, and the sale must be one for export to the country of importation. In most cases, it is not difficult to identify the sale for export.

#### SALE FOR EXPORT

Company A in Korea sells and delivers its washing machines to Company B in Kenya. This is the sale for export, and the price Company B agrees to pay is the basis for the customs value of the merchandise.

Company B may intend to re-sell the machines to its customers in Kenya. These subsequent sales do not affect the customs value because they are not sales for export which triggered the export of the goods from Korea. The sale from Company B to its Kenyan customers is a domestic sale.

Transaction value does not require that the sale take place in the country of exportation. The seller can be located in any country – even the same country as the buyer. What is required is that the sale involve an international transfer of goods. Thus, the seller may ship the goods to the country of importation from a third country or from no country at all (i.e. a fishing vessel on the high seas, or an oil rig outside territorial waters)!

#### TWO QUESTIONS FOR THE EXPERTS

Here are two real cases where the sale for export may not be so obvious. How would you decide these cases?

*"Successive sales"*

An importer places an order for goods with a foreign middleman. The middleman in turn contracts with a foreign factory to fill the order and to ship the goods direct to the importer.

Which sale may be considered the sale for export? Is it the sale between the importer and the middleman? Or is it the sale between the middleman and the foreign factory? Or can both sales be considered "sale[s] for export"?

*The tourist trader*

Here, the importer – who may be a tourist or a "shuttle trader" – travels to another country, where he anonymously purchases and takes delivery of goods on the foreign market (a used car, for example). He then returns home with the goods, or perhaps he has them shipped to himself.

Is the importer's purchase of the goods in the foreign market a "sale for export"? Or was that foreign purchase a purely domestic sale, and not proper basis for transaction value?

For the answers, see p. 88.

If transaction value must be based on the price paid or payable "*when* sold for export," will the customs value be affected if the buyer and seller renegotiate the price *after* the goods are exported? For example:

- to compensate for failure to ship the goods to the buyer by the date specified in the sales contract, the seller rebates a portion of the purchase price to buyer;
- the goods are found on importation not to conform to contract specifications, so the seller reduces the price charged to the buyer;
- the seller reduces the price for the imported goods because the buyer subsequently made large purchases of the same goods (a "retroactive volume discount").

Generally, the price paid or payable for the goods "when sold for export" establishes the transaction value of the goods; therefore, a renegotiation of that price subsequent to exportation would not be taken into account. But it is important to distinguish a post-exportation renegotiation from a price determined after exportation by means of a previously agreed price formula. For example, if the buyer and seller included in their contract a means to calculate price based upon date of actual delivery (e.g. "the contract price shall be reduced for every week of delay by an amount equal to 0.5 percent of the total value of the goods whose delivery has been delayed …"), that price formula might be used to derive a transaction value, as we have seen in our discussion of "deriving a price" above.

### 2.1.4 "… ADJUSTED IN ACCORDANCE WITH THE PROVISIONS OF ARTICLE 8"

Normally the full transaction value of the goods is reflected in the seller's invoice, which the importer is usually required by national legislation to present to Customs.

**WHY ARTICLE 8? (IN THE WORDS OF THE NEGOTIATORS)**

"We start in Article 1 by stating that the price paid or payable for the imported goods shall be accepted as the basis for determining the customs value provided that the buyer and seller are not related. Here we make an assumption that if the buyer and seller are not related then the price made between them is one which is determined by the market forces and is an acceptable one for valuation purposes. **We recognize, of course, that buyers and sellers may be tempted to arrange the transaction so that the price itself reflects only a small element of the value of the goods and that the remainder is transferred between them by some indirect method. We have, therefore, provided, in [Article 8 of the Agreement] of our draft, for certain additions to be made to the price paid or payable if these have not been included in the basic price**. But the basic concept is that provided the price paid or payable fully reflects everything which the buyer has to pay to get the goods then that is accepted as the basis for the customs value."

Statement made by the Commission of the European Communities (MTN/NTM/W/126 (November 21, 1977)).

In more complex transactions, however, the invoice price may not include all payments the buyer made or costs he incurred to acquire the goods. For example, the invoice may not disclose that the buyer is required to pay a royalty to a third party in order to import goods manufactured under a patent, or that the buyer supplied the seller with free manufacturing inputs or services needed for production, or that the buyer will make additional payments to the seller when he resells the goods after importation.

**Article 8** of the Agreement is designed to ensure that certain specific kinds of costs of producing and delivering the imported goods to a buyer are reflected in customs value, regardless of how the parties may have structured their particular transaction.

## 2.2 REQUIRED ADDITIONS TO PRICE

### 2.2.1 GENERAL CONSIDERATIONS

**Article 8** lays out specific rules to define the kinds of additional payments and costs that must be included in transaction value, and under what conditions (see Figure 5 for an example).

Each **Article 8** adjustment has its own peculiarities which customs and traders should understand, and which are discussed below. There are, however, two restrictions that apply to Article 8 generally.

First, and perhaps obviously, customs should not add an amount to the invoice price (and charge duty again) if the seller already included the charge for the Article 8 element in the price of the goods. For example, a seller may

SR MEMORY CARD PRODUCTION INC.

**INVOICE**

555 Forget -Me-Not Road
Geneva, Switzerland
Phone 555-777-555 Fax 555-777-557

INVOICE #MMMC55553
DATE: MAY 12, 2007

**To:**
WTO Workshop Inc.
First Street
Geneva, Switzerland

**SHIP To:**
Same Address

**COMMENTS OR SPECIAL INSTRUCTIONS:**

*How to Calculate Transaction Value – ARTICLE 8 ADDITIONS TO PRICE*

| QUANTITY | DESCRIPTION | UNIT PRICE | TOTAL |
|---|---|---|---|
| | PRICE PAID OR PAYABLE | × | ××,×× |
| | *Plus* | | |
| | + COMMISSIONS AND BROKERAGE, OTHER THAN BUYING COMMISSIONS | × | ××,×× |
| | + COST OF CONTAINERS IN WHICH THE IMPORTED GOODS ARE SHIPPED | × | ××,×× |
| | + COST OR VALUE OF ANY "ASSISTS" | × | ××,×× |
| | + ROYALTIES AND LICENSE FEES | × | ××,×× |
| | + VALUE OF ANY "PROCEEDS" | × | ××,×× |
| | + COST OF INTERNATIONAL TRANSPORT OF IMPORTED GOODS (IF MEMBER COUNTRY CHOOSES) | × | ××,×× |
| | *minus* | | |
| | – POST IMPORTATION CHARGES | × | ××,×× |
| | | Total | **= TRANSACTION VALUE** |

Thank you for your business!

Figure 5 Article 8 assists

have bundled into one sales invoice amount both the commission owed to his agent and the price of the imported goods themselves. Whether the declared price includes the Article 8 element or not is largely a problem of proof: if customs has doubts, the importer may be required to demonstrate that the sale price was inclusive of these charges.

Second, any addition to price under Article 8 must be based on "objective and quantifiable data."

*Article 8(3)*

> 3. Additions to the price actually paid or payable shall be made under this Article only on the basis of objective and quantifiable data.

If customs is not able to obtain sufficient information to quantify these costs accurately, whether from the importer or otherwise, then the adjustment cannot be made. In that case, transaction value cannot be used, and the next method of valuation must be considered.

The **Interpretative Note to Article 8(3)** provides one example where it may not be possible to establish accurately the value of an Article 8 element:

> [A] royalty is paid on the basis of the price in a sale in the importing country of a litre of a particular product that was imported by the kilogram and made up into a solution after importation. If the royalty is based partially on the imported goods and partially on other factors which have nothing to do with the imported goods (such as when the imported goods are mixed with domestic ingredients and are no longer separately identifiable, or when the royalty cannot be distinguished from special financial arrangements between the buyer and the seller), it would be inappropriate to attempt to make an addition for the royalty. However, if the amount of this royalty is based only on the imported goods and can be readily quantified, an addition to the price actually paid or payable can be made.

The Article 8 condition that adjustments be made only "on the basis of objective and quantifiable data" can also be read as a limitation on customs discretion. That is, if the importer provides documentation that establishes the amount he actually paid for packing, for example, that number should be used, regardless of how much customs may think the packing is worth.

### Test your knowledge – "Objective and quantifiable evidence"

What happens if the buyer makes a royalty payment to the seller, but is unable to tell customs the amount of the royalty payment?

Example: Buyer agrees to pay "the usual royalty" but customs has no information about how much a "usual" royalty is for that industry, or how it might be calculated.

Should customs make an estimate of the royalty to calculate customs value?

For the answers, see p. 90.

### 2.2.2 Commissions and Brokerage

> ***Article 8(1)(a)(i)***
>
> 1. In determining the customs value under the provisions of Article 1, there shall be added to the price actually paid or payable for the imported goods:
>
> (a) the following, to the extent that they are incurred by the buyer but are not included in the price actually paid or payable for the goods:
>
> (i) commissions and brokerage, except buying commissions;

International sales transactions can involve one or more intermediaries who assist the buyer or seller in the purchase of the goods. These intermediaries – known variously as "agents," "middlemen," or "brokers" – can provide any number of services to the buyer or seller to facilitate sales, such as contacting customers, marketing products, or supporting sales negotiations.

*(a)* *Buyer's agent – typical duties*

- finds goods for the buyer
- communicates buyer's needs to the seller
- obtains samples of the goods for the buyer to inspect
- inspects goods/factory to ensure production quality
- assists buyer in negotiating best price
- assists buyer in arranging transport of goods
- consolidates shipments from different sellers
- prepares invoices for all goods purchased

*(b)* *Seller's agent – typical duties*

- looks for customers for seller
- solicits and transmits orders to potential buyers for seller
- keeps and shows samples of seller's goods
- arranges transport, insurance, storage of goods for seller
- assists seller prepare export documents
- assists seller prepare export invoices

As a general rule, if the buyer pays a commission or brokerage fee to an intermediary in connection with the purchase of the imported goods, that amount must be added to the price of the goods. There is, however, an important exception to this rule: the fee or *buying commission* that a buyer pays to his own agent to assist in the sale is excluded.

Why should the Agreement exclude buying commissions from customs value? When the buyer pays a fee to the seller's agent, it might be thought of as a kind of indirect payment to the seller: by making the payment, the buyer relieves the seller of a debt that the seller would otherwise have to pay. For that reason, the buyer's payment of selling commissions is considered part of the transaction value of the imported goods. On the other hand, when the buyer pays his own agent (or concludes the sale entirely "in-house," through his own employees), the seller receives no direct or indirect monetary benefit.

A second rationale that has been offered is that the exclusion of buying commissions from dutiable value serves to equalize costs between small or medium-size companies and larger enterprises. That is, a larger trader may have the resources to establish its own office in exporting countries for purchasing purposes, whereas a small company may be required to employ a local buying agent. By excluding buying commissions paid to such agents, the Agreement does not penalize the smaller enterprise for that choice of business operation.[16]

How to distinguish a buyer's agent from a seller's agent? Whether the agent is one or the other may not be apparent from import documentation. Often it will require examination of the actual role the intermediary played in the transaction. In order to prove the agent's role in a transaction, customs administrations may require the importer to present the contract or agency agreement between the buyer and his representative which spells out the functions and responsibility of the agent.

**SIGNS YOU ARE *NOT* THE BUYER'S AGENT**

1. The buyer does not control your activities
2. You are related to the seller (typically, a company related to the seller would be acting as the seller's agent)
3. You take title and bear risk of loss to the imported goods (you may be an independent buyer/re-seller, rather than anyone's agent)
4. You don't need approval from the buyer to conclude a sales contract with the seller (you are probably an independent buyer/re-seller)
5. You invoice the seller for your commission (you are probably a seller's agent)

A buyer's agent acts on behalf of and primarily for the benefit of the buyer rather than the seller or independently, on his own behalf. Thus, the **Interpretative Note to Article 8** defines a buying commission as "fees paid by an importer to the importer's agent for the service of representing the importer abroad in the

[16] WTO, Committee on Customs Valuation, *Minutes of the Meeting of 27 March 2002*, at 18, G/VAL/M/26 (May 21, 2002) (Statement of Japan). The US representative observed that, in her country's experience, approximately 90 percent of cases involving buying agents pertained to textile exports, and the vast majority of these exporters were small and medium size enterprises. *Ibid.*

purchase of the goods being valued." The main factor distinguishing a buying agent is the right of the buyer to control the activities of the agent, particularly in the negotiation and purchasing process.

Finally, the Agreement provides that the addition for the commission paid to the seller's agent should be included in the transaction value only "to the extent incurred by the buyer." In other words, a commission paid to the seller's agent is included in the transaction value only if the buyer makes that payment. It may happen that, for example, a seller agrees to cover part or all of that cost (which might otherwise be shifted to the buyer) in order to make the sale. In such cases, if the buyer does not reimburse the seller for the payment, that amount should not be included in customs value.

### 2.2.3 Containers and packing

> ***Article 8(1)(a)(ii) and (iii)***
>
> 1. In determining the customs value under the provisions of Article 1, there shall be added to the price actually paid or payable for the imported goods:
>
> (a) the following, to the extent that they are incurred by the buyer but are not included in the price actually paid or payable for the goods: …
>
> (ii) the cost of containers which are treated as being one for customs purposes with the goods in question;
>
> (iii) the cost of packing whether for labour or materials;

Normally, the cost of packaging is included in the invoice price for imported goods, just as when you buy goods at the market you pay one price for the goods, as packaged. It is possible, however, that a seller might separately invoice the buyer for the costs of containers in which the imported goods are shipped, or for the costs of packing the goods.

**Article 8** requires an addition to the declared price of any cost incurred by the buyer for "containers which are treated as being one for customs purposes with the goods in question," as well as "the cost of packing the goods, whether for labour or for materials" (see Figure 6).

The customs treatment of containers mentioned in Article 8 is a rule of tariff classification that is found in another international instrument, the Harmonized Commodity Description and Coding System. The Harmonized System provides that normal, non-reusable packaging should be classified under the same tariff category as the imported goods they contain.

COSTS of PACKING

| Materials | Labor |
|---|---|
| • bags | • sealing boxes |
| • blister packs | • vacuum packing |
| • boxes – retail and export | • put on racks |
| • crates | • environmental conditioning |
| • pallets | |
| • bubble wrap | |
| • straw | |
| • Styrofoam chips | |

Figure 6 Packing costs

**HARMONIZED SYSTEM CONTAINER CLASSIFICATION RULE**

"In addition to the foregoing provisions, the following Rules shall apply in respect of the goods referred to therein:

... packing materials and packing containers presented with the goods therein shall be classified with the goods if they are of a kind normally used for packing such goods. However, this provision is not binding when such packing materials or packing containers are clearly suitable for repetitive use."

*Source*: General Rules for the Interpretation of the Harmonized System (GRI) 5(b).

Thus, if Harmonized System rules require packaging to be classified under the same tariff provision as the goods, then any separate payment the buyer makes for the cost of the packaging should be added to the price of the goods to obtain the customs value. Conversely, if the container is one of the reusable types that is required to be separately classified (reusable metal cylinders for transporting gas, for example), its cost is not added to the price of the goods (but it may be subject to valuation and duty assessment in its own right, depending upon the rules of the particular country).

Of course, if the cost of containers or packing is already included in the price, or the buyer did not incur this cost, it is not to be added, for the reasons previously discussed.

### 2.2.4 Assists

> ***Article 8(1)(b)***
>
> 1. In determining the customs value under the provisions of Article 1, there shall be added to the price actually paid or payable for the imported goods:
>
> ...
>
> (b) the value, apportioned as appropriate, of the following goods and services where supplied directly or indirectly by the buyer free of charge or at reduced cost for use in connection with the production and sale for export of the imported goods, to the extent that such value has not been included in the price actually paid or payable:
> (i) materials, components, parts and similar items incorporated in the imported goods;
> (ii) tools, dies, moulds and similar items used in the production of the imported goods;
> (iii) materials consumed in the production of the imported goods;
> (iv) engineering, development, artwork, design work, and plans and sketches undertaken elsewhere than in the country of importation and necessary for the production of the imported goods;

*(a) General principles*

Where a seller receives free-of-charge the materials, tools or "know-how" that he requires to produce exported goods, the seller will naturally be in a position to accept a lower price (and pay a lower duty) for the finished product than if he had to purchase or produce these inputs himself.

**Article 8** of the Agreement thus provides that if the buyer has provided certain production inputs – generally known in customs parlance as "assists" – free or at a reduced cost, then the value of the assist should be factored into customs value.

There can be any number of legitimate business reasons why a buyer would provide these assists free to the seller:

- *Example*: The buyer supplies the foreign manufacturer with parts or components to ensure that the finished product meets the buyer's quality standards.
- *Example*: The buyer provides the foreign manufacturer with parts or components, as he is able to acquire these parts/components on better terms.
- *Example*: The buyer supplies the foreign manufacturer with the design that he wants the manufacturer to use in producing dresses or other clothing items.

- *Example*: The buyer supplies the foreign manufacturer with a proprietary item (a computer chip, for example) that is incorporated in the finished product (a computer).

Assists might be thought of as a kind of indirect payment which a buyer makes to a seller. That is, a buyer might supply the seller with the tools, dies, designs, etc. required to manufacture the imported goods, or he could pay the seller separately to acquire these production inputs. In either case, the buyer relieves the seller of a cost or debt the seller would otherwise incur in order to produce the imported goods. For that reason, the Agreement requires the cost or value of these production inputs to be included in transaction value.

Generally, two questions must be answered when dealing with an import involving assists:

1. whether a service or product that the buyer provides a manufacturer falls within one of the Article 8 assist categories and, if so,
2. what amount should be added to the invoice price to account for the assist; in other words, what is the cost or value of the assist?

### *(b) Assists – categories and conditions*

#### (i) The four assist categories

**Article 8** defines four categories of assists. These are:

1. Materials, components, parts and similar items incorporated in the imported goods.
   For example, raw materials (fabric, metal or plastic sheet, chemicals, etc.), parts and components (fasteners, electrical components, automobile subassemblies, etc.) or semi-finished articles that a producer might require for manufacture of imported goods.
2. Tools, dies, molds and similar items used in production of the imported goods.
   All variety of hand and power tools, and production machinery supplied by the buyer would fall under this category.
3. Merchandise consumed in the production of imported goods.
   Various products or materials that are used in production but would not necessarily be identifiable in the final product (in contrast to parts/components), such as chemical catalysts, fuels, lubricants or Freon used in manufacture of semiconductors.
4. Engineering, research, development, design work, and plans and sketches *undertaken elsewhere than in the country of importation* and necessary for the production of the imported goods.

> This covers certain types of "know-how" a buyer may provide a seller in order to produce the imported goods. It includes specifications for manufacture, product design and testing, construction of product prototypes and models, artwork, blueprints, schematics and other drawings that are used in the production process.
>
> What is NOT covered by this provision are costs of basic research that a buyer may supply to the seller. The GATT negotiators specifically intended to distinguish "research" from "development" activity, by excluding the costs of the former but including the costs of the latter in customs value.[17] As recounted by the GATT Secretariat:
>
> > The secretariat has also consulted those present during the negotiation of the Agreement to discover what more can be said about the intentions of the drafters in regard to this provision … [R]esearch was considered by the negotiators in some detail and the decision to exclude it from the list of adjustments contained in Article 8.1(b)(iv) was a deliberate one, based on the following considerations: (a) it is virtually impossible to apportion research costs to specific imported goods; and (b) research costs are generally charged to the accounting period in which incurred as a general overhead, that is, a general expense, and not the time in which the actual manufacturing of the good may be taking place. These considerations only arose where research costs have not been included in the price actually paid or payable and when considering whether, in certain circumstances, such costs should be added to the price actually paid or payable as one of the adjustments permissible in order to determine the customs value of a good under the transaction value method. Of course, where research costs, as one element in the general costs of production of a good, are already included in the price actually paid or payable, research will form part of the customs value under the transaction value method.[18]

WTO Members agreed that the cost or value of development, engineering, artwork, etc. could be excluded from the customs value if the work is undertaken in the country of importation. This distinguishes this assist from all others (where geographic origin is not important).

[17] Under accounting definitions, "research" is "[o]riginal and planned investigation undertaken with the prospect of gaining new scientific or technical knowledge or understanding," while "development" is the "[a]pplication of research findings or other knowledge to a plan or design for the production of new or substantially improved materials, devices, products, processes, systems or services prior to the commencement of commercial production or use." International Accounting Standard (IAS) No. 38.

[18] Committee on Customs Valuation, *The Term "Development" in Article 8.1(b) (iv) of the Agreement on Implementation of Article VII: Note by the Secretariat*, VAL/W/24/Rev.1 (January 10, 1985). On the basis of that negotiation history, the GATT Valuation Committee issued decision 5.1, reflecting the GATT parties' understanding that the term "development" excludes "research."

**WHY SHOULD COSTS OF ENGINEERING AND DESIGN BE EXCLUDED FROM CUSTOMS VALUE IF UNDERTAKEN IN THE COUNTRY OF IMPORTATION?**

It may seem strange that the Agreement requires customs value to include the cost or value of production inputs (tools, parts and components or other materials) that an importer provides to the foreign manufacturer, but excludes any engineering and design work the importer undertakes in his own country. Both are costs of production of the imported product, and would seem to be equally essential.

One reason relates to national tariff policy. Customs tariff rules in a number of WTO Member countries exempt from customs duties the cost or value of national-origin *materials* incorporated in the imported product. To incentivize the development of domestic technical *service* industries, WTO Members may have wished to provide equivalent tariff treatment to national-origin design and engineering by exempting the cost or value of such services from customs value of the import.*

* See WTO Committee on Customs Valuation, *Minutes of the Meeting of 27 March 2002*, G/VAL/M/26 (paragraph 1.24ff), where the economic rationale for this exclusion is the subject of extended discussion.

**(ii) Conditions for additions to price**

Assuming that the buyer has provided the foreign manufacturer with one of these four kinds of production inputs, the cost or value of the assist must be added only if:

1. It is not already included in the price paid or payable.
   Of course, if the importer has already included the cost or value in the price declared to customs, no addition is made.
2. The buyer supplied the assist free of charge or at a reduced cost.
   If supplied at a reduced cost, an addition will be made only to the extent of the reduction. For example, if the buyer sells a tool or mold to the foreign manufacturer at a discount ($500 instead of $1,000) because, for example, the seller may use the tool for other purposes, then the "assist" is in the amount of the discount ($500).
3. The assist was supplied directly or indirectly by the buyer.
   *Example*: An Italian buyer directs its subsidiary located in Canada to supply the screws and bolts to the US manufacturer to use in producing the tractors shipped to Italy. This assist is supplied indirectly by the buyer.
4. The goods or services must be for use in connection with the production and sale for export of the imported goods.
   Thus, the cost or value of general purpose plant and office equipment not used for production should not be included in transaction value (e.g. heating and air conditioning, office machines – such as typewriters, calculators, photocopiers – fork-lift trucks and conveyors).

Similarly, the cost or value of post-importation technical services or market research, or other such studies for purposes of a price quotation, which are not necessary to produce the imported good, are not to be added to the price.

The four assist categories are exclusive. That is, the cost or value of any other kind of goods or services that an importer may supply to a foreign seller is NOT to be added to the invoice price (unless, of course, it meets the requirements of some other Article 8 category).

*Example*: An importer supplies building materials to the foreign producer to enable him to build administrative offices. Since the building materials are not used to produce exported goods, they do not fall within the Agreement's definition of any of the four assist categories. Therefore, the cost or value of the building materials should not be included in the transaction value of the goods the manufacturer sells the importer.

### *(c) Assists – valuation and apportionment*

Once it has been determined that the buyer supplied an assist to the manufacturer, an amount must be added to the price of the goods to reflect the assist's value. This often involves two aspects: (i) assigning the correct monetary value to the assist, and (ii) apportioning that value to the products the manufacturer made using the assist.

#### (i) Valuing the assist

Assigning the correct value to an assist depends entirely on how it was acquired by the importer:

- If the assist is acquired from a seller not related to the importer, then the value of the assist is the cost of acquisition (i.e. the sale price).
- If the assist was produced by the importer or someone related to him or, if purchased from a related source, its value is the cost to produce it.

The value of an assist, whether based on acquisition cost or cost of production, should also include transport costs to the place where the exported goods are manufactured as well as any duties and taxes that are not refunded.

This is broad guidance, and does not deal with many FAQs, such as …

**Q. What if the buyer provided the manufacturer with equipment that the buyer had previously used in other operations?**

A. If the importer sends used tools, dies or molds to the seller for use in manufacture, then the value of the equipment is original cost of acquisition or production, adjusted downward to reflect the use.

**Q. What if the buyer rented the equipment he supplied to the manufacturer?**

A. The value of the assist is the cost of the lease or rental.

**Q. What if the buyer repaired or customized a tool before sending it free to the manufacturer?**

A. If assist has been repaired or modified, value should reflect the cost of repairs or modifications

**Q. What if the buyer simply copied the design drawings from a publicly available source?**

A. If the design documents are in the public domain, their value is only the cost to obtain copies.

**Q. What if the buyer supplied design work to the seller, but some of the design work was done in the country of importation, and some outside?**

A. In cases where production of the element in question involves a number of countries over a period of time, the adjustment should be limited to the value actually added to that element outside the country of importation.

**(ii) Apportionment**

The tools, equipment or other assists supplied by the buyer will often be used by the manufacturer to produce hundreds or more units of the imported product. The manufacturer may deliver some portion to the buyer in later shipments, keep and sell other units in his own market, or ship still other units to customers in other countries.

This presents the issue of "apportionment." The value of the assist must be allocated in a reasonable way over the manufacturer's entire production. A "reasonable" allocation might include:

- allocate the full cost of the assist to the first shipment imported
- allocate the full cost of the assist over quantity of units produced up to first shipment
- allocate the full cost of the assist over the anticipated production. Generally, the method of allocation will be that requested by the importer, provided that:
  - the method of apportionment is in accordance with generally accepted accounting principles (GAAP) and
  - the importer can produce documentary evidence (if necessary) to justify the method.

### Test your knowledge – apportionment of assists

An Italian importer sends the US manufacturer special tools required for manufacture of sports cars. The Italian importer purchased the tools from a specialty shop in Italy for $1,000 and delivered them free of charge to the US manufacturer. The tools have a useful life of forty cars.

The US manufacturer uses the tools to produce forty cars. He intends to ship twenty cars to Italy, and twenty to Canada, to the Italian company's subsidiary.

The first consignment (five cars) arrives in Italy. What should the importer declare to Italian customs authorities as the customs value?

For the answers, see p. 91.

### (d) *Royalties and license fees*

> ***Article 8(1)(c)***
>
> 1. In determining the customs value under the provisions of Article 1, there shall be added to the price actually paid or payable for the imported goods:
>
> ...
>
> (c) royalties and licence fees related to the goods being valued that the buyer must pay, either directly or indirectly, as a condition of sale of the goods being valued, to the extent that such royalties and fees are not included in the price actually paid or payable;

**Article 8** requires "royalties and license fees" that are paid by the buyer as a condition of the sale of the imported goods to be included in transaction value.

The phrase "royalties and license fees" usually describes the compensation that is paid for rights to use some form of intellectual property, such as patents, trade secrets, trademarks, or copyrights.[19] Royalties or license fees may also be paid for rights to other intangible assets, such as franchise or exclusive marketing rights. Often, the amount of a royalty or license fee is calculated on the basis of the number of patented (or trademarked or copyrighted) units that the licensee manufactures, sells or uses, or on the percentage of the profits the licensee realizes in the sales. These fees might also be calculated as fixed payments per unit of time.

More information about intellectual property rights generally can be found at the Intellectual Property gateway page on the WTO website (www.wto.org/english/tratop_e/trips_e/trips_e.htm).

A customs valuation issue arises when these royalties or licensee fees are paid in connection with an import transaction. For example, a buyer may pay a fee for the exclusive rights to sell the imported goods within a particular geographical area and/or to use the seller's trademark on the imported goods. Or, a buyer may pay a royalty for rights to use an invention imported from the

[19] An Interpretative Note to Article 8 thus states: "royalties and license fees referred to in paragraph 1(c) of Article 8 may include, among other things, payments in respect to patents, trade marks and copyrights."

seller. A more challenging, but not uncommon, example is when a buyer pays a license fee for patents and know-how required to manufacture and sell finished goods using, in part or in whole, raw materials or components imported from the licencor.

**IP LICENCING ARRANGEMENTS**

*Patent license*: A pharmaceutical company may licence a foreign company to produce medicines under a patented process for sale in that foreign market. In return, the foreign company agrees to pay a royalty or fee of 3 percent of profits on sales.

*Trademark license*: The same pharmaceutical company may authorize the foreign company to sell the medicine under the well-known trademark of the pharmaceutical company, in return for an additional royalty payment.

*Copyright license*: An owner of a book or record or film may authorize a foreign company to copy and sell in that foreign market the book, record or film.

Under the **Annex III.6** definition of transaction value, "*all* payments actually made or to be made as a condition of sale of the imported goods by the buyer to seller, or by the buyer to a third party to satisfy an obligation of the seller" are to be considered part of the price of the goods. Thus, the customs valuation problem presented by royalties or license fees is whether they are in fact part of the consideration the buyer pays for the goods themselves, as opposed to *bona-fide* rights apart from and in addition to ownership of the imported goods.

To settle these questions, **Article 8** sets out three separate conditions that must be met before a separate royalty or license fee paid by the buyer is added to customs value:

### (i) Condition 1: the payment must be "related to the goods being valued"

The royalty or license fee must be related to the imported goods.

If the imported goods are themselves the subject of the license, then the payment is clearly "related to the goods being valued." For example, a royalty is "related to the goods being valued" if the imported goods themselves bear the licenced trademark or are manufactured using a licenced patent or know-how.

The more difficult questions can arise when the imported goods are subject to further manufacture, assembly or mixing in the importing country, and the payment is due on the sale of the finished product.

For example, a royalty may be paid on the number of units of medicine tablets produced or sold in the importing country using a patented active ingredient imported from the licencor. In such cases, a close examination of the licencing and sales agreements is required to determine the relationship between the royalty and the imported goods. It may be that, where the processing operations change the identity of the imported goods, the royalty paid on the finished product can no longer fairly be said to "relate to the goods under valuation" but to a new and different product.

**IS THE ROYALTY RELATED TO THE GOODS UNDER VALUATION?**

| YES | NO |
|---|---|
| Buyer pays seller a royalty for each box of juice he produces in the importing country. The juice is made by simply diluting with ordinary water a patented concentrate the buyer imported from the seller. | In an audit, customs finds that the buyer paid the seller a royalty for know-how required to manufacture automobile engines in the country of importation using domestic and imported parts. Customs is considering whether this royalty should be added to value of hoses imported from the seller for use in the production of the cars. |
| **CONCLUSION**: Royalty IS related to the imported concentrate. | **CONCLUSION**: Royalty is NOT related to the imported parts and materials, but to the finished goods made in the importing country. |
| See WCO Advisory Opinion 4.4. | US Customs Ruling 547761 (March 14, 2002). |

An **Interpretative Note** identifies one kind of payment that is not added to transaction value: "charges for the right to reproduce the imported goods in the country of importation shall not be added." This may apply to cases where the importer is charged for rights to duplicate the original – such as copies of an imported master audio or video tape – as well as rights to reproduce the concept or idea of the original in other goods, such as the use of an imported prototype in domestic production of goods.[20] In these kinds of cases, it might

[20] This is the interpretation of the US customs administration, for example:

> [t]he right to reproduce denotes that an idea or an original work is incorporated in, or reflected by, the imported merchandise, and the right is reserved to reproduce that idea or work in other merchandise by using the imported merchandise. The concept of the right to reproduce relates only to the following classes of merchandise: originals or copies of artistic or scientific works; originals or copies of models and industrial drawings; model machines and prototypes; and plant and animal species.

19 Code of Federal Regulations Sec. 152.103(h) (2009). The WCO Technical Committee's Commentary 19.1 is to similar effect.

be said that such payments are not for the imported goods but for other goods (the goods "reproduced" from the imported original).

### (ii) Condition 2: the buyer must pay, directly or indirectly, as a condition of sale

The question that must be answered here is: could the buyer purchase the imported goods without paying the royalty? If not, the royalty amount is paid *for* the goods, and must be added to the price.

The terms of the sales and licencing agreements may answer this question directly by, for example, explicitly providing that the failure to pay the royalty shall terminate the seller's obligation to deliver the goods. More likely, however, the contract terms will not be dispositive, and an examination of all the facts and circumstances surrounding the transaction will be required to determine whether the sale of goods is dependent on payment of the royalty.

The answer to the question may turn on the type of intellectual property rights involved, as well as whether the payment is made to the seller or to a third party. For example, if the royalty is paid for rights to a patent necessary to manufacture the imported goods, it is likely a condition of sale, because the goods could not be produced and exported to the buyer if the patent fee is not paid.

On the other hand, payments made for rights related to the marketing or distribution of goods *after* importation might be excluded from the customs value. This is suggested by the **Interpretative Note to Article 8(1)(c)**:

> [p]ayments made by the buyer for the right to distribute or resell the imported goods shall not be added to the price actually paid or payable for the imported goods if such payments are not a condition of the sale for export to the country of importation of the imported goods.

In this scenario, the buyer may pay a fee for the right to be the exclusive distributor of the goods within a particular territory. Or, the buyer may pay for the right to use a trademark in connection with the resale of the goods in the importing country.

Because the fee or royalty is related to rights of resale of the goods after importation, the buyer may be able to import the goods from the seller without paying the royalty. As always, this conclusion depends on the facts of the particular case. If the licencor is an unrelated third party it is more likely the payment is not a condition of sale. If the licencor is the seller or related to the seller, it is more likely that there is a dependency between the royalty payment and transfer of the goods. In such cases, the licencor may be in a position to prevent the sale if the buyer fails to make the payment.

**(iii) Condition 3: the payment is not already included in the price actually paid or payable**

This condition simply repeats the general conditions applicable to all Article 8 adjustments. Simply stated, the same payment should not be counted twice in customs value.

**TEST YOUR KNOWLEDGE – ROYALTIES AND LICENSE FEES**

1. A UK company grants a US company an exclusive license to manufacture, use and sell its patented automobile switchgears. In return, the US company agrees to pay a royalty equal to 50 percent of the net revenue it earns from sales of the switchgears it manufactures and sells in the United States. To aid the US company in manufacture, the UK company provides technical information and instructions, as well as models or prototypes of the automobile switchgears.
   Upon importation of these prototypes into the United States, the importer claims that the price paid or payable should <u>not</u> include the royalty payment. Is he right?
2. A US company manufactures medicines under a patent license from a Canadian research company. The US company sells the finished medicines to a company in Italy. The sale price does not include a royalty, but the US company requires the Italian company to pay the fee directly to the Canadian research company, the patent owner. Upon importation of the medicines into Italy, should customs add the royalty fee to the sale price?
3. An Italian firm buys a set of phonograph records of a musical performance from a US manufacturer. The recording is of a Canadian musician. When the Italian firm resells the records in Italy, Italian law requires payment of a royalty of 3 percent of the sale price to the Canadian musician. The payment does not accrue to the manufacturer directly or indirectly, nor does the US manufacturer make the payment a condition of the export sale. Should customs add the royalty payment to the price the Italian firm paid for the imported records?

For the answers, see p. 91.

## 2.2.5 PROCEEDS

*Article 8(1)(d)*

1. In determining the customs value under the provisions of Article 1, there shall be added to the price actually paid or payable for the imported goods:

...

(d) the value of any part of the proceeds of any subsequent resale, disposal or use of the imported goods that accrues directly or indirectly to the seller.

**Article 8** requires any "proceeds" associated with the resale or use of imported goods which accrue to the seller to be included in transaction value.

What are these "proceeds"? Proceeds arise in transactions where the seller will receive some portion of the revenue or profits that the buyer realizes on resale, disposal or use of the goods after importation.

> **Proceeds v. Consignments**
>
> Remember – transaction value requires an export sale, and therefore cannot be used if the goods are imported on consignment.
>
> In transactions involving proceeds, the importer is not a consignee. He has purchased and takes title to the imported goods. The parties have simply agreed to delay payment of the full purchase price until revenue is generated on resale, distribution or use of the imported goods.

This might occur, for example, where imported goods are new or experimental in nature and the market price is not established, or perhaps the seller wishes to ease the buyer's cash-flow difficulty. A common use is in the video movie rental business, where the purchase price of the movie is very high, the rental charges low, and the popularity of the movie among consumers uncertain. Whatever the motive, the proceeds are as much a part of the price for the goods as if the buyer agreed to a single payment up front.

Proceeds should not be confused with dividends or any other payments made by the buyer to the seller that do not directly relate to the imported goods.

Dividends are payments made against the overall profit realized by a given company, rather than profit realized on sale of a given product.

A practical difficulty concerning transactions involving proceeds is the amount of these kinds of payments may not be known until some time after goods have been imported and released by customs for sale in the country. As we shall see in section 4.2, below, in these kinds of situations, where customs is unable to make a final valuation determination at the time the goods are presented for customs clearance, **Article 13** of the Agreement requires customs to release the goods to the importer, subject to the importer's guarantee of payment of the duties that may be owed once valuation is finalized. A transaction involving proceeds is a typical case where this "conditional release" procedure is used to delay the final valuation.

The question may arise, however, "how long must customs wait after the importation to receive the information necessary to finalize customs value?" The answer depends on whether the resale, use or disposal of the goods occurs within the time frame allowed under national legislation for delay of final valuation.

**National legislation – proceeds**

*Example*: A buyer contracts to import a new product. Not knowing whether the product ultimately will sell in the United States, the buyer agrees to pay the seller initially $1 per unit with an additional $1 per unit to be paid upon the sale of each unit in the United States. **Assuming the resale price in the United States can be determined in a reasonable period of time, the transaction value of each unit would be $2. Otherwise, the transaction value could not be determined for want of sufficient information.**

*Source*: US Customs regulation (19 C.F.R. 152.103(g) (emphasis added).

As stated in **Article 8.3** of the WTO Customs Valuation Agreement, the adjustments for proceeds can be made only on the basis of objective and quantifiable data. If such data cannot be found within the delayed period – or at all – then the transaction value method cannot be used, and the next valuation method must be considered.

**Test your knowledge – proceeds**

1. An Italian company purchases pharmaceutical products from a US manufacturer. The Italian company agrees to pay the US manufacturer $10,000 for the products upon importation, plus 5 percent of its gross sales proceeds realized on the imported goods in Italy over one year. Should the 5 percent payment be added to the price of the goods ($10,000)? What problems do you foresee with this kind of transaction?
2. The Italian company is the subsidiary of the US manufacturer. At the end of the financial year, the Italian company remits to the US company 75 percent of its net profit realized over that year. Should you add this amount to the price of the pharmaceutical products in order to calculate the transaction value?

For the answers, see p. 92.

### 2.2.6 International transport costs

*Article 8(2)*

2. In framing its legislation, each Member shall provide for the inclusion in or the exclusion from the customs value, in whole or in part, of the following:
(a) the cost of transport of the imported goods to the port or place of importation;
(b) loading, unloading and handling charges associated with the transport of the imported goods to the port or place of importation; and
(c) the cost of insurance.

The Agreement provides WTO Member countries the option of including or excluding from customs value some or all international transport costs and associated loading, handling, and shipping insurance charges. Most Members have chosen to include these transport costs in customs value. Whichever option a country chooses, the Agreement requires that the choice be positively reflected in its legislation.

It may seem curious that an Agreement which is intended to promote "greater uniformity" in customs valuation specifically allows Members to treat transport costs differently. Largely, the anomaly is due to WTO Members' wishes to carry over into the Agreement the treatment given transport costs under their respective predecessor valuation systems.[21] As noted in our discussion of the history of the Agreement in section 1.2, while the ninety plus countries applying the Brussels Definition of Value prior to the adoption of the GATT Valuation Code included the costs of international transport in customs value, a small but important group of countries, including the United States, Australia, and New Zealand, used an f.o.b.-based valuation system.[22]

The transport and related costs that can be included are part or all of the "cost[s] … to the port or place of importation." WTO Members are free to define for themselves what is meant by "place of importation." For example, a country may define the importation point as the land frontier where the goods first cross the border of the country, and thereby exclude the cost of transport from the border to the place of unloading or where the first customs office is situated.

Alternatively, the port or place of importation might be the inland Customs point where the goods are first reported, and thus the cost of the inward journey from the frontier would be included in the customs value.

In any event, the Agreement makes clear that any charges related to transport after the point or place of importation – regardless how it is defined by the country – are to be excluded from customs value if they can be distinguished from the price of the goods.

[21] "We have also recognized that at present some systems are based on a c.i.f. concept and some on an f.o.b. basis. Whilst it would be clearly desirable to establish a single approach we have taken the view that, at least in these negotiations, it is unlikely that we shall all be in a position to agree either on f.o.b. or on c.i.f. as a unique basis. We have therefore made provision for those countries which wish to apply the rules on a c.i.f. basis, to add to the price of the goods, to the extent that it is not already included, the transport costs." GATT Multilateral Trade Negotiations Group "Non-Tariff Measures" Sub-Group "Customs Matters," *Statement Made by the Commission of the European Communities at the Meeting of the Sub-Group of November 15, 1977*, MTN/NTM/W/126 (Nov. 21, 1977).

[22] See Chapter 1 above, text accompanying note 34.

**TEST YOUR KNOWLEDGE – TRANSPORT CHARGES**

If the seller provides the transport free, at no charge to the buyer, must the cost of the transport nevertheless be included in customs value?

For the answers, see p. 92.

### 2.2.7 NO OTHER ADDITIONS

The Article 8 list of additions to price that is described in this chapter – sellers' commissions, assists, royalties and proceeds, etc. – is exclusive. That is, these and only these Article 8 payments and costs may be added to the price paid or payable for the goods.

| *Article 8(4)* |
|---|
| 4. No additions shall be made to the price actually paid or payable in determining the customs value except as provided in this Article. |

However, this statement should be understood in the context of the expansive definition of the "price paid or payable" under the Agreement, discussed in section 2.1, above, which is:

> all payments actually made or to be made as a condition of sale of the imported goods, by the buyer to the seller, or by the buyer to a third party to satisfy an obligation of the seller.

Under this definition, any payment that a buyer makes, if it can be shown to be a condition of sale of the imported goods, is not an "addition to price"; it is part of the price itself.

What are the additional payments or services provided by a buyer that were intended to be excluded from transaction value by Article 8(4)? Some suggestion might be found in the negotiation history of the Agreement, where various proposals were made to expand the list of Article 8 additions, but were ultimately rejected by the GATT parties. These rejected proposals for Article 8 additions included:

- advertizing by the buyer in the country of importation
- warranty and guarantee services provided by the buyer in the country of importation
- ADP or accounting services provided by the buyer to the seller
- costs of storing goods in the country of exportation.[23]

[23] GATT Multilateral Trade Negotiations Group "Non-Tariff Measures" Sub-Group "Customs Matters," *Customs Valuation – Revision*, MTN/NTM/W/175/Rev.1 (November 6, 1978) (revised negotiating text).

Some WTO Members have thus explicitly provided in their national legislation that costs for these kinds of services provided by the buyer shall not be added to the transaction value.[24]

## 2.3 WHEN TRANSACTION VALUE CANNOT BE USED

> ***Article 1(1)(a)–(d)***
>
> 1. The customs value of imported goods shall be the transaction value … provided:
>
> (a) that there are no restrictions as to the disposition or use of the goods by the buyer other than restrictions which:
>
> (i) are imposed or required by law or by the public authorities in the country of importation;
>
> (ii) limit the geographical area in which the goods may be resold; or
>
> (iii) do not substantially affect the value of the goods;
>
> (b) that the sale or price is not subject to some condition or consideration for which a value cannot be determined with respect to the goods being valued;
>
> (c) that no part of the proceeds of any subsequent resale, disposal or use of the goods by the buyer will accrue directly or indirectly to the seller, unless an appropriate adjustment can be made in accordance with the provisions of Article 8; and
>
> (d) that the buyer and seller are not related, or where the buyer and seller are related, that the transaction value is acceptable for customs purposes under the provisions of paragraph 2.

The alternatives to the transaction value method under the Agreement can be used only if "the customs value of goods cannot be determined under the provisions of Article 1." As we have seen, the transaction value method is primary, and is used by customs administrations in practice to value the great majority of import transactions. In some transactions, however, a transaction value may simply not exist or, even if there is a transaction value, it cannot be used as a reliable basis for customs valuation.

The starting point for the transaction value method is the price paid or payable for the imported goods when "*sold* for export." If there is no sale, then there can be no transaction value, and one of the alternative valuation

[24] For example, the EU customs legislation provides that "all activities relating to advertising and promoting the sale of the goods in question and all activities relating to warranties or guarantees in respect of them" undertaken by the buyer, even if the buyer is obligated under an agreement with the seller to provide these services, shall not be considered indirect payments included in transaction value. Article 149, Commission Regulation (EEC) No. 2454/93 of 2 July 1993.

methods must be used. The typical cases where goods are exported without a sale include:[25]

- Gifts, samples and promotional items shipped free of charge to the buyer.
  In these kinds of transactions, there is no price paid by the buyer for the goods (they are free), and therefore no sale takes place.
- Goods shipped on consignment.
  In a consignment transaction, the exporter will ship goods to a commission agent in the country of importation, who will try to find a buyer. However, the goods remain the property of the exporter (at least, until the agent is successful), so there is no sale for export.
- Goods shipped by parent company to branch offices.
  A sale requires a buyer and seller. Generally, branch offices are not considered legal entities separate from their parent company. In these transactions, it is as if the seller is shipping the goods to himself.
- Goods imported under hire, lease or loan.
  These goods remain the property of the exporter; ownership or title to the goods does not pass to the importer. Accordingly, there is no sale.

In addition, a transaction value cannot be determined where customs does not have the information necessary for the appraisement, whether from the importer or other sources. For example, "objective and quantifiable data" is required by **Article 8.3** in order to make an addition under Article 8 to the price; if such data are missing, then an addition cannot be made and a transaction value cannot be calculated. Similarly, under the WTO Ministerial **Decision Regarding Cases Where Customs Administrations Have Reasons to Doubt the Truth or Accuracy of the Declared Value** (discussed in section 4.3, below), if customs is not satisfied that the importer's declaration is truthful and accurate, it may reject the use of transaction value.

Finally, apart from these implicit restrictions on use of Article 1, **Article 1(1)(a)–(d)** expressly disallows the use of a transaction value in four specific situations, as follows:

1. the buyer is subject to certain restrictions on his use or disposition of the imported goods which substantially affect the value of the goods
2. the sale or price is subject to some condition or consideration for which a value cannot be determined with respect to the goods being valued

[25] These examples appear and are further elaborated in the Technical Committee's Advisory Opinion 1.1, "The Concept of 'Sale' in the Agreement."

3. proceeds accrue to the seller when the buyer resells, disposes of or uses the imported goods, and the appropriate adjustment to the sale price cannot be made
4. the sale is between a related buyer and seller, and the parties' price is not acceptable for customs purposes.

In the main, these might be understood as transactions that involve conditions such that a price paid for the goods cannot be determined accurately or that the declared price cannot be considered an acceptable representation of the "actual value" of the goods within the meaning of GATT Article VII (that is, a "price ... in the ordinary course of trade under fully competitive conditions").

These express limitations on the use of transaction value are discussed in turn below.

### 2.3.1 Restrictions on distribution and use of goods

**Article 1(1)(a)** provides that the transaction value method cannot be used if the buyer is subject to certain "restrictions as to the disposition or use of the goods."

Why not use transaction value when these kinds of restrictions are present? If a seller imposes restrictions on how or where or to whom the buyer can use or resell the imported goods, would not the price the parties negotiate take into account the impact of the restrictions, and thus reflect the (possibly diminished) market value of the goods?

There is no mention of the rationale underlying this provision in the written record of GATT valuation negotiations. However, it may have to do with doubts about the *bona fides* of such sales.[26] In commercial law, a "sale" is commonly defined as the passing of title to the goods from the seller to the buyer for a price.[27] By taking title to the goods, the buyer obtains ownership and the

[26] This is the rationale that appears to have been the accepted by the government of the United States, one of the main participants in the Tokyo Round negotiations on valuation, as indicated by proceedings in the US Congress at the time. See US Congress House Report No. 317, 96th Cong., 1st Sess. 82 (1979) ("The Committee understands that the purpose of these limitations is to insure that a particular transaction is bona fide and 'at arm's length' before the transaction value standard will apply."). In fact, the text of Article 1(1)(a) of the Agreement appears to have been taken, with some modification, from the pre-existing US value law. Under that US law, an export sale price for imported goods could be used as the basis for customs value provided such goods were "freely sold ... or offered for sale." That US law further provided that if the purchaser were subject to "restrictions as to the disposition or use of the merchandise" the goods could not be considered "freely sold," unless those restrictions were of a type that "(i) are imposed or required by law, (ii) limit the price at which or the territory in which the merchandise may be resold, or (iii) do not substantially affect the value of the merchandise to usual purchasers at wholesale." 19 US Code 1401a(f)(1) (1976).

[27] For example, this definition of a sale appears in the "Uniform Commercial Code," which is a common basis of commercial legislation in the United States.

right to use or dispose of the goods as he chooses, subject to requirements of local laws and regulations. However, if these usual ownership rights do not pass to the buyer or are substantially restricted – whether due to the terms of the sales contract or otherwise – then there is a question whether the transaction can be considered a genuine "sale," as that term is normally understood in commercial practice.

It is important to note that this restriction in the Agreement on the use of transaction value has a narrow application. In particular, the Agreement defines three exceptions to the prohibition which may cover many or most cases where restrictions on rights of resale or use on imported goods appear in practice. Under these exceptions, transaction value may be applied, if the restrictions on use or disposition of the goods:

- are imposed or required by law or by the public authorities in the country of importation;
  These might include safety, health or environmental controls on use of a product, or consumer labeling or conditions as to time and place regulated products can be sold (e.g. alcohol, firearms, etc.).
- limit the geographical area in which goods can be resold; *or*
  See the sample contract clause (above).
- do not "substantially affect" the value of the goods.

**RESTRICTIONS ON RESALE**

APPOINTMENT. Seller hereby appoints Reseller, and Reseller accepts such appointment, to act as a non-exclusive reseller of Products only to Customers located in the Territory. Sale of Products to other resellers or Reseller's affiliates is strictly prohibited. Reseller will only sell the Products in face-to-face transactions from physical store outlets located in the Territory, and will not market or sell the Products using any Internet site or mail order catalog without specific written authorization by Handspring.
TERRITORY. "Territory" means the United States of America.

*Sample sales contract clause*

The practical application of this last exception may be the most challenging: how does one determine whether a restriction on resale or use "substantially affect[s]" the value of the imported goods?

A commentary issued by the Technical Committee suggests that this must be a case-by-case determination. A number of factors may be considered, but the relative importance of each must depend upon the circumstances of the particular transaction:

> These factors include the nature of the restriction, the nature of the imported goods, the nature of the industry concerned and its commercial practices, and whether the effect on the value is commercially significant. Since these factors may vary from case to case, it would not be proper to apply a fixed criterion in this respect.[28]

The commentary further suggests that one should consider whether the restriction is "usual" for the industry concerned. This suggestion also appears in an **Interpretative Note to Article 1**, which provides the following example:

> Among restrictions which would not render a price actually paid or payable unacceptable are restrictions which do not substantially affect the value of the goods. An example of such restrictions would be the case where a seller requires a buyer of automobiles not to sell or exhibit them prior to a fixed date which represents the beginning of a model year.

The restriction described in the Interpretative Note does not prevent the importer from reselling the imported cars, but only imposes a delay on the time of resale for reasons that are not inconsistent with marketing practices in that industry. If this kind of restriction is "usual" in the industry concerned, then it cannot be said to "substantially affect" the value of the imported goods.

### Test your knowledge – do these sales restrictions prevent use of transaction value?

1. Mr. X purchases a dangerous chemical from abroad. He applies for an import license for this chemical and the government grants the license only on the condition that Mr. X use the chemical for the purposes stated in his application. Does this restriction on Mr. X's use of the imported chemical mean that transaction value cannot be used?
2. Mr. T has invented a chemical product that can be used as a cleaning product or as a food additive. Mr. X wishes to buy the chemical to use as a cleaning product in France. Mr. T has a patent in France for the product for both uses but he sells the product to Mr. X only for use as a cleaning product. Mr. X cannot use the product in France as a food additive without infringing Mr. T's patent. Does this restriction on Mr. X's use of the imported product mean that transaction value cannot be used?
3. The XYZ Charity purchases a new car from abroad for a nominal fee. The sale, however, is subject to the restriction that the imported car may be used only for charitable, non-commercial purposes. Can the imported car be valued on the basis of the transaction value (the nominal fee paid by XYZ)?

For the answers, see p. 93.

[28] Technical Committee, Meaning of the Term "Restrictions" in Article 1.1(a)(iii), Commentary 12.1, in *WCO Compendium*.

### 2.3.2 Price subject to condition

**Article 1(1)(b)** of the Agreement states that transaction value cannot be used in sales where: "The sale or price is … subject to some condition or consideration for which a value cannot be determined with respect to the good being valued."

This expresses – again – the requirement that the elements of transaction value must be "quantifiable." Clearly, if the consideration given by the buyer in exchange for the goods cannot be quantified, it will not be possible to determine the price of the goods accurately.

The examples provided in the **Interpretative Notes** indicate that this prohibition was intended to cover so-called "countertrade" transactions and "tie-in" sales. See **Interpretative Note to Article 1, paragraph 1(b)**.

#### COUNTERTRADE

A means of trading, whereby the exporter is required to accept goods or other instruments of trade in part or whole payment for his sales. This allows the buying country to save foreign currency. Countertrade is thus used by countries experiencing foreign exchange shortages. Countertrade may take different forms, including barter, buy-back or compensation, counterpurchase, offset requirements, swap, switch, evidence or clearing accounts. As a means of payment, countertrade is not encouraged by international and multinational financial institutions as the price-setting mechanisms underlying such transactions frequently lack transparency.

1. Barter is the oldest and simplest method of countertrade by which goods are exchanged against other goods of equivalent value. It is the only way of undertaking trade with no or little money involved. As it does not involve the use of money, it is often used by countries with blocked currencies.
2. Counterpurchase is one of the most common forms of countertrade. Under this arrangement, the exporter undertakes to buy goods from the importer or from a company nominated by the importer, or agrees to arrange for their purchase by a third party, within a specific period (usually one to five years). Both parties pay for their purchases in cash (at least in part) but commit themselves, by signing a "protocol" contract, to fulfil the purchase counter obligation. The goods being sold in exchange are typically unrelated but may be equivalent in value.
3. In offset, the exporter agrees to use goods produced in the importer's country as an input of the products being sold, and up to an agreed percentage of the original sale. In a direct offset, the exported goods are an integral part of the final product, and the agreement involves a co-production arrangement based on the transfer of production technology to the importing country. In an indirect offset the selling country agrees to purchase unrelated products from the importing country.
4. In a compensation or buy-back deal, exporters of equipment, technology, or even entire plants, agree to purchase a certain percentage of the output of the facility as payment.

5. Switch is a complex form of barter, involving a chain of buyers and sellers in different markets and countries, based on the multilateral clearance of bilateral trade imbalances. A specialized countertrade house will typically buy (at a discount) from country A the value of its bilateral trade surplus with country B, and sell it at full value to company or country C, which has a bilateral trade deficit with party A. The trading house will often have to take title to certain goods, which it then has to sell against hard currency.

*Source*: UNCTAD/WTO International Trade Center Glossary on Trade Financing Terms (2000) (www.intracen.org/tfs/docs/glossary/ce.htm).

A tie-in sale occurs where the price for imported goods is subject to the buyer's agreement to purchase other goods from the seller or another person.

### Tying arrangements

"The producer of a desired product may sell it only to those who also buy a second product from him. The manufacturer of color film, for example, might sell it only to those who buy black-and-white film from him. In the customary terminology, the manufacturer 'ties' the sale of the 'tying' product (color film) to sales of the 'tied' product (black-and-white film). Such a tying arrangement might be reflected in a formal agreement, a refusal to continue selling color film to those who buy their black-and-white film elsewhere, or a package sale requiring the buyer to take both products simultaneously."

Phillip Areeda, Antitrust Analysis, 438–39 (1967).

In such cases, the price of the imported goods is influenced by another transaction. The price the buyer pays for the goods he wants may be lower than if he were able to purchase them separately, but the price of the "tied" goods may be higher. The extent to which one transaction influences the price of the other may not be possible to quantify.

There is an important caution in the **Interpretative Note to Article 1(1)(b)**, however: "conditions or considerations relating to the production or marketing of the imported goods," whether or not "quantifiable," do not preclude the use of the transaction value method (emphasis added). In particular:

> [t]he fact that the buyer furnishes the seller with engineering and plans undertaken in the country of importation shall not result in rejection of the transaction value for purposes of Article 1.
>
> Likewise, if the buyer undertakes on the buyer's own account, even though by agreement with the seller, activities relating to the marketing of the imported goods, the value of these activities is not part of the customs value nor shall such activities result in rejection of the transaction value.

As noted previously, the cost or value of advertizing or similar activities that the buyer undertakes on his own account to prepare the market for the imported goods, even if they benefit the seller, shall not be included in the transaction value of the imported goods. See section 2.1, above.

In the case of engineering and design plans that a buyer might be required under the sales contract to supply to the seller, **Article 8** of the Agreement provides that the cost or value shall not be included in customs value if the design work is done in the country of importation. See section 2.2 above, concerning the additions to price required by Article 8.

Consequently, whether or not the cost or value of such marketing activities or engineering plans can be quantified should have no bearing on customs value.

### 2.3.3 PROCEEDS

**Article 1(1)(b)** of the Agreement states that the transaction value method cannot be used if any "... part of the proceeds of any subsequent resale, disposal or use of the goods by the buyer will accrue directly or indirectly to the seller, unless an appropriate adjustment can be made in accordance with the provisions of Article 8."

As discussed in section 2.2 regarding the **Article 8** additions to price, "proceeds" – or payments that a seller receives on the resale, distribution or use of the goods after importation – must be added to the price of the goods when determining a transaction value. And as also discussed, **Article 8.3** requires that the addition for proceeds or any other Article 8 element must be based on "objective and quantifiable data." Accordingly, if "objective and quantifiable data" are not available to allow the adjustment for proceeds, it is implicit in Article 8.3, and explicit here in Article 1(1)(b), that a transaction value cannot be calculated.

Why does the Agreement single out proceeds here? Surely if the appropriate adjustment cannot be made for *any* Article 8 element, the transaction value method cannot be used?

The special focus on proceeds in Article 1 may be due to the unusual customs administrative problem they present. As noted in our discussion of Article 8 proceeds, because the amount of the proceeds will not ordinarily be known at the time the importer presents the goods to customs, there must be a delay in final valuation until the goods are resold and the proceed amount is realized. If the proceed amount cannot be calculated because, for example, the buyer is unable to resell the goods within a reasonable time after importation, the appropriate adjustment cannot be made under Article 8, and the next method of valuation under the Agreement must be considered.

### 2.3.4 Related-party transactions

Perhaps the most important situation in which transaction value cannot be used is where the buyer and seller are related to each other, and that relationship has influenced the price of the imported goods.

In an arm's-length transaction – one where the buyer and seller do not have any ownership or control of the other, but are each motivated by self-interest to maximize their own profit – the price negotiated represents the market value of the goods.

On the other hand, related-party transactions may not take place under fully competitive conditions and, therefore, the parties' price may have been determined by other than market considerations. These other considerations may be entirely legitimate, such as a desire to reduce tax liability as much as possible, to gain a foothold in a new market, or for other commercial reasons. This does not mean that related parties tend to avoid paying duty, but that pricing decisions between them can be affected by the financial or other interest each has in the other.

For these reasons, and the increasing importance of intra-firm transactions in world trade, valuation of related-party transactions is given special and detailed treatment under the WTO Customs Valuation Agreement.

#### The importance of related-party trade

"Beginning in the 1970's and accelerating in the 1980's, the world economy entered a second phase of development – what is now typically referred to as a phase of 'globalization'. Rapid advances in information technologies and communications, together with the systematic reduction of global trade barriers, have allowed global firms to break up the production process and to locate its various components in different markets around the world. The surge in foreign investment flows represents the most unique feature of the globalization phase. Trade is no longer the sole or even the main vehicle for delivering products and services across borders; investment has become an even more powerful force for integration, as transnational corporations extend their global reach by establishing a direct presence in foreign markets. The cumulative assets of foreign investment have trebled since 1987 – to over US $3 trillion – while the annual sales which these assets generate have overtaken the value of world trade.

But trade is also growing as more and more crossborder transactions take place within companies or their affiliates, and as more and more trade encompasses all phases of the production process – from components and services, to design and engineering. Intrafirm trade within transnational corporations or related partners now accounts for about two-thirds of world trade. And trade as a share of global output has more than tripled since 1950 – from 7 to over 22 per cent. Businesses now trade to invest and invest to trade – to the point where both activities are increasingly part of a single strategy to deliver product across borders."

*Source*: former WTO Director General Renato Ruggiero, Address to the International Industrial Conference (IIC) (September 29, 1997).

### (a) Definition of related parties

**Article 15(4) and (5)**

4. For the purposes of this Agreement, persons shall be deemed to be related only if:

(a) they are officers or directors of one another's businesses;
(b) they are legally recognized partners in business;
(c) they are employer and employee;
(d) any person directly or indirectly owns, controls or holds 5 per cent or more of the outstanding voting stock or shares of both of them;
(e) one of them directly or indirectly controls the other;
(f) both of them are directly or indirectly controlled by a third person;
(g) together they directly or indirectly control a third person; or
(h) they are members of the same family.

5. Persons who are associated in business with one another in that one is the sole agent, sole distributor or sole concessionaire, however described, of the other shall be deemed to be related for the purposes of this Agreement if they fall within the criteria of paragraph 4.

**Article 15** of the WTO Customs Valuation Agreement defines the "related parties." This definition, which seems to have been taken from the pre-Tokyo Round US value law (and which can also be found in the WTO Agreements on Dumping and Countervailing Measures) is not necessarily the same as those used for tax or securities laws, or even in ordinary business parlance.[29]

Under the Agreement, a buyer and seller are considered "related" only if their relationship can be characterized by one of the following eight definitions:

| Family | Members of same or affiliated business enterprises | Financial/legal control |
|---|---|---|
| The buyer and seller are members of the same family | The buyer and seller are legally recognized partners in business | A person owns, controls or holds 5 percent or more of the outstanding voting stock of both buyer and seller |

[29] The pre-GATT Code valuation law of the United States thus defined related parties as:

"(A) Members of a family, including brothers and sisters (whether by the whole or half blood), spouse, ancestors, and lineal descendants;
(B) Any officer or director of an organization and such organization;
(C) Partners;
(D) Employer and employee;
(E) Any person directly or indirectly owning, controlling, or holding with power to vote, 5 per centum or more of the outstanding voting stock or shares of any organization and such organization; and
(F) Two or more persons directly or indirectly controlling, controlled by, or under common control with, any person." (19 US Code §1401a(g)(2) (1976).)

| Family | Members of same or affiliated business enterprises | Financial/legal control |
|---|---|---|
| | The buyer is the employer of the seller, or *vice versa* | The buyer directly or indirectly controls the seller, or *vice versa* |
| | The buyer and seller are officers or directors of one another's businesses | Both buyer and seller are directly or indirectly controlled by a third person<br>Buyer and seller together directly or indirectly control a third person |

Any other relationship between buyer and seller is not in itself a reason to question the use of transaction value. Perhaps most importantly, **Article 15(5)** of the Agreement expressly provides that a sale to a sole agent or sole distributor is NOT considered a related party transaction *unless* the seller and his sole agent/distributor also have one of the eight relationships defined above.

### (i) Family

A buyer and seller are considered related for purposes of the Agreement if they are members of the same family. Clearly, when two members of the same family deal with one another in a sale transaction, there is a strong possibility that the usual, competitive market conditions will not prevail.

A question that is left to individual WTO Members to define in their national legislation or practice is "who is family?" Here is one example:

#### WHO ARE "MEMBERS OF THE SAME FAMILY"? NATIONAL LEGISLATION

Persons shall be deemed to be members of the same family only if they stand in any of the following relationships to one another:

- husband and wife
- parent and child
- brother and sister (whether by whole or half blood)
- grandparent and grandchild
- uncle or aunt and nephew or niece
- parent-in-law and son-in-law or daughter-in-law
- brother-in-law and sister-in-law.

*Source*: Article 143(1)(h), Commission Regulation (EEC) No. 2454/93 of July 2, 1993.

**(ii) Members of the same or affiliated business enterprises**

A buyer and seller are considered related if they are legally recognized partners in business or they are employer and employee.

A business partnership is a legal entity created under commercial law. The Agreement leaves to each WTO Member to define the conditions (if any) under which a business partnership would be recognized under that Member's laws.

A buyer and seller are related if they are **officers and directors of one another's businesses**. This refers to the case of the "interlocking directorate," where both the buyer and seller participate either as executive managers or as directors of each other's business. For example, the chief executive officer of the seller may also act as the president of the buyer. In such positions, that individual can influence or manipulate pricing decisions of one business to the advantage of the other.[30]

**(iii) Financial/legal control**

The previous definitions discussed largely concern relationships involving individuals (employment, family members, partners, directors and officials of businesses). In terms of trade volumes, the more important relationships are those that involve related companies or other related legal entities, such as transfers between a parent and subsidiary company or transfers between affiliates within the same corporate family.[31]

The WTO Valuation Agreement sets out two different tests to determine whether a transfer of goods between two entities shall be considered a related-party transaction: one based on stock ownership; the other based on a concept of "control."

**Stock ownership:** A buyer and seller are related if a **third person directly or indirectly owns, controls, or holds 5 percent or more of the outstanding voting stock of both the buyer and seller**. This definition describes the case where the buyer and seller are members of the same corporate family. One person or entity (the corporate parent) is in a position to exercise influence both on the buyer and seller as a result of an ownership interest it has in each of them. (As the **Interpretative Note to Article 15(4)** makes clear, a "person" could include a legal person, such a company or other business entity, which

[30] Strictly speaking, the definition would deem the director or officers of the two interlocking firms to be related, as opposed to the firms themselves. As such, the definition has limited reach, as it would seem unlikely as a practical matter that directors would sell to each other as individuals, rather than conclude the sale through their respective companies. However, in such cases, the two firms might be considered related under the broader concept of control (see Control concept, below).

[31] For example, nearly 30 percent of all US exports are made to a foreign consignee that is owned by, or who owns, the US exporter. Press Release, US Department of Commerce, US Goods Trade: Imports and Exports by Related Parties 2007 (May 9, 2008) at www.census.gov/foreign-trade/Press-Release/2007pr/aip/related_party/.

owns or controls the buyer and seller, which themselves might also be such business entities.)

Why is voting stock of 5 percent important? Although not said in the Agreement, it was likely intended to mark the boundary between a pure portfolio-type investment, where the investor is interested only in the financial returns from investment in a business, from a direct investment which the investor makes for purposes of exercising management control. This same 5 percent standard appears, for example, in US securities laws, where certain disclosures are required by anyone seeking to acquire more than 5 percent of a company's securities because such offers are considered an effort to gain control of the company. Compare also the OECD/IMF definition of a direct investment.

> ***Direct investment***: is a category of international investment made by a resident entity in one economy (direct investor) with the objective of establishing a lasting interest in an enterprise resident in an economy other than that of the investor (direct investment enterprise). "Lasting interest" implies the existence of a long-term relationship between the direct investor and the enterprise and a significant degree of influence by the direct investor on the management of the direct investment enterprise ... Ownership of 10 percent of the ordinary shares or voting stock is the guideline for determining the existence of a direct investment relationship. An "effective voice in the management", as evidenced by an ownership of at least 10 percent, implies that the direct investor is able to influence, or participate in, the management of an enterprise; absolute control by the foreign investor is not required. (IMF/OECD Glossary of Foreign Direct Investment Terms (1996))

**Control concept:** Stock ownership does not cover all business arrangements whereby one business may be in a position to exert influence over the pricing or other commercial or strategic decisions of another firm. For example, consider these cases:

- The majority shareholder of company S (the seller) is also a director of company B (the buyer).
- Company S (the seller) directs, under a management contract, the day-to-day operations of independent company B (the buyer).
- Company B (the buyer) is a franchisee of company S (the seller).
- Company S (the seller) is the majority creditor of company B (the buyer) or holds a mortgage against its assets.
- Company S (the seller) and Company B (the buyer) together form a joint venture company, Company C, which is the ultimate consignee of the imported goods.

In these kinds of cases – where there is not a relationship in terms of a stock ownership, family, employment etc. – the buyer and seller might nonetheless be considered related **if** one person or entity "directly or indirectly control[s]" the other, or if both directly or indirectly control or are controlled by a third party.

The **Interpretative Note to Article 15** provides the following definition of "control":

> For purposes of this Agreement, one person shall be deemed to control another when the former is legally or operationally in a position to exercise restraint or direction over the latter.

There is no "bright-line" or set of quantitative criteria that can be applied here. What is required by the definition is a case-by-case examination of the circumstances of a particular relationship to determine whether there is control of the nature described in the Interpretative Note.

Perhaps the clearest – and most common – case of legal control within the meaning of the Interpretative Note is the parent-subsidiary corporate relationship, where one firm fully owns or has a controlling interest in the other, and is thereby "legally … in a position to exercise restraint or control" by, *inter alia*, appointment or removal of management or directors of the subsidiary.

Other cases may require closer examination. For example, a seller may be "operationally in a position" to restrain or direct the buyer where the seller's president also acts as the chief operating officer of the buyer. On the other hand, where the president of the exporter is just one of a seven-member committee that directs the buyer, each with an equal vote, the requisite control has been found not to exist, and the buyer and seller therefore not related.[32]

Buyers and sellers typically enter into contracts for sale of goods, and contracts by their nature impose legally-enforceable obligations (i.e. deliver goods within specified period, pay the agreed price, use specified means of transport, etc.). In some cases, one party may be in a stronger bargaining position than the other – such as a franchisor of well-known/high demand trademark products – and the terms and conditions may be one-sided as a consequence. Does the fact that a seller (or buyer) can enforce performance of a sales contract mean that he is "legally … in a position to exercise restraint or control" over the other within the meaning of the Interpretative Note? If so, would not *all* transactions between buyers and seller under contract be considered related-party transactions?

A Technical Committee Explanatory Note answers no:

> It can be concluded that it is not the intent of the Agreement to create a relationship out of every contract or agreement which of their very nature establish legal rights or obligations enforceable under national laws. Therefore the wording of the Interpretative Note to Article 15.4(e)

[32] This was the decision of the US customs administration in Ruling Letter 543425 (September 28, 1985).

> must normally be taken to apply to situations which go beyond usual buyer/seller or distribution agreements and involve a position to exercise restraint or direction in respect of essential aspects relating to the management of the activities of the other person.[33]

A companion Technical Committee Case Study finds that "essential aspects relating to management" include decisions about changes in management personnel, or ownership or voting control, or location of the business. A sales and distribution contract that provides the seller with rights to approve these kinds of decisions by the buyer evidences the kind of control required by the Interpretative Note to Article 15.[34]

### (iv) Sole agent/distributor/concessionaire

**Article 15(5)** emphasizes that a sale to a sole agent or distributor or concessionaire (hereinafter, "sole agent") is not to be considered related-party transaction *unless* the seller and his sole agent fall within one of the eight relationships defined above.

The main purpose of this provision is to distinguish clearly the treatment of sole agents under the WTO Agreement from the treatment of such agents under the BDV.

Generally, an agent or distributor has rights to sell the foreign supplier's goods within a specified geographic region.[35] If the right is "sole," the foreign supplier cannot appoint another agent to sell his good in the same territory.[36] Agents and distributors generally bear their own marketing and sales costs and risks. In compensation, an agent is usually paid a commission on the supplier's sale price of the imported goods, while a distributor is compensated in the form of the resale margin over the price paid to the supplier.

Under the BDV, discounts or other reductions in price granted to "sole agents" or "sole concessionaires" were required to be included in dutiable value. The BDV rationale was that such "privileged" discounts would not be found in a "normal price," i.e. an open market sale between a buyer and seller independent of each other.[37]

[33] WCO, Explanatory Note 4.1: Consideration of Relationship under Article 15.5, Read in Conjunction with Article 15.4 (July 1998).

[34] WCO, Case Study 11.1: Application of Article 15.4(e) Related Party Transactions (July 1999).

[35] A difference between an agent and a distributor is that the agent is authorized by the supplier to enter into sales agreements with customers, on the seller's behalf, but does not take title to the goods. A distributor purchases the imported goods from the foreign seller, and resells the products on to his own customers.

[36] See Cleaver Fulton Rankin, *Agency and Commercial Agents Regulations*, www.investni.com/agency_and_agents.pdf. If the agent or distributor also has "exclusive" rights, then the supplier himself is also prohibited from making direct sales into the territory.

[37] World Customs Organization, *The Brussels Definition of Value and the GATT Valuation Agreement: A Comparison* (1985), 9.

The WTO Valuation Agreement adopts the contrary view – that a distribution or agency contract, even with exclusive rights, is consistent with a normal, arm's-length commercial arrangement. Thus, as **Article 15(4)** indicates, a sole agency or distributor arrangement is no longer, by itself, sufficient to establish that the agent and his supplier are related.

This view of sole agents was resisted both in the Tokyo and Uruguay Round negotiations by a number of developing countries.[38] More recently, the sole agent problem has been described as one of implementation: the difficulty – particularly for customs administrations with limited resources – in obtaining the contract and other commercial documentation necessary to determine whether a sole agent is in fact "controlled" by the foreign seller within the meaning of the Interpretative Note definition.[39]

As noted in section 1.2, the Uruguay Round negotiations produced a WTO Ministerial Decision to prompt the Technical Committee to conduct studies in order to assist developing countries in dealing with the sole agent issue. In response, the Technical Committee has produced a case study on sole agents,[40] as well the revised explanatory note and case study on related parties mentioned in the previous section. Nevertheless, the Agreement's treatment of sole agents continues to be a source of contention.[41]

### *(b) Related parties – tests*

**Article 1(2)** of the WTO Customs Valuation Agreement sets out a structured framework for the analysis of related-party transactions. It requires customs to test the declared price with a series of questions and exchange of communications with the importer, as follows:

[38] In the Tokyo Round, developing countries took the position that the Agreement text "did not deal adequately … with the question of sole agents and distributors" and proposed (without success) that developing countries be permitted to treat these entities as related parties under the Agreement. GATT Multilateral Trade Negotiations, Group "Non-Tariff Measures" Sub-Group "Customs Matters," *Meeting of 3 April 1979*, MTN/NTM/67 (April 5, 1979) (Summing up by chairman of the negotiating subgroup). The Uruguay Round discussions on sole agents are described in section 1.2.

[39] "Article 15.5 put the burden of proving a relationship on the customs administration. It was unlikely that the customs administration in the importing country would have access to pertinent business documentation on contracts that would be necessary to prove such a relationship." WTO, *Report of the Committee on Customs Valuation to the Trade Negotiations Committee on the Implementation-Related Issues in Accordance with Paragraph 12 of the Ministerial Declaration*, G/VAL/49 at 6 (November 25, 2002) (Secretariat summary of rationale for proposal to treat sole agents as related parties).

[40] WCO, Case Study 9.1: Sole Agents, Sole Distributors and Sole Concessionaires.

[41] See G/VAL/49 at 6 (November 25, 2002) (India proposal to modify the agreement provisions on sole agents).

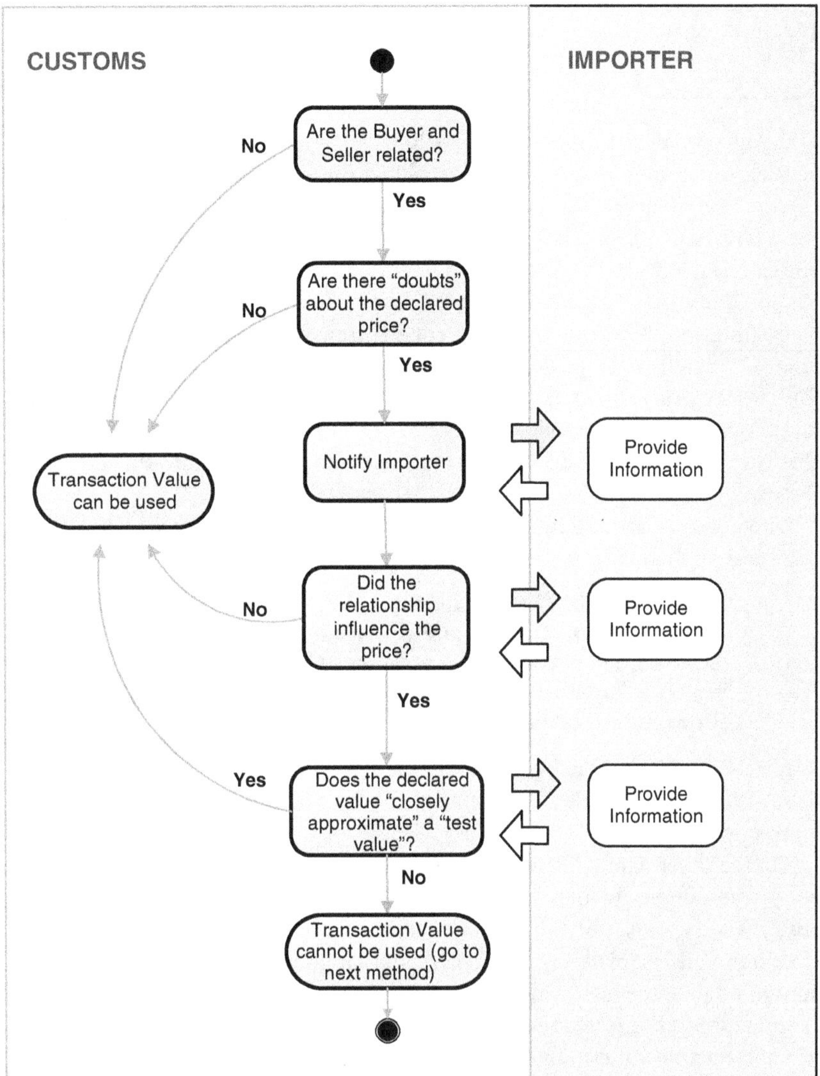


Figure 7 Analysis of a related-party price

A buyer and seller are related if their relationship is one defined in **Article 15** of the Agreement. See discussion of "Definition of related parties," above.

Are there "doubts" about the declared price?

The Agreement does not permit customs to reject a declared price simply because the buyer and seller are related. Based on available information, whether supplied by the importer or obtained from other sources, customs must have some grounds for finding that the buyer and seller's relationship influenced the price.

Nor does the Agreement require that customs examine *every* related-party transaction before it can accept the transaction value. Given the volume of related-party trade, it would be impractical for customs to do so. Rather, the Agreement intends that customs select for examination those related-party transactions "[w]here there are doubts about the acceptability of the price." See **Interpretative Note to Article 1, Paragraph 2** (below).

There may in fact be related-party transaction values about which customs will have no doubts:

> For example, the Customs administration may have previously examined the relationship, or it may already have detailed information concerning the buyer and the seller, and may already be satisfied from such examination or information that the relationship did not influence the price. (**Interpretative Note to Article 1, Paragraph 2**)

Similarly, if identical or similar goods were previously imported, customs may be satisfied that the declared value is consistent with those accepted in the prior transactions.

On the other hand, customs may have doubts about the validity of related-party transactions involving new or unknown traders, or where a declared customs value is significantly less than transaction values customs found in prior transactions involving identical or similar goods. It also would be consistent with the Agreement if customs relied upon risk management to select for examination those related-party transactions that present a higher probability of unacceptable values, and allow the low-risk traders or transactions to pass without further review.

Notify Importer

If customs does have doubts that the price was affected by the relationship, **Article 1(2)** of the Agreement requires that customs communicate those grounds to the importer, and that the importer be given a reasonable opportunity to respond. If the importer so requests, customs must provide this communication in writing.

An importer can justify a transaction value challenged by customs by either of two means:

1. the declared price (transaction value) can be used if the circumstances surrounding the transaction demonstrate that the parties' relationship did not play a role, or
2. whether the relationship influenced the price or not, the price that the parties settled on is nearly equivalent – "closely approximates" – the transaction value of similar or identical goods.

"Circumstances of sale" and "test values" are alternatives: the importer need establish or meet only one of them.

Did the relationship influence the price?

Customs is required to accept a related-party price if the circumstances surrounding the transaction show that the buyer and seller, although related, buy and sell from each other as if they were not. The Agreement leaves to the discretion of the customs authority the kinds and sources of information it may take into account to determine whether the relationship influenced the price.

An **Interpretative Note** suggests three proofs that an importer could offer to demonstrate an acceptable price:

1. the price had been settled in a manner consistent with the normal pricing practices of the industry in question, or
2. the price was settled in a manner consistent with the way the seller settles prices for sales to buyers who are not related to him, or
3. the price is adequate to ensure recovery of all costs plus a profit that is representative of the firm's overall profit realized over a representative period of time in sales of goods of the same class or kind.

Does the declared value "closely approximate" a "test value"?

Even if the price was influenced by the parties' relationship, the importer may nevertheless establish that the price is acceptable if it "closely approximates" a test value. A test value is one that customs had previously accepted for imports of identical or similar goods. In the words of the Agreement:

> [a transaction value in a sale between related parties] shall be accepted … whenever the importer demonstrates that such value closely approximates one of the following, occurring at or about the same time:
> i. the transaction value in sales to unrelated buyers of identical or similar goods for export to the country of importation
> ii. the customs value of identical or similar goods as determined under the provisions of Article 5 [deductive value]
> iii. the customs value of identical or similar goods as determined under the provisions of Article 6 [computed value].

Typically, therefore, when customs searches for test values, three questions must be answered:

1. Are the goods in the prior shipment "identical" or "similar" to the goods under valuation?
   The question whether one shipment of goods is "identical" or "similar" to another is exactly the same question that arises under the second and third methods of customs valuation. See the discussion of identical and similar goods in section 3.1, below.
2. Does the transaction value declared by the importer "closely approximate" a test value?
   A test value can be used to support the importer's declared value even if it is not the exact same price. The importer's declared transaction value must only "closely approximate" the value of the prior shipment.
   An **Interpretative Note** makes the point that a large difference in prices of goods in some industry sectors may not be commercially significant, while small price differences for other types of goods may well be significant. Thus, in determining whether the declared value "closely approximates" a previously accepted customs value, customs should consider factors such as:

- The nature of the goods (e.g. perishables, high-tech goods, novelty items with short-interest span, etc.).
  Apples are apples, but the price for week-old apples presumably will be lower than the price for fresh apples. The same may be true for novelty or seasonal items.
- The nature of the industry (e.g. high tech, video games and toys, chemicals, etc.).
  Competitive conditions differ between industries. Certain industries compete on price, and therefore the range of market prices generally will be small. Other industries compete on innovation or brand

name (e.g. toothpaste), where there may be a greater range of market prices.

- The season in which imported (e.g. fruits and vegetables, wearing apparel, seasonal activity equipment such as tennis and skiing, etc.).

These factors will vary from case to case. Therefore, it would be wrong to apply a rule across-the-board to all commodities that, for example, one price will be considered to "closely approximate" another if there is no more than a 5 percent difference between the two.

In addition, the Agreement accepts that a low related-party value can be said to "closely approximate" a higher customs value that was previously accepted by customs *if* the difference in price is shown to be due to any of the following reasons:

- differences in commercial level (wholesale, retail, consumer, sales)
- differences in quantity levels (bulk shipments v. individual items)
- differences in **Article 8** elements (assists, transport costs)
- differences in seller's costs in sales to unrelated parties versus sales to related parties (i.e. marketing costs, market research, etc.).

For example, the related party price might involve a wholesale quantity, while the higher-price "test-value" shipment may have been a retail quantity. Where the price difference is demonstrated to be due to a usual wholesale discount, the related-party price might be accepted as a "close approximation." Similarly, in a WTO Member country which includes the costs of international transport in customs value, the declared goods may have been shipped by ocean, whereas the previously accepted values may have included (usually more expensive) air freight charges.

3. Does the declared value "occur at or about the same time" as the test value?

   The test value must "occur" at or about the same time as the transaction value between the related parties. When a test value can be said to "occur" is not altogether clear under the terms of the Agreement, and WTO Members have developed different interpretations. Some Members use the time of export. Other Members use the time of export if the test value is a transaction value, but use time of sale if the test value is a deductive value and time of import if it is a computed value.[42]

[42] GATT Committee on Customs Valuation, Time Standard for Test Values under Article 1.2(b) of the Agreement, VAL/W/18 (April 29, 1983).

Regardless of the point in time used as the reference (the date of export or otherwise), the Agreement provides that transactions taking place "at *or about*" that date may be considered. Prices can change simply because of the passage of time; therefore, the closer in time the prior shipment, presumably the more accurate a reflection of the market value of the imported goods. Of course, because market conditions are different between industries and products, it may be appropriate to consider only transactions occurring within a short period of time for some types of goods (for example, perishable goods) but a longer period for others. Therefore, the Agreement sets out a flexible standard, and leaves the implementation to the discretion of individual WTO Members in their national laws and procedures.

### (c) *Transfer pricing and customs valuation*

"Transfer pricing" refers to the allocation by multinational corporations of their profits among members of the corporate group for tax purposes.[43] Other factors being equal, a corporation will normally choose to shift its profits to countries with lower tax rates, and to report low earnings in countries with higher rates. Manipulation of the transfer price – the price paid for goods exchanged across borders between members of the corporate group – is a means by which the multinational can reduce its worldwide tax burden.

For example, a producer located in a country that imposes high taxes on earnings might establish a low transfer price for goods it ships to a related distributor located in a country with low tax rates. The producer is subject to tax on the minimal profit it earns on the sale to the distributor (i.e. the difference between its costs and the low transfer price). The distributor will earn a larger share of the overall profit (i.e. the difference between the low transfer price and the resale price to the purchaser in the country of import), but those profits will be subject to a low rate of tax.

National tax authorities have concerns similar to customs administrations about abuses of related-party pricing – although customs authorities are normally concerned that the declared price may be *understated* to avoid duty, while the tax authority's concern is that the price may be *overstated* to avoid tax on earnings. And, parallel to the WTO Valuation Agreement, Article 9 of the OECD Model Tax Convention establishes an international standard – the "arm's length" principle – that is used by tax authorities and multinationals to establish acceptable transfer prices for purposes of taxation.

[43] J. Neighbor, "Transfer Pricing: Keeping it at Arm's Length," *OECD Observer* (2002); OECD, *Transfer Pricing Guidelines for Multinational Enterprises and Tax Administrations* (2001).

The "arm's-length" principle simply means that a transfer price should be the same as if the two companies involved were two independents, rather than part of the same corporate group. This principle is further elaborated in the OECD Transfer Pricing Guidelines, which defines several methods that can be used to establish an acceptable transfer price. These include:

- "Comparable uncontrolled price method" – the "arm's-length" principle is satisfied if the transfer price is equivalent to a price in a *comparable* transaction between unrelated parties in *comparable* circumstances.
- "Resale price method" – an acceptable transfer price can be established by subtracting from the price at which the distributor resells the imported goods to an independent purchaser an "appropriate gross margin," i.e. a margin covering a distributor's profit and expenses equivalent to that you would find in *comparable* transactions with or between independent enterprises.
- "Cost plus method" – the transfer price can be determined by adding to the costs incurred by the producer or supplier of the goods an "appropriate cost plus markup" to allow the producer or supplier an "appropriate profit," i.e. a profit margin found in *comparable* transactions with or between unrelated parties (the "cost plus" method).

What impact does a transfer pricing determination by the national tax authority have on customs value? Can information that justifies a tax transfer price also justify a customs transaction value between related parties?

The uses to which transfer-pricing information may be put in related-party examinations is a matter for national customs administrations. But there are obvious similarities in the purposes and methods of the OECD Guidelines and the WTO Valuation Agreement. On the other hand, there are also differences which may bear on the relevance of transfer-pricing information in a customs related-party examination.

One important difference is the factors used to determine whether a related-party transaction is comparable to a transaction between independents. The WTO Valuation Agreement focuses on similarity of imported goods in determining whether one transaction is comparable to another; that is, whether the goods are "identical" or "similar" or "the same class or kind." Under OECD Guidelines, tax authorities will consider the economically significant conditions of the transactions in full, and particularly "the functions performed by the parties (taking into account assets used and risk assumed), the contractual terms, the economic circumstances of the parties, and the business strategies pursued by the parties." Thus, a sale of imported toasters by a distributor who takes on responsibility for advertizing and marketing (which impacts his expenses and profit margin) is not directly comparable for tax purposes to a sale of identical toasters by another distributor who does not perform these functions or assume these risks.

Given these overlapping but distinct methods, customs administrations have considered transfer pricing information to be relevant to determining the acceptability of related-party price, but not conclusive. In the words of one customs administration:

> Based on these considerations, [the US customs administration] has ruled that the fact that the importer's transfer pricing methodology satisfies one of the [tax] methods is not determinative of whether it is an acceptable transaction value for customs purposes. Rather, a related party transaction value will be considered acceptable only if it satisfies either the circumstances of sale test or closely approximates one of the test values as provided in customs value law …
>
> [But customs] recognizes that in some cases, the underlying facts and the conclusions reached in an APA[44] or transfer pricing study[45] may contain some relevant information about the circumstances of sale and thus may be considered in applying the circumstances of sale test. For example, they may contain pertinent information about how the related parties transact business and may include information about sales of similar products to unrelated purchasers. The weight given to the facts and conclusions in an APA or transfer pricing study depends in large part on the particular circumstances presented and the transfer pricing methodology used.[46]

## TEST YOUR KNOWLEDGE – CIRCUMSTANCES OF SALE

1. A Korean manufacturer sells auto parts to his 35 percent-owned subsidiary in Kenya at $10 per item. An examination of the circumstances of the sale indicates that the Korean manufacturer sells identical goods to unrelated customers in Japan and Mexico at the same price and under same sales conditions. Is the price influenced by the relationship?

44 An APA is an advanced pricing arrangement. This is an "arrangement that determines, in advance of controlled transactions, an appropriate set of criteria (e.g. method, comparables and appropriate adjustments thereto, critical assumptions as to future events) for the determination of the transfer pricing for those transactions over a fixed period of time. An advance pricing arrangement may be unilateral involving one tax administration or multilateral involving the agreement of two or more tax administrations." OECD, *Transfer Pricing Guidelines*, at G-1.

45 A study prepared by the multinational to support its transfer price. These "generally include a description of intercompany transactions, the company's transfer pricing methodology, a discussion of … transfer pricing methods and the selection of the best method, and conclusions regarding the arm's length nature of the intercompany pricing." US Customs and Border Protection, *What Every Member of the Trade Community Should Know About: Determining the Acceptability of Transaction Value for Related Party Transactions* (April 2007), 14.

46 *Ibid.* at 15–16.

2. A company in Ghana sells cocoa to its subsidiary in Norway at $1,500 per short ton. An examination of the circumstances of the sale indicates that this price is based on the published prices on the London Commodity Exchange for cocoa. Is the price influenced by the relationship?
3. The president of an exporter is also one of a seven-member governing committee which controls the importer. An examination of the circumstances of the sale reveals that each member of the importer's governing committee has an equal vote, and none of the other members of the importer's governing committee is associated with the exporter. Is the price influenced by the relationship?

For the answers, see p. 93.

## 2.4 ANSWER KEY

### TEST YOUR KNOWLEDGE – CAN TRANSACTION VALUE BE USED?

*Pricing formulae*

Question 1. Transaction value is the primary method of value under the Agreement, and should be used where possible. In this case, a transaction value cannot be determined at the time of importation. However, customs could allow the goods to be released under Article 13 of the Agreement, which allows goods to be withdrawn from customs (under guarantee, if necessary), and the final value assessed later, when all necessary information is available. Of course, if objective and quantifiable data is not made available, the transaction value method must be rejected and the next method of value should be considered.

*Package deals (one price for several items)*

Question 2. There is a price paid or payable for the goods so transaction value can be used. Customs will have to apportion the price among goods that are classifiable under the different tariff categories. Guidance on methods of apportionment in these kinds of cases is provided in Technical Committee's Commentary 8.1. "Treatment of Package Deals," reprinted in *WCO Compendium.*

*Barter deals*

Question 3. In a strict barter exchange of *x* goods for *y* goods there is no price paid or payable, and transaction value cannot be used. Customs must consider the next method of value. Other cases of barter situations where transaction *could* be used are discussed in the Technical Committee's Advisory Opinion 6.1, "Treatment of Barter or Compensation Deals under the Agreement," reprinted in *WCO Compendium.*

### Test your knowledge – should these payments be included in transaction value?

Question 1. No. These would be considered payments for post-importation services, and are therefore excluded from transaction value.

Question 2. Yes. It could be argued that the "penalty" amount is not a payment *for* the imported goods – and therefore should not be included in transaction value – but a payment *for* the number of items that the buyer did not import to meet the minimum. However, customs administrations have considered this to be a kind of "price formula" where the buyer and seller agree to a provisional price for the imported goods, which is subject to adjustment up or down based on factors determined after importation. Price formulae can be used as the transaction value because the definition of transaction value includes the price actually paid or *payable*.

If you wish to read more about the use of price formulae for transaction value, see Commentary 4.1 of the Technical Committee, "Price Review Clauses," reprinted in *WCO Compendium*.

Question 3. A warranty is a guarantee for the goods that are imported. Accordingly, the Technical Committee, and a number of customs administrations, take the position that the buyer's payment to the seller for the warranty is part of the transaction value of the imported goods, even if separately invoiced.

A different result might be possible if the buyer and seller have a separate legal agreement for the warranty (apart from the sales agreement for the goods) and the warranty agreement can be shown to have been optional; that is, not imposed on the buyer by the seller as a condition of sale of the goods.

If you wish to read more about customs valuation issues presented by warranties, see the Technical Committee's Case Study 6.1 ("Insurance Premiums for Warranty") and Commentary 20.1 ("Warranty Charges"), both of which are reprinted in *WCO Compendium*.

### Two questions for experts

#### *1. Multi-tier transactions*

Where there are successive sales prior to importation, most customs administrations take the position that the last sale is the only one which can be considered under Article 1 of the Agreement.

In a 2007 commentary, the Technical Committee confirmed this interpretation: where there are a series of sales, "the price paid or payable for the imported goods when sold for export to the country of importation is the price paid in the last sale occurring prior to the introduction of the goods into the country of importation."[47] In the scenario outlined in the Commentary, the earlier or first sale cannot be used as the basis for customs value.

The Technical Committee's interpretation is based on a close reading of the text of the Agreement, which suggests that the drafters of the Agreement intended that the buyer in the sale to be used for valuation purposes would be the importer located in the country of importation. For example, certain of the Interpretative Notes interchange the term "importer" for "buyer". Also, Article 1(a) refers to restrictions imposed on the "buyer" by authorities in the "country of importation." Finally, unless the last sale is used for valuation purposes, parties could avoid making the Article 8 adjustments that are necessary to reflect in the transaction value "the substance of the entire commercial import transaction" – such as additions to the declared price for goods and services supplied by the purchaser in the country of importation to the foreign manufacturer free or at reduced price.

As a contrary view, certain customs administrations will accept customs value based on an earlier (and, presumably, lower) sale price where the declarant can prove that prior sale led to the export of the goods to the particular country of importation.

For example, the European Union rules provide that the last sale that led to the introduction of the goods into the customs territory (or the last sale taking place in the customs territory before the goods are released for free circulation) should be considered the sale for export, unless the declarant can demonstrate to the satisfaction of the customs authorities that a prior sale qualifies. Article 147, Commission Regulation (EEC) No. 2454/93 of July 2, 1993. The kind of proof that might be presented to support such a claim may include:

> – the goods are manufactured according to EC specifications, or are identified (according to the marks etc. they bear) as having no other use or destination,
>
> – the goods in question were manufactured or produced specifically for a buyer in the EU,
>
> – specific goods are ordered from an intermediary who sources the goods from a manufacturer and the goods are shipped directly to the EC from that manufacturer.

Customs Code Committee (Customs Valuation Section) Commentary No. 7, reprinted in European Commission, Directorate-General Taxation and Customs Union, Compendium of Customs Valuation Texts (January 2007) (available at the website of the EU Customs Directorate, http://ec.europa.eu/taxation_customs/customs/customs_duties/declared_goods/european/index_en.htm).

[47] Technical Committee Commentary 22.1, Meaning of the Expression "Sold for Export to the Country of Importation" in a Series of Sales.

Similarly, the US Customs Service "presumes" that transaction value is based upon the price paid by the importer. The importer who wishes to use a prior sale must provide "complete details of all the relevant transactions and documentation (including purchase orders, invoices, evidence of payment, contracts and other relevant documents). General Notice – Determining Transaction Value in Multi-Tiered Transactions, T.D. 96–87, Vol. 30/31, No. 52/1 Cust. B. & Dec. (January 2, 1997). This may be a difficult burden, where the importer is not a party to that prior sale.

### 2. *The tourist trader*

Under the Technical Committee's Advisory Opinion No. 14, the importer's purchase of the goods – such as a used car – on the foreign market can be considered a "sale for export." That opinion states:

> the fact that the goods are presented for valuation of itself establishes their importation which, in turn, establishes the fact of their exportation. The only remaining requirement then, is to identify the transaction relating thereto...If the importer can demonstrate that the immediate sale under consideration took place with the view to export the goods to the country of importation, then Article 1 can apply.

Advisory Opinion 14.1, Meaning of the Expression "Sold for Export to the Country of Importation," in *WCO Compendium.* The specific case of purchase of a car on the foreign market for export is discussed in Study 1.1, Treatment of Used Motor Vehicles, *WCO Compendium.* As noted in these decisions, the result may be otherwise if the car is used after purchase and prior to importation.

The European Community, in its customs legislation, provides a similar answer to the question: "[f]or the purposes of Article 29 of the Code [the transaction value method], the fact that the goods which are the subject of a sale are declared for free circulation shall be regarded as adequate indication that they were sold for export to the customs territory of the Community."[48]

## Test your knowledge – "objective and quantifiable evidence"

The Agreement is very clear. Where data does not exist, you cannot make the appropriate adjustment to calculate a transaction value and, therefore, cannot use transaction value as a basis for customs value.

[48] Article 147, Commission Regulation (EEC) No. 2454/93 of July 2, 1993.

In the context of royalty and license fees, the interpretive notes describe some specific examples where "objective and quantifiable" data does not exist, and transaction value cannot be used:

- if the payment of the royalty is based partly on the imported goods and partly on other factors which have nothing to do with the imported goods, it would be inappropriate to attempt to make an adjustment for the royalty
- where imported goods are mixed with domestic ingredients and are no longer separately identifiable (and there is therefore no way to apportion the royalty payment to the imported element of the finished goods)
- where the royalty payment cannot be distinguished from special financial arrangements between buyer and seller.

### Test your knowledge – apportionment of assists

The full cost of the tool ($1,000) should be apportioned to the total number of units produced (40 cars), or a cost of $25 per car. The importer then has some choices:

- The importer can allocate the full cost of the tool over the anticipated production. In this case, he would declare $125 ($25 × 5 cars) on the first shipment.
- The importer can allocate the full cost of the tool to the first consignment. The full cost of the assist is $1,000. However, the tool will be used to produce cars exported both to Italy and to Canada. The importer should be permitted to take into account only the production destined for Italy when allocating the cost of the tool. Thus, if the importer chooses to declare to Italian Customs the full cost on the first consignment of five cars, he would declare $500 ($1,000 × 20 ÷ 40), which is the full cost of the tool as it pertains to exports to Italy.

### Test your knowledge – royalties and license fees

Question 1. The importer is likely right, and the payment should not be included in the price of the prototypes. This is because the royalty is not related to the imported goods (the prototypes) but to other goods, namely, those that the US company manufactures and sells in the United States.

Question 2. In this case, the royalty must be added to the sale invoice price because (1) it is related to the imported goods (the goods are made with the patent), (2) it is paid by the buyer (the Italian company) and is a condition for export sale (the US company requires payment of the royalty as a condition of its sale of the medicine to the Italian company), and (3) it is not already included in the invoice price.

Question 3. While the royalty is related to the imported goods, it is not a condition of sale of the imported goods but arises under the laws of Italy upon the resale of the imported goods in Italy. Therefore, it should not be included in the customs value of the imported records.

In this regard, you might note the Interpretative Notes state "payments made by the buyer for the right to distribute or resell the goods will not be added *provided* such payments are not a condition of sale for export to the country of importation of the imported goods."

### Test your knowledge – proceeds

Question 1. Five percent of the Italian company's gross sales proceeds realized on the imported pharmaceutical products will be considered proceeds on resale of the imported goods, and therefore should be added to the price paid for the goods ($10,000). A difficulty here, however, is that the total amount realized on resales payable to the seller will not be known for a year after the import takes place. This means that customs may require legal authority under its national laws to delay final valuation and collection of duty on the goods, as well as to verify, if necessary, the buyer's accounting.

Question 2. In this case, the remittance cannot be considered as proceeds since it represents the flow of dividends or other payments from the Italian buyer to the seller which do not relate to the imported pharmaceutical products. Therefore, this payment is not part of the transaction value of the imported goods.

### Test your knowledge – transport charges

Where a country chooses to include transport in customs value, the Agreement provides it may include "cost of transport" rather than, for example, the amount the buyer actually paid or will pay for the transport. The European Union, for example, requires the cost of transport to be included in customs value even if transport is free or is provided by the buyer, based on freight rates normally applied for the same modes of transport. Article 164(c), Commission Regulation (EEC) No. 2454/93 of July 2, 1993.

## Test your knowledge – do these sales restrictions prevent use of transaction value?

Question 1. Although this is a restriction on Mr. X's ability to use the goods, it is a restriction imposed by government authorities. Therefore, transaction value can be used.

Question 2. This is a restriction on Mr. X's use of the product but the restriction does not substantially impair the value of the imported product to Mr. X. After all, Mr. X imported the product to use it as a cleaning product, not as a food additive.

Question 3. The answer is no, according to the Technical Committee. A restriction "which could have a substantial effect on the value of the imported goods is one that is not usual in the trade concerned." By limiting the buyer's use of the imported car to charitable purposes, the restriction "substantially affects" its value, and thus precludes use of transaction value. *See* Technical Committee, Meaning of the Term "Restrictions" in Article 1.1(a)(ii), in *WCO Compendium*.

## Test your knowledge – circumstances of sale

Question 1. No. Since the Korean manufacturer settles prices in the same manner to unrelated buyers in Canada and Mexico, this would demonstrate that the price was not influenced by the relationship.

Question 2. No. This price is consistent with the normal pricing practice in the industry and shows that the price was not influenced by the relationship.

Question 3. Parties may only be technically related, but not have real control over the other. In this case, the circumstances of the sale suggest that the president of the exporter is not in a position to exercise the requisite degree of control required to influence the price.

# 3

# ALTERNATIVE VALUATION METHODS

## 3.1 TRANSACTION VALUE OF IDENTICAL OR SIMILAR GOODS

### 3.1.1 THE VALUATION PRINCIPLE

The basic principle of **Articles 2 and 3** is that if customs cannot use transaction value to appraise the imported merchandise, then the next best substitute is a transaction value that the customs authorities accepted in a prior transaction involving like goods.

The sole difference between **Articles 2 and 3** is the type of goods that can be considered by customs as the reference. Under **Article 2**, customs must attempt to find a prior importation involving goods that are "*identical*" to those under review. If none is found, customs must proceed to **Article 3** and widen the scope of its search to prior imports of "*similar*" goods.

Where customs is able to find prior imports of identical or similar goods, customs is to apply the transaction value that it accepted for such imports. And, if more than one transaction is found, the lowest value must be used.

*Article 2*

1. (a) If the customs value of the imported goods cannot be determined under the provisions of Article 1, the customs value shall be the transaction value of identical goods sold for export to the same country of importation and exported at or about the same time as the goods being valued.
   (b) In applying this Article, the transaction value of identical goods in a sale at the same commercial level and in substantially the same quantity as the goods being valued shall be used to determine the customs value. Where no such sale is found, the transaction value of identical goods sold at a different commercial level and/or in different quantities, adjusted to take account of differences attributable to commercial level and/or to quantity, shall be used, provided that such adjustments can be made on the basis of demonstrated evidence which clearly establishes the reasonableness and accuracy of the adjustment, whether the adjustment leads to an increase or a decrease in the value.

2. Where the costs and charges referred to in paragraph 2 of Article 8 are included in the transaction value, an adjustment shall be made to take account of significant differences in such costs and charges between the imported goods and the in question arising from differences in distances and modes of transport.
3. If, in applying this Article, more than one transaction value of is found, the lowest such value shall be used to determine the customs value of the imported goods.

*Article 3*

1. (a) If the customs value of the imported goods cannot be determined under the provisions of Articles 1 and 2, the customs value shall be the transaction value of similar goods sold for export to the same country of importation and exported at or about the same time as the goods being valued.
   (b) In applying this Article, the transaction value of similar goods in a sale at the same commercial level and in substantially the same quantity as the goods being valued shall be used to determine the customs value. Where no such sale is found, the transaction value of similar goods sold at a different commercial level and/or in different quantities, adjusted to take account of differences attributable to commercial level and/or to quantity, shall be used, provided that such adjustments can be made on the basis of demonstrated evidence which clearly establishes the reasonableness and accuracy of the adjustment, whether the adjustment leads to an increase or a decrease in the value.
2. Where the costs and charges referred to in paragraph 2 of Article 8 are included in the transaction value, an adjustment shall be made to take account of significant differences in such costs and charges between the imported goods and the in question arising from differences in distances and modes of transport.
3. If, in applying this Article, more than one transaction value of is found, the lowest such value shall be used to determine the customs value of the imported goods.

*When are Articles 2 and 3 applied?*

Customs use of **Articles 2 and 3** as a method of appraisement is limited to those situations where customs value cannot be determined by the transaction value method under **Article 1** – the primary basis of customs value. As we have seen, this means in practice that customs use of the **Articles 2 and 3** valuation methods will mainly occur in three situations, where the transaction value method cannot be used:

1. in a related-party transaction, if customs has found that the relationship influenced the price of the imported goods
2. where the goods have not been imported pursuant to a sale (for example, imports under consignment, lease, gifts, etc.)
3. where, applying the WTO Ministerial **Decision Regarding Cases Where Customs Administrations Have Reasons to Doubt the Truth or Accuracy of the Declared Value**, customs determines that the price declared by the importer or his supporting documents are unreliable, or does not otherwise have sufficient information to compute a transaction value.

### 3.1.2 What are identical and similar goods?

The definitions of "identical" and "similar" goods are found in **Article 15** of the Agreement.

"Identical" goods are those:

> which are the same in all respects, including physical characteristics, quality and reputation. Minor differences in appearance would not preclude goods otherwise conforming to the definition from being regarded as identical.

"Similar" goods are:

> goods which, although not alike in all respects, have like characteristics and like component materials which enable them to perform the same functions and to be commercially interchangeable. The quality of the goods, their reputation and the existence of a trademark are among the factors to be considered in determining whether goods are similar.

In addition to these criteria, the goods in the prior transaction must have been produced in the same country – that is, they must have been grown, manufactured or mined in the same country as the imported goods – in order to be considered identical or similar.

Whether goods may be considered identical or similar often requires a close examination of the particular products and industry involved. For example, could the articles depicted here be considered "identical" or "similar" within the meaning of the Article 15 definitions?

**Shirt 1**
**Designer Brand X**
100% Silk, Petite sizes, Made in Italy

**Shirt 2**
**Designer Brand X**
100% Silk, Sizes 8 to 14, Made in Italy

**Shirt 3**
**Designer Brand X**
100% Silk, Petite sizes, Made in Italy

**Shirt 4**
**Generic Brand Y**
100% Silk, Petite sizes

Shirt 1 and Shirt 2 would likely be considered "identical" because they have the same physical characteristics – same material and design – bear the same brand name, and are made in the same country. Although the blouses are made up of different colors, patterns, and sizes, these likely are "minor differences in appearance" that would not preclude a finding of identicality.

On the other hand, what if one of the blouses (Shirt 3) carries the label of a well-known fashion designer (Brand X), while Shirt 4 is not branded?

In this case, the blouses may not be considered either "identical" or "similar". In this particular industry, the importance of a fashion label – or "reputation" – may preclude a finding that the otherwise similar dresses are commercially interchangeable.

In other industries, the existence of a trademark may not be determinative. For example, consider whether automobile tyres that are made by different manufacturers, bear different trademarks, and vary in their chemical composition might nevertheless be considered commercially interchangeable, and therefore "similar":

Tire 1

Tire 2

**SPECIFICATIONS FOR TIRE 1**

**Manufacturer – Company Y**
**Brand – Ice™**
Type – Passenger, Winter Radial

Section Width – P185
Aspect Ratio – 60
Rim Size – 14
Load Index – 82
Speed Index – H

**14% Natural Rubber**
Made in Italy

**SPECIFICATIONS FOR TIRE 2**

**Manufacturer – Company X**
**Brand – SureGrip™**
Type – Passenger, Winter Radial

Section Width – P185
Aspect Ratio – 60
Rim Size – 14
Load Index – 82
Speed Index – H

**12% Natural Rubber**
Made in Italy

With the exception of the different trademarks and the small variation in natural rubber content, the tyres are identical: same dimensions, same composition, designed to perform the same functions, and manufactured in the same country. The tyres cannot be considered "identical" within the meaning of Article 15 because of the differences in marks and composition. But, assuming that the minor variation in chemical composition would be considered insignificant in the tyre manufacturing industry and that the two brands have equivalent reputation in the automobile tyre market, these articles may be considered "similar."[1]

A final example – based on a Technical Committee commentary – is a comparison of assembled and unassembled goods. The bicycles depicted below are identical in all respects – same brand, size, materials and design – but Bicycle 1 is fully assembled when imported, while Bicycle 2 is imported disassembled, and requires the ultimate consumer to attach the wheels to the frame.

Bicycle 1 – Assembled

[1] This example was suggested by a US Customs decision under its customs drawback law, in which it was demonstrated that the tyre industry manufacturing standards would consider a 2 percent variation in chemical composition as insignificant, because such minor differences would not affect the commercial interchangeability of the tyre. US Customs Service Ruling Ltr. 221953 (December 28, 1989). A similar example is given in WCO, *Commentary 1.1: Identical or Similar Goods for the Purposes of the Agreement*, which can be found in *WCO Compendium*.

Bicycle 2 – Unassembled

In this case, the Technical Committee's commentary suggests that the two shipments might be considered "identical" because "[a]lthough an assembly operation will normally preclude treating assembled and unassembled goods as identical … when, as in this case, the goods are designed to be assembled and disassembled in the ordinary course of their use, the nature of the assembly operation would not preclude them from being considered identical."[2]

### 3.1.3 Other conditions

Even where customs or the importer finds prior transactions involving identical or similar goods, the Agreement imposes certain requirements regarding the commercial conditions surrounding the prior imports that must be met before they can be used for valuation.

*(a) Identical or similar goods must have been "exported at or about the same time"*

First, for various reasons – such as seasonal factors affecting supply or demand, fluctuations in value of currency, inflation, etc. – prices for goods may change

[2] WCO, *Commentary 1.1: Identical or Similar Goods for the Purposes of the Agreement.*

over time, and not necessarily in an even or predictable manner. To account for these kinds of distortions, **Articles 2 and 3** of the Agreement require that the goods involved in the prior transaction were "exported at or about the same time" as the goods under valuation.

When is an export made "at or about the same time"? This is left to individual countries implementing the Agreement to decide. Some countries include this phrase in their legislation, which allows customs officials to apply the standard flexibly, imposing shorter comparison periods where prices for goods are not stable, for example. Other countries have defined the period – for example, only goods exported within ninety days of date of exportation of the goods under valuation can be considered.

The importation of the identical or similar merchandise can occur before or after the good being valued but it is important to compare the date of exportation.

### *(b) Identical or similar goods should be made by same producer*

Second, **Article 15(2)(e)** of the Agreement requires that customs first try to find and use transactions involving identical or similar goods that were produced by the same producer as those under valuation.

> ***Article 15(2)(e)***
>
> (e) goods produced by a different person shall be taken into account only when there are no identical goods or similar goods, as the case may be, produced by the same person as the goods being valued.

It is possible, for example, that the same producer previously exported product to other purchasers in the same country of importation. However, this is a preference only. If no such prior transactions can be found (i.e. no prior imports recorded involving that producer), then it is permissible for customs to use prior transactions involving identical or similar goods produced by other manufacturers in the same country.

### *(c) Identical or similar goods should be sales at the same level of trade*

Third, the preference in the Agreement is to compare transactions at the same commercial level and substantially the same quantity as the goods being valued. Pricing is often a factor of level of distribution and discounts for volume – the bulk price of 10,000 units of a product will often be less than a retail price for one or a few units of the same product.

Again, this is a preference and not an absolute requirement. If transactions at the same commercial level of trade or in the same quantity cannot be found, the Agreement allows customs to look at transactions involving different quantities or at different trade levels, provided the appropriate adjustment to the price can be made that will reflect those differences. See **Articles 2(1)(b) and 3(1)(b)** of the Agreement.

The **Interpretative Notes to Article 2 and 3** contain an important warning to customs and traders about making these adjustments for trade levels or quantities:

> A condition for adjustment because of different commercial levels or different quantities is that such adjustment, whether it leads to an increase or a decrease in the value, be made only on the basis of demonstrated evidence that clearly establishes the reasonableness and accuracy of the adjustments, e.g. valid price lists containing prices referring to different levels or different quantities.
>
> As an example of this, if the imported goods being valued consist of a shipment of 10 units and the only identical imported goods for which a transaction value exists involved a sale of 500 units, and it is recognized that the seller grants quantity discounts, the required adjustment may be accomplished by resorting to the seller's price list and using that price applicable to a sale of 10 units. This does not require that a sale had to have been made in quantities of 10 as long as the price list has been established as being bona fide through sales at other quantities. In the absence of such an objective measure, however, the determination of a customs value under the provisions of Article 2 is not appropriate.

This condition described in the Interpretative Notes would preclude customs or traders from making assumptions either that quantity discounts are given or the levels at which they are granted. There must be evidence – such as a published wholesale price list – that such discounts are actually offered by the seller as well as the quantity levels at which they are given (or evidence as to how they are calculated).

### *(d) Adjustments for transport charges*

As we have seen, goods can be considered identical or similar only if they have been produced in the same country. However, it is possible that the imported goods under valuation may have been delivered to the country of importation by a different mode of transport (air, sea, rail, truck) or by a different route, or both, than the goods involved in the prior transactions. For example, shipping goods by air transport normally would be more costly than shipping by sea. **Articles 2(2) and 3(2)** of the Agreement allow for an adjustment in customs value in such cases, where these differences have a significant impact on transport costs.

**SR MEMORY CARD PRODUCTION INC.** Price List

555 Forget-Me-Not Road
Geneva, Switzerland
Phone 555-777-555 Fax 555-777-557

***UNFORGETTABLE RRODUCTS!***

DATE: JULY 20, 2010

| DESCRIPTION | SKU | RETAIL PRICE | WHOLESALE PRICE | NOTES |
|---|---|---|---|---|
| Memory Card Standard | SR1000 | $3.00 | $1.50 | |
| Memory Card – Liquid Form | SR1500 | $3.00 | $1.50 | T |
| Memory Master – Standard | SR2000 | $3.00 | $1.50 | |
| Memory Master – Liquid Form | SR2500 | $3.00 | $1.50 | T |
| Memory Jogger – Standard | SR3000 | $3.00 | $1.50 | |
| Memory Jogger – Liquid Form | SR3500 | $3.00 | $1.50 | L |
| Memory Card Standard – Extra Strength | SRX4000 | $4.00 | $2.00 | |
| Memory Card – Liquid Form – Extra Strength | SRX4500 | $4.00 | $2.00 | |
| Memory Master – Standard – Extra Strength | SRX5000 | $4.00 | $2.00 | |
| Memory Master – Liquid Form – Extra Strength | SRX5500 | $4.00 | $2.00 | N |
| Memory Jogger – Standard – Extra Strength | SRX6000 | $4.00 | $2.00 | N |
| Memory Jogger – Liquid Form – Extra Strength | SRX6500 | $4.00 | $2.00 | |

Notes:
T = Top seller
N = New product
L = Limited stock available

**Thank You For Your Business!**

### *(e) Goods incorporating design/engineering assists are not identical or similar*

As we have seen in our discussion of **Article 8** "assists" in section 2.2.4, the costs of engineering, development, artwork, designs or plans and sketches used in the manufacture of imported goods are not included in the transaction value *if* that work is undertaken in the country of importation.

For example, a factory in China contracts to manufacture toys using proprietary designs created and supplied by a buyer in the United States. When the finished toys are exported to the United States, the cost of the design work supplied by the US buyer can be excluded from the transaction value under Article 8.

Clearly, in this scenario, the transaction value of the imported toys does not reflect the actual, commercial value of the goods, as a major cost element – design – has been excluded. **Article 15** of the Agreement thus provides that goods in such transactions, which exclude costs of design or similar costs pursuant to Article 8, cannot be considered "identical" or "similar" to the goods under valuation.

> ***Article 15(2)(c)***
>
> (c) the terms "identical goods" and "similar goods" do not include, as the case may be, goods which incorporate or reflect engineering, development, artwork, design work, and plans and sketches for which no adjustment has been made under paragraph 1(b)(iv) of Article 8 because such elements were undertaken in the country of importation;

*(f) Test your knowledge – identify identical or similar goods*

Roses are imported into Switzerland on February 9, 2007 for the Valentine's Day market. The importer provides customs with the following invoice for the shipment:

**SELLER:**
AGRO ROSE FARMS
ECUADOR

**INVOICE**

INVOICE #1
DATE: FEBRUARY 10, 2007

**BUYER:**
FLORABUNCANCE WHOLESALERS
GENEVA, SWITZERLAND

| DATE OF EXPORT | SHIPPER VIA | F.O.B. POINT | TERMS |
|---|---|---|---|
| **FEBRUARY 8, 2007** | **AIR** | **ECUADOR** | **Due on receipt** |

| QUANTITY | DESCRIPTION | UNIT PRICE | TOTAL |
|---|---|---|---|
| 10,000 | **Fresh cut, "long stem"/50cm, hybrid tea roses, red and yellow color. H.S. code 0603.11** | .45 | 4500.00 |
| | | SHIPPING & HANDLING | **450.00** |
| | | TOTAL DUE | **4950.00** |

Thank you for your business!

Customs value cannot be determined under the provisions of Article 1; therefore, customs value under Article 2 or 3 must be investigated. Customs is aware of four other imports of roses.

Evaluate each of the following invoices for rose shipments, and determine whether the goods described in the invoice can be considered "identical" or "similar" to the February 9, 2007 shipment under valuation.

For the answers, see p. 132.

**SELLER:**
MEERMAN & CO
NETHERLANDS

**INVOICE**

INVOICE #2
DATE: FEBRUARY 1, 2007

**BUYER:**
FLORABUNCANCE WHOLESALERS
GENEVA, SWITZERLAND

| DATE OF EXPORT | SHIPPER VIA | F.O.B. POINT | TERMS |
|---|---|---|---|
| **FEBRUARY 1, 2007** | **AIR** | **AMSTERDAM** | **30 DAYS** |

| QUANTITY | DESCRIPTION | UNIT PRICE | TOTAL |
|---|---|---|---|
| **8,500** | **Long cut, fresh cut hybrid tea roses. Red and yellow. H.S. Code 0603.11** | **.52** | **4420.00** |
| | | SHIPPING & HANDLING | **442.00** |
| | | TOTAL DUE | **4862.00** |

Thank you for your business!

**SELLER:**
AGRO ROSE FARMS
ECUADOR

**INVOICE**

INVOICE #3
DATE: NOVEMBER 15, 2006

**BUYER:**
LAKE GARDEN CENTER
GENEVA, SWITZERLAND

| DATE OF EXPORT | SHIPPER VIA | F.O.B. POINT | TERMS |
|---|---|---|---|
| **November 1, 2006** | **AIR** | **ECUADOR** | **Due on receipt** |

| QUANTITY | DESCRIPTION | UNIT PRICE | TOTAL |
|---|---|---|---|
| **15,000** | **Fresh cut roses; hybrid tea variety 50 cm stems. H.S. Code 0603.11** | **.35** | **5250.00** |
| | | SHIPPING & HANDLING | **52.00** |
| | | TOTAL DUE | **5302.00** |

Thank you for your business!

**SELLER:**
AGRO ROSE FARMS
ECUADOR

**INVOICE**

INVOICE #4
DATE: FEBRUARY 10, 2007

**BUYER:**
LAKE GARDEN CENTER
GENEVA, SWITZERLAND

| DATE OF EXPORT | SHIPPER VIA | F.O.B. POINT | TERMS |
|---|---|---|---|
| **FEBRUARY 10, 2007** | **AIR** | **ECUADOR** | **Due on receipt** |

| QUANTITY | DESCRIPTION | UNIT PRICE | TOTAL |
|---|---|---|---|
| **10,000** | **Fresh cut roses, spray and sweetheart varieties; 35 cm/short stems. H.S. code 0603.11** | **.20** | **3000.00** |
| | | SHIPPING & HANDLING | **300.00** |
| | | TOTAL DUE | **3300.00** |

Thank you for your business!

**SELLER:**
COTOPAXI FARMS
ECUADOR

**INVOICE**

INVOICE #5
DATE: FEBRUARY 10, 2007

**BUYER:**
THE SWISS CORNER GROCERY MARKET
GENEVA, SWITZERLAND

| DATE OF EXPORT | SHIPPER VIA | F.O.B. POINT | TERMS |
|---|---|---|---|
| **FEBRUARY 1, 2007** | **AIR** | **ECUADOR** | **Due on receipt** |

| QUANTITY | DESCRIPTION | UNIT PRICE | TOTAL |
|---|---|---|---|
| **100** | **Fresh cut roses; hybrid tea variety 50 cm stems. H.S. code 0603.11** | **.50** | **50.00** |
| | | SHIPPING & HANDLING | **5.00** |
| | | TOTAL DUE | **55.00** |

Thank you for your business!

### 3.1.4 Implementation challenges

The basic challenge for customs and traders in applying **Articles 2 and 3** is to find prior import transactions involving identical or similar goods.

Foremost is the challenge of locating recent transactions involving identical or similar goods. Customs may not be aware whether or not a particular importer had previous transactions involving identical imports. On the other hand, it may be unlikely that the importer will be in a position to obtain customs values of other traders' imports of the same goods, given that these others may be competitors. In light of those difficulties, the Agreement recognizes that close co-operation between traders and customs will almost certainly be required:

> there should normally be a process of consultation between the customs administration and importer with a view to arriving at a basis of value under the provisions of Article 2 or 3. It may occur, for example, that the importer has information about the customs value of identical or similar imported goods which is not immediately available to the customs administration in the port of importation. On the other hand, the customs administration may have information about the customs value of identical or similar imported goods which is not readily available to the importer. A process of consultation between the two parties will enable information to be exchanged, subject to the requirements of commercial confidentiality, with a view to determining a proper basis of value for customs purposes.

See **General Introductory Commentary**, WTO Customs Valuation Agreement.

Customs valuation databases – if organized with the level of product specificity required to identify identical or similar goods – may also usefully assist in this process. (With regard to use of valuation databases, see the Technical Committee's "Guidelines on the Development and Use of a National Valuation Database as a Risk Assessment Tool," discussed in sections 4.3 and 4.5, below.)

As is clear from the examples given, the question of identicality or similarity of goods is highly product specific. It is a judgment that depends upon both qualitative (quality and reputation) and quantitative (physical characteristics, component materials) factors. Moreover, the relative commercial importance of a particular feature – color, trademark, packaging – will vary from one product to another.

Effective application of **Articles 2 and 3** therefore requires of the customs officer an understanding of the particular industry and market, such as the conditions of supply and consumption – what product features are significant, which factors are important to consumers – in order to make the relevant product comparisons. Again, this will ordinarily require customs to co-operate closely with their importers, as the latter have the product and market expertise required for these judgments.

**TRANSACTION VALUE OF IDENTICAL OR SIMILAR GOODS METHODS: IN BRIEF**

- Typically used to value consignment shipments, related-party transactions, or where the importer's price declaration is unreliable or incomplete.
- In place of the importer's declared price, customs assigns the value it accepted for previous imports of identical or similar (commercially interchangeable) goods.

- The prior imports must have been manufactured in the same country – preferably by the same manufacturer – and exported at or about the same time as the goods under valuation.
- Adjustments in value can be made where the goods under valuation and prior imports were shipped in different quantities or levels of trade, or traveled by different mode of transport or over different distances.

## 3.2 Deductive value method

***Article 5***

1. (a) If the imported goods or identical or similar imported goods are sold in the country of importation in the condition as imported, the customs value of the imported goods under the provisions of this Article shall be based on the unit price at which the imported goods or identical or similar imported goods are so sold in the greatest aggregate quantity, at or about the time of the importation of the goods being valued, to persons who are not related to the persons from whom they buy such goods, subject to deductions for the following:
   - (i) either the commissions usually paid or agreed to be paid or the additions usually made for profit and general expenses in connection with sales in such country of imported goods of the same class or kind;
   - (ii) the usual costs of transport and insurance and associated costs incurred within the country of importation;
   - (iii) where appropriate, the costs and charges referred to in paragraph 2 of Article 8; and
   - (iv) the customs duties and other national taxes payable in the country of importation by reason of the importation or sale of the goods.

   (b) If neither the imported goods nor identical nor similar imported goods are sold at or about the time of importation of the goods being valued, the customs value shall, subject otherwise to the provisions of paragraph 1(a), be based on the unit price at which the imported goods or identical or similar imported goods are sold in the country of importation in the condition as imported at the earliest date after the importation of the goods being valued but before the expiration of 90 days after such importation.

2. If neither the imported goods nor identical nor similar imported goods are sold in the country of importation in the condition as imported, then, if the importer so requests, the customs value shall be based on the unit price at which the imported goods, after further processing, are sold in the greatest aggregate quantity to persons in the country of importation who are not related to the persons from whom they buy such goods, due allowance being made for the value added by such processing and the deductions provided for in paragraph 1(a).

In simple terms, deductive value is the price at which the importer sells the imported goods to his customer in the country of import *minus* his markup for profit and other expenses related to sale and delivery of the goods to his customer.[3]

The principle underlying this method is that if these post-import costs can be deducted from the importer's resale price, the net amount will reflect the value of the goods at the border.

A deductive value can be based on the resale of the imported goods themselves, or on the resale of previously-imported identical or similar goods. As a practical matter, however, it may most often be based upon the importer's resale price of the goods that are under valuation or, possibly, the importer's second shipment will be valued on the basis of his resale price of his first shipment. Information concerning imports and resales of identical or similar goods by other importers may not be as readily available.

### 3.2.1 Importer's option – bypass deductive value

**Article 4** of the Agreement gives the importer the option to bypass the deductive value method of valuation in favor of the computed value method. The importer might exercise this option if foreign production cost information is more easily available to him than information on resale costs, or perhaps in expectation of a more favorable valuation under the computed value method. Whatever the motive, the Agreement makes clear the choice is left solely to the importer. Of course, if customs finds that it cannot value goods under the computed value method, it must return to the deductive value method to attempt a valuation.

### 3.2.2 Deductive value conditions

The price at which the imported goods are resold in the country of importation is the starting point in the deductive value calculation. Therefore, it is important that this domestic sale upon which the deductive value will be based is as representative of actual market value as possible. For that reason, the

[3] As a matter of historical interest, the deductive value provisions are largely taken from "United States Value" method that is found in the pre-Tokyo Round law of the United States, which similarly provided for valuation based on price at which the imported or similar goods are sold in the market of the importing country in "usual wholesale quantities" (defined in the US law as the "price for one quantity in an aggregate volume which is greater than the aggregate volume sold at the price or prices for any other quantity"), less the same deductions described in Article 5 of the Agreement. 19 US Code §1401a(c) (1976).

Agreement imposes certain technical requirements to ensure the integrity of the resale transaction. These are:

- the sale must be the first commercial sale that takes place after importation to a person who is not related to the buyer

First Sale After Importation

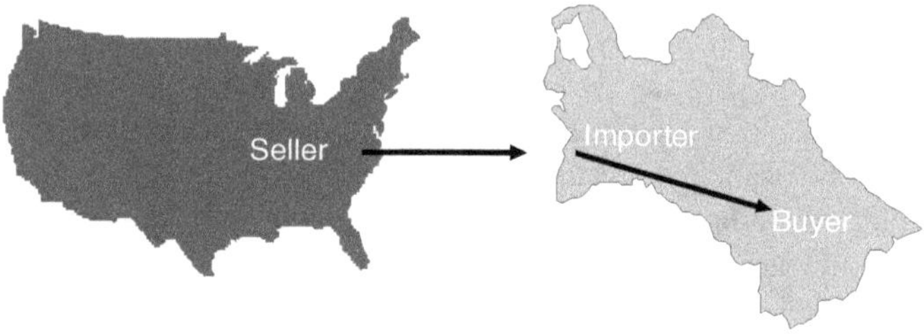


Sale from Importer to Domestic Unrelated Buyer

A sale by the importer to a buyer related to him cannot be used for deductive value because of the possibility that the price will have been distorted by the relationship.

- the buyer in the importing country cannot have supplied the foreign seller with an "assist"

  "Assists," which are defined in **Article 8** (see section 2.2.4, above), are certain items required for manufacture of the imported goods that are supplied by the buyer to the seller free of charge or at reduced cost. These items may be parts, components, tools, or designs needed to make the imported product. Where the buyer supplies these production inputs to the seller free, presumably the buyer would pay the importer a lower price for the finished goods than otherwise would be the case.
- the resale price used for valuation must be the unit price at which the imported goods (or identical or similar goods) are sold "in the greatest aggregate quantity"

  This qualification ensures that a commercially representative price is used as the basis for customs value, and would preclude an importer from arranging a sale of one or two units of an import shipment at an artificially low price, in order to establish a low deductive value (and pay less duty) for the bulk of the shipment.

- the resale in the importing country must take place "at or about the time" the goods under valuation are imported (see Figure 8). Only if no such sales take place may customs value be based on later sales, but in no event may consideration be given sales that occur more than ninety days after importation.

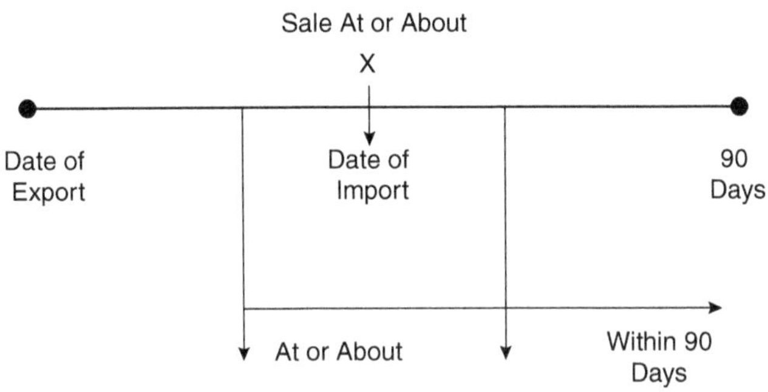


Figure 8 Sale at or about the time of importation

### 3.2.3 The deductive value calculation

| | |
|---|---|
| • Resale price ............................................................ | 1000 |
| • Usual commission *or* usual profit and general expenses....... | – 100 |
| | 900 |
| • Usual transport, insurance and associated costs incurred in the country of importation............................................ | – 25 |
| | 875 |
| • International transport charges/costs............................... | – 50 |
| | 825 |
| • Customs duties/import taxes.......................................... | – 9 |
| • DEDUCTIVE VALUE................................................. | = 816 |

### 3.2.4 Deduction for commissions or profit/general expense

Remember why the alternative valuation methods, such as the deductive value method, are used: most often, it is either because the imported goods were shipped "on consignment" – and therefore no export sales transaction occurred that could be used for transaction value – or the goods were imported by a firm or person related to the foreign seller, and customs found that the parties' relationship influenced the export price.

In the case of a sale on consignment, the importer typically acts as a selling agent and receives a commission when he sells the imported goods to a customer. Usually this commission is a percentage of the sale price, which is intended to cover the agent's costs plus a profit. In that case, the amount of the commission must be deducted from the sale price to derive the customs value.

On the other hand, in the case where customs has rejected a related-party transaction value, the importer will have title to the goods – although at a price that is not acceptable for customs valuation purposes – and may resell them in the country of importation, ordinarily with a markup to reflect his profit and costs in marketing the goods. In such cases, the importer's profit and sales expense must be deducted from the resale price to obtain the customs value.

As the Agreement makes clear, however, customs shall deduct *either* an amount for commissions *or* an amount for profit and general expenses: not both. It would not be consistent with the Agreement, for example, to deduct both a commission and the importer's marketing expenses.

The amount of deduction should be equivalent to the "usual" commission or "usual" profit/general expenses (taken as a whole) found in sales of goods of the "same class or kind." The concept of goods of the "same class or kind" is introduced here for the first time, but will also appear under computed value method.

> **Same class or kind**
>
> "In this Agreement 'goods of the same class or kind' means goods which fall within a group or range of goods produced by a particular industry or industry sector, and includes identical or similar goods."
>
> **Article 15(3)** WTO Customs Valuation Agreement

Goods of the "same class or kind" are imported goods that are produced by the same industry or industrial sector, regardless of country of origin. The concept therefore encompasses a broader set of products than the "identical" or "similar" goods, and might include, for example, all goods classified under the same tariff number. However, in determining whether goods are of the same class or kind, an **Interpretative Note** requires customs to consider "the narrowest group or range of imported goods of the same class or kind, which includes the goods being valued, for which the necessary information can be provided."

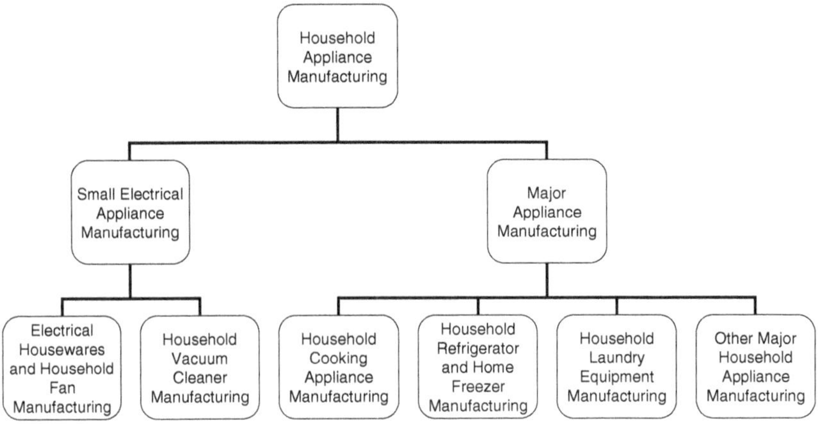


*Source*: North American Industry Classification System (2007)

Figure 9 Same class or kind: industry/industry sectors

Why should the Agreement allow the deduction for a commission or profit/general expenses found in sales of goods of the "same class or kind" rather than sales of identical or similar goods? The reason may be that this commission or profit/expense margin is compensation for the activity of selling, and the amount is more likely determined by the activity and risks that the distributor undertakes than the nature of the goods sold. Whether a distributor sells small domestic appliances like toasters or mixers, the commission or profit/expenses margin on resale is likely to be the same regardless of the type of product. On the other hand, if the types of goods sold are very different (i.e. they are goods of different industries, such as household appliances and automobiles), the risks and functions of the distributor – and therefore his compensation amount – are not likely comparable.[4]

What commissions or profits/general expenses are "usual" is not the kind of information that a customs administration routinely collects or to which it typically has access. The **Interpretative Note to Article 5** lightens customs' burden in large measure somewhat by allowing customs to rely on the importer's figures to make the deduction for usual profit and general expenses, unless

[4] See OECD, *Transfer Pricing Guidelines for Multinational Enterprises and Tax Administrations* (2001), II–5, which offers this rationale in connection with transfer pricing "resale price method," the tax parallel to the WTO Valuation Agreement deductive value method.

customs finds the importer's figures inconsistent with those of other sales in the country of importation of imported goods of the same class or kind:

> It should be noted that "profit and general expenses" referred to in paragraph 1 of Article 5 should be taken as a whole. The figure for the purposes of this deduction should be determined on the basis of information supplied by or on behalf of the importer unless the importer's figures are inconsistent with those obtained in sales in the country of importation of imported goods of the same class or kind. Where the importer's figures are inconsistent with such figures, the amount for profit and general expense may be based upon relevant information other than that supplied by or on behalf of the importer.

### 3.2.5 Deduction for costs of transport in country of importation

Determination of usual costs of transport in the country of importation includes freight and related costs – handling, inspection, unloading, forwarders fees, etc. – required to move the goods from the point of importation to delivery to the customer.

### 3.2.6 Deduction for international transport charges

In those few WTO-country Members who have elected, under **Article 8(2)** of the Agreement, to exclude costs of international transport in customs value, a deduction from the resale price must also be made for actual international freight, insurance and associated handling charges.

### 3.2.7 Deduction for customs duties and national taxes

Customs import duties and national taxes (VAT, for example) payable on the goods by reason of importation or sale must be deducted.[5] The arithmetic is as follows:

| | |
|---|---|
| Resale Price | $98 |
| *Less* deductions | |
| (other than customs duties) | $23 |
| Equals | =$75 |

If import duty is 6.5 percent, then deductive value is calculated:

$$\frac{\$75}{1.065} = \boxed{\$70.42}$$

[5] Anti-dumping or countervailing duties on the imported goods also would be considered customs duties or national taxes that should be deducted. See Technical Committee Advisory Opinion 9.1.

### 3.2.8 Superdeductive value – goods processed after importation

The foregoing discussion concerns the situation where the imported goods are resold as is – in the same condition in which they are imported. But what of the case where the imported goods are further processed after importation prior to resale? For example, imported cars are rust-proofed and detailed prior to resale.

**Article 5(2)** provides the importer with the option of using deductive value under the same conditions, provided an allowance can be made for the value added to the imported product as a result of the post-importation processing or manufacture. This amount would then be another cost deducted from the resale price:

Super Deductive Value Calculation

| | | |
|---|---|---|
| • Resale price | | 1010 |
| • ***Value added by processing or manufacture in importing country*** | – | 10 |
| | | 1000 |
| • Usual commission *or* usual profit and general expenses | – | 101 |
| | | 899 |
| • Usual transport, insurance and associated costs incurred in the country of importation | – | 25 |
| | | 874 |
| • International transport charges/costs | – | 50 |
| | | 824 |
| • Customs duties/import taxes | – | 9 |
| • DEDUCTIVE VALUE | | = 815 |

### Test your knowledge – identifying the relevant unit sale price

The seller offers the buyer a discount based on the volume (number of units) purchased. The buyer takes advantage of this volume discount to make a number of separate purchases from the seller over a three month period, as follows:

| | Quantity | Price | Unit price |
|---|---|---|---|
| 10 days ago | 1,400 | $60,480 | $43.20 |
| 12 days ago | 495 | 23,424 | 48.00 |
| 19 days ago | 975 | 44,460 | 45.60 |
| 30 days ago | 500 | 23,280 | 48.00 |
| 42 days ago | 475 | 18,000 | 48.00 |
| 55 days ago | 1,950 | 90,000 | 36.00 |
| 60 days ago | 485 | 20,880 | 48.00 |

Which of these sales should be used as the resale price for calculating a deductive value?

For the answers, see p. 133.

## 3.3 COMPUTED VALUE METHOD

*Article 6*

1. The customs value of imported goods under the provisions of this Article shall be based on a computed value. Computed value shall consist of the sum of:

(a) the cost or value of materials and fabrication or other processing employed in producing the imported goods;
(b) an amount for profit and general expenses equal to that usually reflected in sales of goods of the same class or kind as the goods being valued which are made by producers in the country of exportation for export to the country of importation;
(c) the cost or value of all other expenses necessary to reflect the valuation option chosen by the Member under paragraph 2 of Article 8.

2. No Member may require or compel any person not resident in its own territory to produce for examination, or to allow access to, any account or other record for the purposes of determining a computed value. However, information supplied by the producer of the goods for the purposes of determining the customs value under the provisions of this Article may be verified in another country by the authorities of the country of importation with the agreement of the producer and provided they give sufficient advance notice to the government of the country in question and the latter does not object to the investigation.

### 3.3.1 THE CONCEPT

**Article 6** of the Agreement sets out the methodology for constructing a customs value based on the cost of production of the imported goods.

This computed value is calculated by *adding* the foreign manufacturer's production costs and his profit and general expenses, as well as international transport and associated costs, if the WTO Member importing country includes such costs in customs value.

**Computed Value Calculation**

| | |
|---|---|
| • Cost or value of materials + manufacturing or other fabrication...................................................... | 900 |
| • Usual profit & general expense for goods of same class or kind, made by producers in same country, for export to the country of importation.......................... | + 100 |
| | 1000 |
| • International transport charges/costs........................ | + 50 |
| • COMPUTED VALUE.......................................... | = 1050 |

Computed value may be the least frequently used and most challenging method of valuation for customs administrations. Verification of a computed value requires customs officials in the importing country to examine the foreign manufacturer's cost data. This can present customs with difficulties of different languages, different record-keeping and accounting systems and principles, as well as the costs inherent in conducting a verification audit in a foreign country.

For these reasons, WTO Members recognized that use of computed value depends on co-operation of the foreign producer which, as a practical matter, means that its use will be limited to cases where the buyer and seller are related.

Article 6 provides the foreign manufacturer with certain protections. If customs in the importing country wishes to verify the foreign manufacturer's cost data, Article 6 requires that they obtain the agreement of the foreign producer, as well as notify in advance the producer's government and obtain their acquiescence to the verification visit. The foreign manufacturer has the right to refuse to furnish the necessary data or to refuse verification, and no penalty or punishment can be assessed on a business that refuses to co-operate.

XYZ Corporation Schedule of cost of goods manufactured Year ended December 31, 2008 (in 000's)

| | | |
|---|---|---|
| Direct materials: | | |
| Beginning inventory, January 1, 2008 | $150 | |
| Direct materials purchased | *400* | |
| Cost of direct materials available for use | 550 | |
| Ending inventory, December 31, 2008 | (*25*) | |
| Total direct materials used | | $525 |
| Direct labor | | 200 |
| Factory overhead: | | |
| Property taxes | 5 | |
| Depreciation: factory equipment | 15 | |
| Depreciation: factory building | 25 | |
| Utilities: factory | 20 | |
| Insurance: factory | 10 | |
| Indirect manufacturing labor | 100 | |
| Indirect materials | *30* | |
| Total factory overhead | | *205* |
| Total manufacturing costs | | 930 |
| Add: Beginning work-in-process inventory, January 1, 2008 | | *50* |
| | | 980 |
| Less: Ending work-in-process inventory, Dec. 31, 2008 | | (*10*) |
| Cost of goods manufactured | | 970 |

### 3.3.2 THE COST OR VALUE OF MATERIALS AND PROCESSING

These are the manufacturing costs – materials, labor and overhead – that a producer incurs in the production of the imported goods.

Generally, manufacturing costs include:

- direct labor (e.g. the wages and benefits paid to assembly or production line employees)
- direct materials (e.g. raw materials, parts, or components incorporated in the imported goods) and
- manufacturing overhead, such as indirect labor (e.g. salaries or wages and benefits paid to plant supervisors, factory maintenance and janitorial staff or other factory workers not directly involved in production), indirect materials (e.g. additives, catalysts or other kinds of materials that are consumed in production of the goods), depreciation of the factory building and the production equipment, electricity used to operate the factory equipment, insurance, taxes on the factory property, etc.

*However*, with the qualifications noted below, the Valuation Agreement does not dictate what cost elements must be included as "materials and fabrication" costs in a computed value, or how such costs must be calculated or allocated to imported goods. Rather, as stated in an **Interpretative Note**, customs shall accept the producer's accounting of its materials and processing costs as the basis for the computed value calculation *provided that* his accounting is in accordance with "generally accepted accounting principles" applicable in the country of production.

**MANUFACTURING COSTS – USE PRODUCER'S ACCOUNTS IF CONSISTENT WITH GAAP**

2. The "cost or value" referred to in paragraph 1(a) of Article 6 is to be determined on the basis of information relating to the production of the goods being valued supplied by or on behalf of the producer. It is to be based upon the commercial accounts of the producer, provided that such accounts are consistent with the generally accepted accounting principles applied in the country where the goods are produced.

Interpretative Note to Article 6

(For further discussion of "generally accepted accounting principles," please see section 4.3.3, *below*).

Two exceptions to this principle on use of the producer's accounts appear in the **Interpretative Note to Article 6**. First, the cost of containers and packing of the imported goods must be added to the computed value, if the producer has not included these costs in his accounting.

Second, the value of any "assist" listed in **Article 8(1)(b)** that the buyer provides to the manufacturer must be likewise added as a material or processing cost, if not already included in the producer's accounting. As you may remember from the discussion of Article 8 in section 2.2.4, "assists" are:

- materials, parts and components incorporated in the imported goods
- tools, dies, moulds used for production
- materials consumed in production and
- engineering, development, artwork, design work that is undertaken outside the country of importation.[6]

If these assists are provided by the buyer free of charge, their value may not be reflected in the producer's accounts. However, as these items would normally

[6] If design or similar work supplied by the buyer is produced in the country of importation, then the cost of that design work is added to computed value only to the extent the producer is charged for the work.

be reflected as a producer's direct or indirect material or manufacturing overhead costs, their cost must be included in the computed value.

### 3.3.3 An amount for profit and general expenses

In addition to the manufacturing costs just discussed, a producer will normally incur selling and general administrative costs in connection with production and export of the goods.

Selling expenses include sales salaries, sales commissions, marketing and advertising costs, and shipping/delivery expenses. General administrative expenses, which relate to the general management of the business, include such items as office salaries, office supplies, depreciation on office equipment, etc. Possibly, some of these general administrative costs may have been already accounted by the producer in his books as a manufacturing cost; for example, the producer may have included a charge for utilities or property taxes that covers both the factory floor and administrative offices as manufacturing overhead. An **Interpretative Note** thus provides that "general expenses ... covers the direct and indirect costs of producing and selling the goods for export *which are not included [as a manufacturing cost] under* paragraph *1(a) of Article 6*" (emphasis added).

These selling and general administrative expenses, plus an amount for the producer's profit, would normally be covered by the producer's sale price to the importer.

**Article 6(1)(b)** thus requires an amount for profit and general expense to be included in the computed value of the imported goods. In determining the amount of profit and general expense to be added, the Agreement requires customs to accept the information supplied by the producer, unless there is some evidence the amount is not equal to that "usually" found in sales of goods of the "same class or kind" to the same country of importation.

**Non-manufacturing costs – Use producer's accounts unless inconsistent with sales of goods of same class or kind**

The "amount for profit and general expenses" referred to in paragraph 1(b) of Article 6 is to be determined on the basis of information supplied by or on behalf of the producer unless the producer's figures are inconsistent with those usually reflected in sales of goods of the same class or kind as the goods being valued which are made by producers in the country of exportation for export to the country of importation.

Interpretative Note to Article 6

The phrase "goods of the same class or kind" has the same meaning as that which appears in the deductive value method (see discussion at section 3.2, above); that is goods which fall within a group or range of goods produced by a particular industry or industry sector, and includes identical or similar goods.

In the case of a computed value calculation, only goods that are produced in the same country where the imported goods are manufactured can be considered of the same class or kind.

As was also the case in deductive value calculations, the profit and general expense is to be taken as a whole in determining whether it is usual. That is, as long as the total amount is usual, an unusually high or low profit element (considered alone), for example, does not preclude use of computed value.

What is a "usual" profit and general expense for goods of the same class or kind may depend upon the particular commercial circumstances of the transaction. The Interpretative Notes illustrate this point with some specific scenarios:

**"USUAL" PROFIT AND GENERAL EXPENSE**

Where the producer can demonstrate a low profit on sales of the imported goods because of particular commercial circumstances, the producer's actual profit figures should be taken into account provided that the producer has valid commercial reasons to justify them and the producer's pricing policy reflects usual pricing policies in the branch of industry concerned. Such a situation might occur, for example, where producers have been forced to lower prices temporarily because of an unforeseeable drop in demand, or where they sell goods to complement a range of goods being produced in the country of importation and accept a low profit to maintain competitivity. Where the producer's own figures for profit and general expenses are not consistent with those usually reflected in sales of goods of the same class or kind as the goods being valued which are made by producers in the country of exportation for export to the country of importation, the amount for profit and general expenses may be based upon relevant information other than that supplied by or on behalf of the producer of the goods.

Interpretative Note to Article 6

What if there are no other sales of goods made in the producer's country of the same class or kind and exported to the same country of importation? In that case, at least one national customs administration has taken the view that the producer's reported sales and general expense figures can be accepted as "usual" if the producer's books are prepared in accordance with generally accepted accounting principles applicable in the country of production.[7]

[7] See e.g. US Customs Ruling Letter 546801 (November 5, 1998).

### 3.3.4 THE (ACTUAL) COSTS OF INTERNATIONAL TRANSPORT

Where the WTO importing country chooses to include international transportation costs in customs value, then these costs must also be added to derive the computed value. See the discussion on addition of international transport costs to price under the **Article 8**, in section 2.2, above.

## 3.4 FALL-BACK METHOD

*Article 7*

1. If the customs value of the imported goods cannot be determined under the provisions of Articles 1 through 6, inclusive, the customs value shall be determined using reasonable means consistent with the principles and general provisions of this Agreement and of Article VII of GATT 1994 and on the basis of data available in the country of importation.
2. No customs value shall be determined under the provisions of this Article on the basis of:

(a) the selling price in the country of importation of goods produced in such country;
(b) a system which provides for the acceptance for customs purposes of the higher of two alternative values;
(c) the price of goods on the domestic market of the country of exportation;
(d) the cost of production other than computed values which have been determined for identical or similar goods in accordance with the provisions of Article 6;
(e) the price of the goods for export to a country other than the country of importation;
(f) minimum customs values; or
(g) arbitrary or fictitious values.

3. If the importer so requests, the importer shall be informed in writing of the customs value determined under the provisions of this Article and the method used to determine such value.

### 3.4.1 THE VALUATION PRINCIPLE

The five methods of customs valuation – from transaction value through computed value – should provide a customs value for imported goods in nearly all transactions. However, because the WTO Agreement is intended to be a comprehensive system of valuation, it must have a fail-safe – a "fall-back" valuation method – that will produce a valuation result where the other methods cannot be used. These cases may be unusual but they do arise. Some examples:

- Article 7 has been used to value damaged goods that have been returned to the manufacturer in the importing country for repair.[8]
- Article 7 may be used to value articles – such as automobiles – that are purchased and used by individuals for a period of time abroad before arrival to the country of importation.[9]
- Article 7 has also been used to value goods that are returned to a customer in the importing country after being repaired abroad.[10]

In all of these cases, the imported goods were not the subject of an export sale, and the alternatives to the transaction value method were either inapposite in the circumstances or not available due to lack of information.

**An Article 7 scenario**

- Waste is imported for disposal. The importer is paid a fee by the exporter for the disposal service.
- The imported waste was not the subject of a sale for export (therefore, transaction value is not applicable)
- There are no previous imports of identical or similar waste (therefore, transaction value of identical or similar goods is not applicable)
- The waste is not imported for sale but for disposal/destruction (therefore, deductive value is not applicable)
- Information regarding the "production" of waste is not available (therefore, computed value is not applicable)

[8] The US customs administration, for example, has applied Article 7 where damaged goods imported for repair were not the subject of an export sale (title to the goods remained with the purchaser abroad); there were no prior imports of identical or similar goods in such damaged condition; the goods were not resold in the United States; and, the original cost and sales records related to the returned used goods were not available. See, e.g. US Customs Ruling Letter HQ563407 (April 13, 2006).

[9] See Canada Customs and Revenue Agency Memorandum D13–10–2, *Used Automobiles, Motor Vehicles, and Other Vehicles* (March 30, 2001). Article 7 may be applied to second-hand automobiles imported by individuals for personal use, where the car was delivered to the purchaser abroad more than thirty days before the date of importation. In such cases, the imported goods cannot be considered the same as those "sold for export," given the extended use abroad prior to importation; the goods are imported for the importer's own use, not resale; and, used goods are not produced or manufactured as such, thus precluding use of computed value. Unless other imports of used cars can be found that are identical or similar, which is doubtful, use of the fall-back method is appropriate.

[10] Under the European Union's Customs Code, the customs value of goods temporarily exported for repair may be considered "an amount equal to the repair costs, provided that those costs represent the only consideration" that the importer pays to the foreign repair facility and that payment is "not influenced by any links" between the importer and that foreign facility. Article 153, Council Regulation (EEC) No. 2913/92 (October 12, 1992).

The negotiating history suggests two competing concerns underlay the drafting of Article 7. On the one hand, where all the prescribed methods of value fail, customs officers must be given sufficient discretion to work out a customs value in the circumstances of the particular transaction. On the other hand, in the absence of transparency and standards to guide that discretion, there is the danger of arbitrary decision-making and "fictitious" valuations.

**ARTICLE 7 – INTENT OF NEGOTIATORS**

"We expect that the majority of valuation cases will be settled by the application of [the previous valuation methods defined in the Agreement] but we have to recognize that there will be cases where this will not happen. We therefore have to provide what one might call a fall-back method and here we looked at a number of possible alternative approaches. Our aim was to limit so far as possible the scope for arbitrary decisions by customs officials and we came to the conclusion that the current Canadian approach of determining the value in a legal instrument (an order made by a Minister, a regulation) was the best way of limiting the scope for arbitrariness by officials ...

... Furthermore, we believe it important to try to prescribe certain limits so as to avoid arbitrary or fictitious values. You will see that we have proposed that the value established under the provisions of this Article should be based on objective criteria relevant to the circumstances of the particular sale or other transaction and that it should have due regard to the principles and general provisions of the code. Furthermore, we propose that the reasoning by which the value is arrived at should be set out in the legal instrument so as to give the buyer the possibility of challenging the decision in the courts."

*Source*: Commission of the European Communities, MTN/NTM/W/126 at 5 (November 21, 1977).

Article 7 thus provides customs authorities with the discretion to devise their own valuation method as needed to fit the particular circumstances of an import transaction, when all other methods fail. However, that discretion is not unbounded: the means that customs chooses to determine the value must be "reasonable" and "consistent with the principles and general provisions of the Agreement and GATT Article VII," and the method used must be made transparent (i.e. the customs officer must explain it to the importer, in writing, if requested).[11]

[11] As is clear from the quoted excerpt of the Statement made by the European Commission, the original proposal for Article 7 would have required a high level official, such as a Minister, to issue a legal instrument defining the valuation method used in each Article 7 case. Obviously, this requirement was not adopted in the final text of Article 7, which does not require that level of formality. However, Article 7 does capture the principle that the "reasoning by which the value is arrived at" should be set out in writing, so that it can be challenged in court by the importer if necessary.

In addition, to avoid the practical difficulties of Customs overseas verifications, Article 7 provides that the value must be based on information that is available in the country of importation.[12]

The **Interpretative Notes** and Technical Committee opinions provide some guidance as to what methods of valuation under Article 7 might be considered "reasonable" and "consistent with the principles and general provisions of the Agreement and GATT Article VII":

- Customs should use one of the previous five methods defined in the Agreement but apply "reasonable flexibility" or looser interpretation of requirements in order to arrive at a customs value for the imported goods.

  For example, the **Interpretative Note** suggests that when using the transaction value of identical or similar goods, one could consider identical or similar goods that are exported within a broader time frame or that are produced in countries other than the country of exportation. Or, when using the deductive value method, one might consider sales made more than 90 days after the importation.
- Customs should consider flexible application of the previous methods in the sequential order given in the Agreement, starting with transaction value.[13]
- To the "greatest extent possible" a customs value determined under Article 7 should be based on previously-determined customs values.

**Article 7 "Reasonable flexibility"**

A catering company agrees with an airline to supply pre-packaged food for use in domestic flights. The machine used to package foods is unique and expensive so the catering company leases a machine for three years. The average life of the machine is three years. The monthly rental is 2,000 per month.

There is no sale and there are no identical or similar goods. Nor was there a resale of the goods (and therefore deductive value method is not available). A reasonable method to flexibly interpret transaction value may be to use the full rental fee which represents the lifetime of the machine (36 months × 2,000) as the customs value.

Source: Technical Committee, Treatment of Rented or Leased Goods, Case Study 4.1, in *WCO Compendium*

[12] That is, the data must be available to, and verifiable by, customs in the importing country. As long as those criteria are met, the original source of documents and information used could be foreign. See Technical Committee, Use of Data from Foreign Sources in Applying Article 7, Advisory Opinion 12.3, in *WCO Compendium*.

[13] Technical Committee, Advisory Opinion 12.2: Hierarchical Order in Applying Article 7, in *WCO Compendium*.

### 3.4.2 PROHIBITED VALUATION METHODS

In exercising this "flexibility," customs must act consistently with the principles of the Agreement and GATT Article VII. **Article 7** thus expressly prohibits the use of a specified list of valuation methods that are incompatible with these principles. As mentioned in the discussion of the history of the Agreement (see section 1.2), most of the methods proscribed by Article 7 are those that were used by governments prior to the Tokyo Round as "secondary" valuation methods (i.e. applied when the invoice price was not an acceptable basis for valuation) and were found objectionable by other GATT contracting parties. These include:

*(a) The selling price in the country of importation of goods domestically produced*

This recalls the protectionist "American Selling Price" (ASP) valuation method that was designed to equalize differences in costs of production between imported and domestically produced goods. Such systems, which are as trade inhibiting as tariffs or similar measures, violate the GATT Article VII:2 prohibition against valuation based on the price of merchandise of national origin.

*(b) A system which provides for the acceptance for customs purposes of the higher of two alternative values*

Certain pre-Tokyo Round valuation systems (e.g. Australia, South Africa) valued merchandise on the basis of invoice price or current price of the goods in the market of the exporting country, whichever was higher. These are said to create uncertainty because traders cannot predict in advance the customs valuation of their goods.[14]

*(c) Price of goods on the domestic market of the country of exportation*

The objection to the "domestic value" method, which was applied by a number of countries in the years prior to the Tokyo Round, was that prices prevailing

[14] See GATT Multilateral Trade Negotiations, *Part 2 of the Inventory of Non-Tariff Measures: Customs and Administrative Entry Procedures, Note by the Secretariat*, MTN/3B/2 (February 12, 1974). See also GATT Contracting Parties Ninth Session, Review Working Party II on Tariffs, Schedules and Customs Administration, *Articles V, VII, VIII, and IX: Report by the Technical Group on Customs Administration to Review Working Party II*, W.9/155 (January 24, 1955), in which GATT Working Party rejected a proposed amendment to Article VII to prohibit use of "higher of two values" but observed that "[i]t was, however, generally agreed that there were valid grounds of objection to a system of valuation which prescribed the adoption of the higher of figures arrived at by alternative criteria where these criteria were of such a nature that the traders concerned could not, in advance, calculate the figures from which the higher would be chosen, since this could constitute a serious impediment to trade."

in the domestic market of the exporting country do not necessarily reflect the prices at which exporters could sell the goods in the international markets generally, or the importing country in particular. Also objectionable was the difficulties and burden placed on exporters in price investigations undertaken in the exporting country.[15]

*(d)* *Cost of production other than computed values which have been determined for identical or similar goods in accordance with the provisions of Article 6 (computed value)*

Article 6 defines a valuation method based on the production costs of the *imported* goods. This provision of Article 7 allows customs to extend Article 6 to determine valuation of the imported goods based on the production costs of *identical* or *similar* goods.

*(e)* *The price of goods for export to a country other than the country of importation*

The defect of this method is the same as the method that bases valuation on the price of goods in the domestic market of the exporting country (see point "c" above).

*(f)* *Minimum customs values*

Official or minimum values were used by a number of countries (particularly, developing countries) prior to the WTO Valuation Agreement to protect domestic industries, among other reasons (see section 1.2 above). Developing countries' continued use of minimum values is subject to reservation and agreement by other WTO members (see section 4.4, below); otherwise, these are prohibited.

*(g)* *Arbitrary or fictitious values*

The phrase "arbitrary or fictitious values" is not further elaborated in the WTO Valuation Agreement. It is taken directly from GATT Article VII:2(a), which provides that:

[15] As noted in section 1.2, developing countries complained that prices in their home markets could be "artificially high[er]" than export prices, due to supply scarcities, structural imbalances and inflationary pressures prevalent in such countries. In smaller countries (e.g. Switzerland) it was claimed that higher prices prevailed than in the international market because quantities sold at home were smaller. See MTN/3B/2 (February 12, 1974).

> The value for customs purposes of imported merchandise should be based on the actual value of the imported merchandise on which the duty is assessed, or of like merchandise, and should not be based on the value of merchandise of national origin or on **arbitrary or fictitious values**.

Given that GATT Article VII sets this contrast between "actual value" (the value of imported goods or like merchandise) and "arbitrary and fictitious values," the phrase has been interpreted to mean a system using values "that are not related to the value of the imported merchandise in question or of like imported merchandise."[16] So, for example, a valuation method based on prices of goods manufactured in the importing country, has been considered arbitrary.

A system that provides full discretion to a customs officer or other government official to fix values of imported goods might be considered "arbitrary," as might a method that fixes a value for all imported goods of a certain kind (i.e. a set price per kilogram of used clothing, regardless of quality, country of origin, export price, etc.).[17]

### 3.4.3 Article 7 and valuation of used goods

The customs valuation of used articles has historically been a particular challenge for customs administrations. Generally, the difficulty lies not in the application of customs valuation principles, but in customs doubts about the truth or accuracy of the declared prices. These doubts may arise because importers of used articles are often individuals rather than commercial entities known to customs; the transactions can be informal and cash based; and the market value of a used article is dependent on its specific condition and therefore can be highly varied. It has been said that used articles, particularly automobiles, are frequently undervalued.

**Importation of used articles: customs valuation – and other – practical difficulties (A WTO Member notification*)**

*[Used tires]*

"The declared values for tyres usually do not represent even 5 per cent of the cost of a new tyre. In addition, the tyres are so worn that they do not meet the safety requirements for this type of product. Particularly, the lack of proper papers and

[16] GATT, Valuation for Customs Purposes: *Questionnaire for the Ninth Session*, L/228 (September 20, 1954).

[17] MTN/3B/2 (February 12, 1974).

the minimum value declared by the importer for such products constitute unfair competition for importers of new articles of this kind."

*[Used clothing]*
"Imports of worn clothing have an adverse impact on the economy and directly affect the development of small- and medium-sized industry engaged in manufacturing clothing and footwear. Furthermore, this sector of our industry, which generates a large number of jobs, is seriously affected by the competition from imports of these products, for which insignificant values are declared and for which the tax authority does not have sufficient human and material resources to determine the real transaction value and thus minimize the adverse effects of cheap imports on domestic production.

Moreover, in a country with six million inhabitants and an economically active population of two million, about 10 per cent are small employers who create approximately five jobs per firm and some manufacture clothing and footwear for the majority of the population not in a position to purchase imported products. They are seriously affected by imports of used products."

*[Used domestic appliances]*
"As for imports of used domestic appliances, many of which have been got rid of in the developed countries because of their negative effect on the ozone layer, Honduras, pursuant to the provisions of the Montreal Protocol, to which we are signatories, is under an obligation to establish measures to help shift consumer preferences to new or used articles that meet environmental protection requirements."

*[Used automobiles]*
"Reference prices are retained for motor vehicles in order to assure fair market play and our population's health and safety for the following reasons:

- These goods are usually supplied through the informal sector, a group which in most instances does not provide proper papers for sales, and virtually no method or concept of value can be applied, thus causing unfair competition for the firms engaged in normal trade in new vehicles.
- Since they are "second-hand" products with a great deal of wear and tear, in most cases they create health problems and environmental contamination, giving rise to conditions that are in no sense beneficial to the quality of life of the inhabitants of developing countries.
- Furthermore, additional measures have to be taken to protect the consumer and the environment, and are also necessary to prevent road accidents, which generally occur because these vehicles are very old models with worn parts."

* *Source*: Statement by Honduras, G/VAL/W/44/Rev.1 (November 16, 1999).

Under the Agreement, if a valid transaction value exists, it should be used as the customs value of the imported goods. This principle applies equally to second-hand goods imported by individuals for their personal use as it does to new goods imported by commercial enterprises for resale or distribution. Of course, customs may reject the declared value as the basis for customs value where it has reasonable doubts as to the truth or accuracy of the importer's declaration or supporting documents, subject to the provisions of the **Decision Regarding Cases Where Customs Administrations Have Reasons to Doubt the Truth or Accuracy of the Declared Value** (see section 4.3, below).

There can be a question whether imported used goods were the same as those "sold for export." As you may recall, the definition of transaction value is the "price actually paid or payable *for the goods* when sold for export." In the case of an automobile, for example, "the goods" purchased by an individual in the country of exportation may not be the same as the goods ultimately imported, if the car is used for a period of time abroad before brought (or driven) to the country of importation. In such cases, can the purchase in the foreign market be used as the basis of transaction value?

According to a Technical Committee study, this is a question that should be "left to the discretion of each [customs] administration because the widely differing situations which may arise in this field do not lend themselves to harmonization of the practices adopted."[18] The Canadian Customs administration, for example, has responded with a "thirty-day rule": if vehicles and boats are imported within thirty days of the date of delivery to the purchaser abroad "a valid sale for export to Canada is considered to have occurred, and any use of the vehicle or boat prior to importation will be regarded as being incidental to delivery of the vehicle or boat to Canada."[19] If more than thirty days have passed, use of the transaction value method based on the sale to the purchaser would not be appropriate.

Where transaction value cannot be used, and the other methods applied in sequence also fail to produce a customs valuation, customs may appraise the imported used automobiles under Article 7. The Technical Committee study suggests how, through a "reasonabl[y] flexibl[e]" application of the Article 1–5 methods, such an Article 7 valuation might be derived:

- *Flexible transaction value*: use the price actually paid or payable for the imported goods, adjusted downward by a depreciation factor determined by the age or odometer reading of the car.
- *Flexible transaction value of identical goods*: use the previously accepted transaction value of identical imported new cars of the same make and model, adjusted downward to take into account the use and condition of the imported car and, possibly, adjusted upward to take into account any accessories/features the used car has that the new car did not (plus the usual Article 2 adjustments for differences in quantity and/or commercial level).

[18] Technical Committee, Treatment of Used Motor Vehicles, Study 1.1, in *WCO Compendium*.

[19] Canada Customs and Revenue Agency Memorandum D13–10–2, *Used Automobiles, Motor Vehicles, and Other Vehicles* (March 30, 2001).

- *Flexible transaction value of similar goods*: same as above, but start with the accepted transaction value of new cars of different make or model (but otherwise similar).
- *Flexible deductive value*: use catalogue of prices of new imported cars of the same make and model sold in the country of importation, with adjustments for depreciation plus the usual deductive value adjustments (i.e. customs duties, inland transport costs, etc.).
- *Flexible deductive value*: use catalogue of prices of used imported cars of the same make and model sold in the country of importation, with adjustments necessary to take into account the particular condition of the imported car, as well as the usual deductive value adjustments.

What is not permitted would be a customs valuation based on a catalogue of (i) prices of new or used cars that are manufactured in the country of importation, or (ii) prices of new or imported cars as offered for sale on the domestic market of the country of exportation.[20]

### Case study

*Valuation of used cars under Article 7*

At a WTO conference, a WTO Member country in Eastern Europe described its methodology for valuation of imported used cars as follows:

"As a rule, customs value of used cars for purposes of assessing customs duty and VAT is based on the price actually paid or payable, plus the value of transport costs and insurance.

As a proof of sale of the imported car, the customs officers may accept any document which contains the following main elements: type, model, price, number of chassis, technical specifications. The document may be: invoice or sales contract, which provides proof of the sale and the price actually paid.

In determining the customs value of the used cars, Customs officials use the SUPERSCHWACKE catalogue as a reference catalogue. This is a catalogue or price list that is published abroad in Germany and which contains the prices of new cars and average prices of used passenger, off-road and light commercial vehicles sold on the German market in the previous 12 years. At the time of customs clearance, the latest issue of SUPERSCHWACKE will be used.

[20] There may be cases, however, where the catalogue price is the same for the domestic market as for export. "For imported used vehicles which are not 'sold for export to Canada,' importers may declare a value for duty by referencing used vehicle valuation guides published in the country of export, which list retail sales values for vehicles in average condition. These values indicate the amount any purchaser can expect to pay for the vehicle, **whether purchased for use in the country of export or for export to Canada**. Examples of such publications are the *US Automobile Red Book – Official Used Car Valuations* and *Parker's Used, New and Trade, Car Price Guide* published in the United Kingdom. The value of any options included in the vehicle being valued which are not included in the basic price of the vehicle as listed in the guide must be added in order to determine the customs value." Canada Customs and Revenue Agency Memorandum D13–10–2 (emphasis added).

Based on the documents submitted for the clearance of a used car (car specifications, invoice and other supporting documents), the customs officer will check the high and low prices in the catalogue SUPERSCHWACKE for the imported vehicle for the appropriate year of production.

If the invoice value falls between the high and low value given in the catalogue, the customs value is determined according to the transaction value method. In this case the customs value is the invoice value together with the transport and insurance costs.

If the declared price of the used car falls below the lower catalogue value, the customs value is determined according to fall-back value method. In this case the customs value is the lower catalogue value increased by the transportation and insurance costs."

Is this valuation methodology consistent with the principles of the WTO Agreement?

For the answers, see p. 134.

## 3.5 ANSWER KEY

### TEST YOUR KNOWLEDGE – IDENTIFY IDENTICAL OR SIMILAR GOODS

*Invoice no. 2, dated February 1, 2007*

These roses from the Netherlands are NOT identical or similar to the goods under valuation, which are from Ecuador. Pursuant to Article 15(d) of the Agreement, "goods shall not be regarded as 'identical goods' or 'similar goods' unless they were produced in the same country as the goods being valued."

*Invoice no. 3, dated November 15, 2006*

Valuation under Article 2 or 3 of the Agreement requires that the identical or similar goods are "exported at or about the same time as the goods being valued." The goods under valuation were exported on February 9, 2007 for the Valentine's Day market, while this shipment was exported on November 1, 2006, more than three months earlier.

The WTO Customs Valuation Agreement standard that goods must be "exported at or *about* the same time" is explicitly flexible. However, a difference of more than three months between the shipments may be too great in an industry, like the cut flower industry, where price is known to be affected by seasonal factors such as higher demand around Valentine's Day and other holidays.

*Invoice no. 4, dated February 10, 2007*

Article 15 of the Agreement defines "Identical Goods" as "goods which are the same in all respects, including physical characteristics, quality and reputation." "Similar goods" are those which "have like characteristics and like component materials which enable them to perform the same functions and to be commercially interchangeable."

The goods described in this invoice involve a different variety of rose than the goods under valuation (spray and sweetheart roses *versus* hybrid tea roses), as well as a different grade of rose (short stem *versus* long stem). In the rose industry, these differences – particularly in grade – are commercially important, and could preclude customs from finding that they are identical or similar to the goods under valuation.

*Invoice no. 5, dated February 10, 2007*

These goods are identical in description to the goods under valuation, were exported at or about the same time, and were produced in the same country. The goods were not produced by the same seller as the goods under valuation (Agro Rose Farms *versus* Cotopaxi Farms), appear to be different commercial levels (a wholesaler *versus* a retail grocery market) and are not sold in the same quantities (10,000 units *versus* 100 units).

Nevertheless, Article 15(e) provides that these goods sold by other producers could be used as the basis for valuation under Article 2, "if there are no identical goods or similar goods, as the case may be, produced by the same person as the goods being valued."

Similarly, Article 2 of the Agreement provides that if qualifying sales at the same commercial level and substantially same quantity cannot be found, other sales can be used, "adjusted to take account of differences attributable to commercial level and/or quantity."

### Test your knowledge – identifying the relevant unit sale price

During this period, 1955 units at a unit price of $48 were sold. This exceeds the aggregate quantity of any other given unit price. Accordingly, the unit price in the greatest aggregate quantity would be $48, and should be used as the basis for deductive value calculation. This is true even though $48 is not the per unit price of the single largest shipment or the most recent shipment.

### Case study – valuation of used cars under Article 7

As we noted in section 3.4 above, customs may reject a declared value where there are "reasonable doubts" about the truth or accuracy of the declaration or supporting documents, and subject to the requirements of the Ministerial **Decision Regarding Cases Where Customs Administrations Have Reasons to Doubt the Truth or Accuracy of the Declared Value**. But, the fact that the declared price falls below a catalogue price would generally not be a sufficient reason – by itself – to reject the declared value, given that the low price may be the result of a discount, or due to changes in market conditions, or due to the condition of the imported car, or due to any of a number of other factors that came into play in the parties' transaction. Moreover, under the facts of the scenario, the substitution of the catalogue price for the declared transaction value might be considered a use of a "minimum value system" prohibited under Article 7.

# 4

# IMPLEMENTATION AND OPERATION

## 4.1 CURRENCY CONVERSION

> *Article 9*
>
> 1. Where the conversion of currency is necessary for the determination of the customs value, the rate of exchange to be used shall be that duly published by the competent authorities of the country of importation concerned and shall reflect as effectively as possible, in respect of the period covered by each such document of publication, the current value of such currency in commercial transactions in terms of the currency of the country of importation.
> 2. The conversion rate to be used shall be that in effect at the time of exportation or the time of importation, as provided by each Member.

Importers are generally required to declare customs value in the importing country's national currency, even though the underlying sales transaction may have been conducted in a foreign currency. This requires the importer to convert the foreign currency – but at what rate?

In the absence of rules, a country could use exchange rates for protective or discriminatory purposes. For example, it could require that importers of certain products use a special (unfavorable) exchange rate, which would inflate the customs value of the imported goods, and therefore the amount of duty and tax the importer must pay.

The WTO Agreement does not dictate use of any particular exchange rate or method of conversion. **Article 9** of the Agreement does, however, impose three requirements designed to promote transparency and predictability. These are:

- the exchange rate used must be that which has been duly published by "competent authorities" (this might be the Central Bank, Treasury Department, or exchange markets)
- the rate must reflect, as effectively as possible, the current value of the foreign currency in commercial transactions in terms of the currency of the country of importation
- the country must use for all imports either the rate that is in effect on the date the goods were exported or the exchange rate in effect at the date of importation.

Commercial rates for currencies change daily (if only by fractional amounts), but to require customs and importers to follow those changes can present significant administrative difficulties, such as disseminating the new rates to all customs offices, or updating tables in declaration processing systems.

The Agreement therefore allows countries to adopt a flexible approach that would permit a customs administration to use periodic rates for valuation purposes. For example, a customs authority might use for an extended period – for a week or even a calendar quarter – the same, unchanging exchange rate for a foreign currency that is "stable" against the national currency, and use a daily rate for less stable currencies. As noted, a periodic rate must reflect "as effectively as possible" the current value of the currency in commercial transaction over the designated period and, in all cases, the rate and its period of application must be published.

## 4.2 IMPORTER PROCEDURAL RIGHTS

The WTO Customs Valuation Agreement requires a good deal of co-operation between importers and customs. The information customs needs for valuation is largely in the hands of the importer: prices paid for goods, contract terms, information on prior sales of similar or identical goods, production costs in the foreign country, or resale costs in the home market, etc. For that reason, the Agreement provides customs with rights to question and obtain information from importers. On the other hand, to ensure fairness and transparency in the valuation process – and thereby encourage greater co-operation between customs and traders – the Agreement also provides importers with certain procedural rights and protections.

These rights and protections, which must be taken into account in WTO Members' legislation, are as follows:

### 4.2.1 Protection of confidential information

*Article 10*

All information which is by nature confidential or which is provided on a confidential basis for the purposes of customs valuation shall be treated as strictly confidential by the authorities concerned who shall not disclose it without the specific permission of the person or government providing such information, except to the extent that it may be required to be disclosed in the context of judicial proceedings.

Customs and other governmental authorities are required to protect confidential information they may receive for purposes of customs valuation, whether from the importer, other persons, or governments. They may disclose this information only if required to do so in a court proceeding, or otherwise with the specific permission of the person or government who provided it.

What is confidential information that customs and other authorities must strictly protect? The Agreement sets out two general standards:

1. information that is "by nature" confidential
2. information that is provided on a confidential basis.

The interpretation of these standards in concrete cases is left to individual WTO Members. Generally speaking, information "by nature" confidential might include the importer's prices, the identity of his suppliers, specific contract terms, or other such financial or commercial information which he would usually not disclose publicly as it would harm him competitively.

### 4.2.2 Right of appeal

*Article 11*

1. The legislation of each Member shall provide in regard to a determination of customs value for the right of appeal, without penalty, by the importer or any other person liable for the payment of the duty.
2. An initial right of appeal without penalty may be to an authority within the customs administration or to an independent body, but the legislation of each Member shall provide for the right of appeal without penalty to a judicial authority.
3. Notice of the decision on appeal shall be given to the appellant and the reasons for such decision shall be provided in writing. The appellant shall also be informed of any rights of further appeal.

Importers – or any other person responsible for payment of duty (such as the surety who guarantees the importer's liability) – must be given a right to appeal adverse customs valuation decisions to a judicial authority, and to receive a written decision.

WTO Members can require that importers take an initial appeal to customs (for example, to customs headquarters against a decision by a local office) or another independent body, such as an administrative tribunal.

The right of appeal must be available without penalty; that is, an importer should not be discouraged from exercising his right of appeal by threat of a fine or penalty. At the time of the negotiations on the GATT Valuation Code, in some countries valuation cases were heard by the criminal courts, where the importer was subject to a fine if he lost.[1]

However, as stated in the **Interpretative Note to Article 11**, payment of normal court costs and lawyers' fees are not considered a "fine" for this purpose (apparently to accommodate those jurisdictions that apply the so-called "English Rule," whereby the loser in civil litigation pays court and legal fees), and the WTO Members may require the payment of the contested duty amount before allowing the appeal.

### 4.2.3 Right to explanation

> *Article 16*
>
> Upon written request, the importer shall have the right to an explanation in writing from the customs administration of the country of importation as to how the customs value of the importer's goods was determined.

Closely linked to the right of appeal is the importer's right to receive an explanation from customs as to how the value was determined. In order to make an effective appeal against a customs decision (or to decide whether to make an appeal), the importer must be told the reasons for the decision.

A written explanation is required from customs only if the importer requests it. If the customs valuation is based on the transaction value that the importer himself declared, no explanation would normally be needed. The explanation is important, however, when customs rejects the declared price and values the imported goods under an alternative method. In these cases, the basis for the valuation, the method of calculation, and/or the information customs takes into account may not be apparent to the importer.[2]

This Article 16 principle is restated, with more specificity, in certain of the other articles of the Agreement concerning use of the alternative valuation methods. In particular, **Article 1(2)(a)** (transaction value method) requires customs to communicate the reasons it believes a declared related-party price should be rejected when it finds the price was influenced by the relationship.

[1] See GATT Multilateral Trade Negotiations Group "Non-Tariff Measures" Sub-Group "Customs Matters," *Customs Valuation*, MTN/NTM/W/20 at 8 (September 29, 1975).

[2] Article 16 appears to have evolved from "draft interpretative note" No. 11 written by the 1971 Committee on Trade in Industrial Products (CTIP) (see chapter 1, text accompanying note 35), which provides: "The customs administration shall explain to the importer or exporter, on his request, how the customs value has been calculated for his goods, particularly in cases where the invoice price is not acceptable, provided the confidentiality of business secrets is safeguarded."

In the negotiations on the GATT Valuation Code, a number of countries proposed that this CTIP principle be included in the new agreement to provide greater transparency where customs uses an alternative valuation method. See MTN/NTM/W/20 at 9–10 (September 29, 1975).

Similarly, where customs applies the fall-back valuation method, **Article 7(3)** requires, if the importer requests, a written explanation of the method used to determine the value. Finally, if customs uses information other than that supplied by the producer to calculate a computed value, an **Interpretative Note to Article 6** requires customs, on request, to inform the importer of the source of the information and the uses to which it is put.

The negotiation history of the GATT Valuation Code suggests that, in addition to promoting transparency and enabling an effective appeal, the requirement of a written explanation in these particular cases was intended as a check on arbitrary customs decisions to reject declared prices in related-party transactions and substitute an uplifted value on a discretionary basis.[3]

### 4.2.4 Publication of laws and decisions

> *Article 12*
>
> Laws, regulations, judicial decisions and administrative rulings of general application giving effect to this Agreement shall be published in conformity with Article X of GATT 1994 by the country of importation concerned.

**Article 12** requires WTO Members to publish "in conformity with" **GATT Article X** all national laws, regulations, judicial decisions and administrative rulings of general application which give effect to the Valuation Agreement.

**GATT Article X** is the general transparency and due process guarantee of the GATT. It essentially requires each WTO Member to:

1. publish its trade-related laws, regulations, rulings and agreements "promptly in such a manner as to enable governments and traders to become acquainted with them" (Article X:1)
2. abstain from enforcing measures of general application prior to their publication (Article X:2) and
3. administer the above-mentioned laws, regulations, rulings and agreements in a uniform, impartial and reasonable manner. In this context, parties are required to institute or maintain tribunals or procedures for

[3] "United States exporters have experienced problems with countries that use the Brussels Definition of Value in applying 'uplifts' whenever the importer and exporter are 'associated in business.' The customs official operating under the BDV fixes a percentage increase on merchandise between related parties or on entries by a buyer having exclusive purchasing rights. This may not always reflect the real costs involved in the transaction. The problem appears primarily related to the failure of customs officials to employ real costs in calculating uplifts and to explain how they arrived at the percentage of uplift. Thus, international rules on customs valuation should reflect CTIP Interpretative Note, No. 11. In other words, customs officials should be required to explain on request to importers or exporters how the customs value has been calculated for their goods." MTN/NTM/W/20 at 10.

the, *inter alia*, prompt review and correction of administrative action relating to customs matters (Article X:3).[4]

The Article 12 (and GATT Article X) publication obligation extends only to trade measures of "general application" as opposed to measures that deal with specific transactions, such as an administrative ruling or court decision on a specific shipment or addressed to a specific company.[5] Moreover, Members are permitted to withhold publication of decisions and other legal measures where necessary for the protection of confidential information.[6]

An early decision of the Valuation Committee requires Members to provide the WTO Secretariat with copies of all national legislation on customs valuation (laws, regulations, etc.) in one of the three WTO languages (i.e. English, Spanish and French).[7] Text of laws and regulations submitted by Members is publicly accessible for examination via the WTO website. Further, **Article 22** of the Agreement requires Members to notify the Valuation Committee of "any changes in its laws and regulations relevant to this Agreement and in the administration of such laws and regulations"; these notifications are likewise publicly available via the website.

WTO Member's valuation legislation can be accessed via the WTO website under the document code G/VAL/N/*.

### 4.2.5 Release under guarantee

> ***Article 13***
>
> If, in the course of determining the customs value of imported goods, it becomes necessary to delay the final determination of such customs value, the importer of the goods shall nevertheless be able to withdraw them from customs if, where so required, the importer provides sufficient guarantee in the form of a surety, a deposit or some other appropriate instrument, covering the ultimate payment of customs duties for which the goods may be liable. The legislation of each Member shall make provisions for such circumstances.

[4] See WTO Negotiating Group on Trade Facilitation, *Article X of GATT 1994 – Scope and Application: Note by the Secretariat*, TN/TF/W/4 at 4 (January 12, 2005).

[5] *Ibid.* (reviewing WTO Appellate Body and Panel interpretations under GATT Article X:1). An administrative ruling might be considered general – and therefore must be published – if it would "establish or revise principles or criteria applicable in future cases."

[6] This is according to GATT Article X:1 ("The provisions of this paragraph shall not require any contracting party to disclose confidential information which would impede law enforcement or otherwise be contrary to the public interest or would prejudice the legitimate commercial interests of particular enterprises, public or private.").

[7] See WTO Committee on Customs Valuation, *Decisions concerning the Interpretation and Administration of the Agreement on Implementation of Article VII of the GATT 1994 (Customs Valuation)*, G/VAL/5 at 5 (October 13, 1995) (in Appendix).

When customs challenges an importer's declared value, the importer is often required to collect and provide supporting sales and other documentation on the transaction, which may or may not be readily available to the importer. Or, the importer may simply not have provided a document (such as a commercial invoice) required for customs clearance. Resolution of these situations can involve complex questions and delay clearance of the goods.

In these or other circumstances where customs is unable to make a final value determination at the time of importation, the Agreement provides importers with the important procedural right to obtain release of their goods from customs subject, if necessary, to the provision of a sufficient guarantee (a bond, a cash deposit, etc.) to cover the potential duty liability. Absent this requirement, the goods could be held by customs at the border, accruing demurrage charges and putting the importer at risk of late delivery to his customer, until the valuation issues are resolved.

## 4.3 CUSTOMS VERIFICATION

### 4.3.1 Right to verify truth or accuracy

*Article 17*

Nothing in this Agreement shall be construed as restricting or calling into question the rights of customs administrations to satisfy themselves as to the truth or accuracy of any statement, document or declaration presented for customs valuation purposes.

Under the Agreement, transaction value – the price that is *actually* paid or payable – is the primary basis for customs valuation. Where an importer, whether due to inadvertence, negligent error or fraud, declares a price to customs that is not the "actual" amount paid or payable, the Agreement does not oblige customs to accept it. Further, **Article 17** of the Agreement reaffirms the rights of customs authorities to question or investigate the truth or accuracy of any declarations or supporting documents submitted by the importer.

This verification right of customs administrations is reiterated in **Annex III, paragraph 6** of the Agreement, which provides:

> Article 17 recognizes that in applying the Agreement, customs administrations may need to make enquiries concerning the truth or accuracy of any statement, document or declaration presented to them for customs valuation purposes. This Article thus acknowledges that enquiries may be made which are, for example, aimed at verifying that the elements of value declared or presented to customs in connection with a determination of customs value are complete and correct. Members, subject

to their national laws and procedures, have the right to expect the full cooperation of importers in these enquiries.

Although this principle of customs control may seem unremarkable, its practical implementation has been a long-standing concern to some customs administrations – particularly those of developing countries. The issue is the burden of proof: to reject transaction value, must customs prove that the invoice price declared by the importer is not correct or incomplete and, if so, what level of proof is required? Since the evidence of the actual amounts paid is within the control of the importer suspected of the fraud, customs may have some difficulty establishing this proof, particularly in the cases where the exporter and importer are acting in collusion.

### *(a) Technical Committee advisory opinions*

Because of these concerns, the Technical Committee in the 1980's clarified customs rights under the Tokyo Round Code through a series of advisory opinions. These opinions held that:

1. the mere fact that a price is lower than the prevailing market price for identical goods is not a basis to reject transaction value, subject to Article 17[8]
2. the Valuation Agreement does not require customs to rely on fraudulent documentation[9] and
3. national laws and regulations, rather than the terms of the Agreement, govern whether customs or the importer bears the burden of proof in the course of the determination of customs value.[10]

Nevertheless, burden of proof remained a concern for developing country members, and a reason at least some did not accede to the Tokyo Round Valuation Code.[11]

### *(b) Uruguay Round Ministerial decision*

The burden of proof question became a major point of negotiation in the Uruguay Round as a result of a proposal by the government of India. India

[8] Technical Committee, Acceptability of a Price below Prevailing Market Prices for Identical Goods, Advisory Opinion 2.1, in *WCO Compendium*.

[9] Technical Committee, Treatment of Fraudulent Documents, Advisory Opinion 10.1, in *WCO Compendium*.

[10] Technical Committee, Application of Article 17 of the Agreement and Paragraph 6 of Annex III, Advisory Opinion 19.1 in *WCO Compendium*; Group of Negotiations on Goods (GATT), Negotiating Group on MTN Agreements and Arrangements, *Communications from the Customs Co-operation Council*, MTN.GNG/NG8/W33 (August 29, 1988).

[11] Group of Negotiations on Goods (GATT), Negotiating Group on MTN Agreements and Arrangements, *MTN Agreements and Arrangements: Special and Differential Treatment for Developing Countries, Note by the Secretariat*, MTN.GNG/NG8/W/2 (May 4, 1986).

proposed that the Agreement should provide "adequate flexibility" to allow customs to shift the burden to the importer to prove the validity of the declared price where the declared price (i) "is less than that noticed in a series of transactions immediately preceding the relevant one" or (ii) "is less than that noticed for transactions involving identical goods imported directly from the country of manufacture."[12]

The terms of India's proposal were not accepted as such. However, the negotiations did produce a WTO Ministerial decision that clarifies the burden of proof question. This is the **Decision Regarding Cases Where Customs Administrations Have Reasons to Doubt the Truth or Accuracy of the Declared Value**. That decision places a responsibility on the importer to provide information or documentation to show that the declared price represents the total amount actually paid or payable where customs has "reasons to doubt" the truth or accuracy of the valuation declaration or supporting documents.

Where Customs has "reasons to doubt" the truth or accuracy of a declaration or supporting documents...

- Customs ***may*** ask the importer for additional information/documentation
- Based on information received (if any) Customs ***may*** reject transaction value *if* it still has reasonable doubts but:
  - Customs ***must*** inform the importer of its reasons for doubts, in writing if requested
  - Customs ***must*** give the importer a reasonable opportunity to respond
  - Customs ***must*** inform the importer in writing of the final decision

The full text of the decision is contained in Appendix 2.

### *(c) "Reasons to doubt"*

What are sufficient "reasons to doubt" to justify customs requiring the importer to provide information? Inconsistencies or irregularities in the documents presented

12 Group of Negotiations on Goods (GATT), Negotiating Group on MTN Agreements and Arrangements, *Communication from India*, MTN.GNG/NG8/W/9 (September 30, 1987). As noted in section 1.2 on the history of the Valuation Agreement, India's proposal was supported by Brazil and a number of other developing countries.

for customs clearance of the goods are obvious "reasons to doubt," but fraud is not always that transparent. The phrase is not further elaborated in the Uruguay Round Ministerial decision.[13] Some light might be shed by placing the decision within the context of customs methods for control of fraud generally.

Modern customs controls, as defined by the Kyoto Convention, emphasize use of post-clearance audit of traders' books and records – rather than movement-based, import-by-import control – and rely upon risk analysis to determine which traders and transactions should be examined and the extent of the examination.[14] The WCO and most WTO Members take the position that intelligence-based risk assessment and post-clearance auditing systems are fundamental to effective customs valuation control.[15]

The goal of risk-based systems is to concentrate customs resources on transactions that present the highest probability of violations, with the gravest impact if not controlled, while allowing the balance of trade to clear customs without intervention. Under a risk-based system, a customs administration will build "risk profiles" or combinations of risk indicators which, based on intelligence, past experience, or probability, identify those transactions that, if presented to customs, should be selected for control. Risk indicators might be a particular commodity code, the country of origin of the goods, the compliance history of the parties involved in the transaction, the customs procedure declared, the type or itinerary of the carrier, etc.

"Reasons to doubt" might thus be considered a kind of "risk profile" that customs has identified, using risk assessment principles, as presenting a high risk of valuation error or fraud. If an import transaction matches such a profile, customs – applying the Uruguay Round Ministerial decision – might thus require the importer to submit additional information or documents to support the declared suspect value.

### 4.3.2 Valuation databases

A "reason to doubt" the truth or accuracy of an importer's declaration might be supported by a finding of a discrepancy between the declared value and historic prices for the same goods. For this purpose – as well as to support appraisement decisions generally where determination of the value of "identical" or "similar" goods is an issue – some customs administrations have developed

[13] The terms of the decision itself appear to have been derived from US customs practices dealing with suspect false invoices. See GATT Committee on Customs Valuation, *Report by the Technical Committee on Customs Valuation Concerning the Effects of False Invoicing on Customs Valuation*, VAL/W/32 (November 7, 1985) (paragraph 17).

[14] Kyoto Convention, Standards 6.4 and 6.6.

[15] See e.g. WTO Committee on Customs Valuation, *Minutes of the Meeting of 30 September – 1 October 2002*, G/VAL/M 31 (October 31, 2002).

valuation databases. These databases store previously accepted customs values and related transaction details, and may also include price information from other sources, such as price catalogues, customs audit results, or price data from pre-shipment inspection companies. With access to the database, customs users can more quickly and precisely cross-check suspect declarations or obtain values required for the application of Article 2 or 3 of the Agreement.

In 2004, the Technical Committee issued guidelines on the use of valuation databases for the benefit of national customs administrations.[16] The guidelines are a response to the WTO Ministerial Doha Mandate "to identify and assess practical means" to address developing country concerns about valuation fraud.[17] The guidelines contain recommendations on the source of data to be included, confidentiality of data, the age of records to be kept, and the potential uses of the database. In addition, the guidelines address concerns expressed by some WTO Members that valuation databases might be misused, for example, to substitute previously accepted prices for the declared price, or as a means to establish a system of minimum values.

**WCO GUIDELINES**

*Use of valuation databases as a risk assessment tool*

*Customs officials may*:

- (generally) control transactions based on differences with the valuation database only if other risk factors are present
- use the database to perform cross-checks to target specific import declarations for examination

*Customs officials should not*:

- reject declared values based solely on differences with database value(s)
- substitute database prices for declared values
- use database prices as a mechanism to establish minimum values
- disregard the requirements of Article 13 of the Agreement (allowing release of imported goods under guarantee) in order to employ a valuation database
- rely solely on a valuation database to assess the truth or accuracy of the declared value.

16 WTO, Committee on Customs Valuation, *Technical Committee on Customs Valuation – Response to the Terms of Reference for the Work of the Technical Committee on Customs Valuation in Connection with Concerns on the Accuracy of the Declared Value: Supplement*, G/VAL/54/Suppl.1 (October 13, 2004) (includes text of the WCO's "Guidelines on the Development and Use of a National Valuation Database as a Risk Assessment Tool").

17 WTO Committee on Customs Valuation, *Terms of Reference for the Work of the Technical Committee on Customs Valuation in Connection with Concerns on the Accuracy of the Declared Value*, G/VAL/51 (December 11, 2002).

With regard to customs use of historic prices as a basis for finding "reasons to doubt" a declared price, the Technical Committee's guidelines state that, a difference between the declared price and historic prices for the same goods is not by itself a reliable indicator of potential risk with respect to the truth or accuracy of the declared value (unless, perhaps, it is an abnormally large discrepancy). This is because differences in prices, including substantial declines, are a part of international trade. However, price differences can be used, if in combination with other risk factors, to target import shipments for control.

The full text of the Technical Committee's valuation database guidelines is set out in Appendix 4.

**Case study**

*Use of valuation databases*

The following valuation practice is reported to be used by an Asian country: Customs officials check the price declared by the importer against their valuation database. If the declared price is significantly lower than the average price for goods previously imported under the same tariff classification code, customs officials may ask the importer for additional documents or information to support the declared price. Pending determination of final valuation, customs will allow conditional release of the goods, provided the declarant submits a guarantee or deposit in an amount equivalent to the duty and taxes estimated on the basis of the average price from the valuation database.

If the importer is unable to satisfy customs request for the supporting documents or information within sixty days, customs will reject the declared price and, citing Article 7 of the Agreement as the basis for valuation, collect customs duties and taxes based on the amount of the conditional release deposit or guarantee (i.e. based on the average value for the goods given by the valuation database).

Question:

Is this use of valuation database prices to assess value consistent with the principles of the Agreement?

For the answers, see p. 155.

### 4.3.3 Generally accepted accounting principles

A general Interpretative Note to the Agreement requires customs authorities to "utilize information prepared in a manner consistent with **generally accepted accounting principles**" in the country which is appropriate for the Article in question.

In other words, customs may not reject cost or value data submitted by an importer on the basis of the accounting method by which that information was prepared, if the preparation was in accordance with the generally accepted accounting principles or "GAAP."

**Generally accepted accounting principles – Definition**

1. "Generally accepted accounting principles" refers to the recognized consensus or substantial authoritative support within a country at a particular time as to which economic resources and obligations should be recorded as assets and liabilities, which changes in assets and liabilities should be recorded, how the assets and liabilities and changes in them should be measured, what information should be disclosed and how it should be disclosed, and which financial statements should be prepared. These standards may be broad guidelines of general application as well as detailed practices and procedures.

*Source*: Interpretative Notes – General Note.

The intention is that customs authorities use the same standards in evaluating cost or value submitted by importers that business enterprises generally use when preparing their financial statements and accounting records. This obligation might be said to evidence, again, one of the fundamental principles of the Agreement: customs valuation should be based to the greatest possible degree on commercial documents and commercial practice.[18]

Because there is not as yet complete international harmonization of accounting standards, one country's "generally accepted accounting principles" may not be the same as those of another country. The **Interpretative Notes** thus provide that the GAAP used for customs valuation purposes must be "appropriate" to the method of valuation under the Agreement.

For example, if the submitted data is the manufacturer's profit and general expense under the Article 6 computed value method, customs must evaluate the submission against the GAAP of the country of production, where the manufacturer is located. On the other hand, if the question concerns the distributor's profit and general expense under the Article 5 deductive value method, the appropriate GAAP would be those of the country of importation, where the distributor resells the goods.

Questions about consistency with accounting principles arise most often in the following scenarios:

- Determination of the cost or value of materials and fabrication under the computed value method (Article 6)

  As noted in our discussion of Article 6, whether a particular cost incurred by a producer should be included in a computed value is

[18] This principle is reflected directly in the Preamble to the Agreement (customs value should be based on "simple and equitable criteria consistent with commercial practices"). See also section 1.2.1, text accompanying note 35, above (Committee on Trade's draft valuation principle 6: "valuation systems … should be based to the greatest possible degree on commercial documents").

to be determined on the basis of the "commercial accounts of the producer, provided that such accounts are consistent with the generally accepted accounting principles applied in the country where the goods are produced."

- Determination of the cost or value of an assist provided by the buyer to the seller (Article 8)

  The method of apportionment of the cost or value of an assist to the imported goods – whether on the first import transaction, over a series of transactions, or over the useful life of the asset, etc. – must be in accordance with GAAP, as is noted in the Interpretative Note to Article 8 (see also discussion on assists in section 2.2.4, above).

  Similarly, GAAP may be relevant in determining whether the declared cost or value of an assist is appropriately calculated. For example, GAAP should define whether the claimed value of a used tool, die or mould supplied by the buyer to the manufacturer reflects an appropriate method and rate of depreciation.

### 4.3.4 Exchange of information between customs administrations

With the exception of the computed value method, declared customs values should be verifiable by customs, in most cases, on the basis of commercial records available in the country of importation, where the duty is paid, the goods are located, and the persons legally responsible for the transaction can be found.[19] Thus, the payments that a buyer makes for the imported goods, the value of assists supplied by the buyer to the foreign manufacturer, the proceeds of sales earned in the importing country, etc. should be reflected in the business and banking records of the buyer in the country of importation.

Nevertheless, there can be instances where customs administrations may require information regarding the transaction from the foreign seller or manufacturer in the country from which the goods originated or were exported. An obvious case is where goods are valued under the computed value method, where foreign production costs are at issue. Under the other valuation methods,

[19] As indicated in the historical record, reliance on records in the country of importation was a fundamental principle guiding development of the Agreement: "[t]he determination of customs value should be based to the greatest possible degree on commercial documents which are available in the country of importation and relate to the goods … [this] springs from the practical need to be able to check statements in the country in which the duty is paid. Checks which can only be made outside the country of importation can be inconclusive and vexatious." GATT Multilateral Trade Negotiations Group "Non-Tariff Measures" Sub-Group "Customs Matters," *Customs Valuation: Addendum*, MTN/NTM/W/20/Add.9 (February 17, 1976).

however, records and declarations of the foreign seller also may be useful to the customs administration in the importing country. In particular, this information may be required in specific cases where fraud is suspected in order to compare, for example, the buyer's declaration of the price paid for imported goods with the seller's bills and actual receipts.

There is not – as yet – a legal obligation or mechanism in the Agreement itself that requires customs administrations' co-operation in these verifications. The Uruguay Round Ministerial **Decision Regarding Cases Where Customs Administrations Have Reasons to Doubt the Truth or Accuracy of the Declared Value** recognizes only that "[i]t is entirely appropriate in applying the Agreement for one Member to assist another on mutually agreed terms."[20] But, these mechanisms can be found in other international legal instruments.

### *(a) Bilateral/regional mutual assistance agreements*

One common mechanism for exchange of information is the customs-to-customs "mutual assistance agreement." Under these bilateral or regional agreements, customs administrations define the conditions under which they will exchange information required for enforcement of their customs laws. These agreements may provide, for example, a formal request and response mechanism whereby customs in the importing country can obtain from the exporting country customs administration the export declarations, invoices, shipping documentation etc. which may be needed to validate the importer's declaration or investigate cases of suspected value fraud.

The WCO's "Model Bilateral Agreement on Mutual Administrative Assistance in Customs Matters" provides a template for use by national authorities in their bilateral negotiations. It is available on the WCO website at www.wcoomd.org.

[20] WTO Committee on Customs Valuation, *Marrakesh Ministerial Decisions and Texts Relating to Customs Valuation*, G/VAL/1 (April 27, 1995). This WTO ministerial encouragement of co-operation between Member countries' customs administrations was apparently in response to developing country "practical difficulties" in combating valuation fraud. See Group of Negotiations on Goods (GATT), Negotiating Group on MTN Agreements and Arrangements, *Agreement on Implementation of Article VII: Submission by Brazil*, MTN.GNG/NG8/W/57 (November 22, 1989):

> "6. Apart from … questions related [to] lack of resources and consequently infrastructure in developing countries, the absence of an international and accessible data bank and the somewhat limited cooperation afforded by many trading partners in supplying information (to allow for the determination of the relationship between importer and exporter, for the comparison of prices etc.) is of equally great concern to Brazilian customs authorities.
>
> 7. Brazil therefore considers that the Negotiating Group should examine … ways of improving the mechanisms for technical cooperation and exchange of information within the agreement."

### (b) Nairobi Convention

The leading multilateral customs mutual assistance agreement is the 1977 Nairobi Convention.[21] Annex II of the Convention provides for exchange of valuation information. Where a customs authority in the importing country has "good reason to believe that a serious Customs offense has been committed," it may request from customs in the exporting country information related to the transaction such as the commercial invoice, export declaration, price lists, trade catalogues, etc. – provided both countries are members of the Convention and have accepted the Convention's valuation annex.

The Nairobi Convention has a limited number of adherents, few of which are developed countries.[22] Its reach is also limited by the fact that a customs administration is permitted under the Convention to decline requests for assistance that it determines would infringe the "sovereignty, security or other substantial national interests or prejudice the legitimate commercial interests of any enterprise, public or private."

### (c) Doha Decision on exchange of information

Following the 1998 WTO Geneva Ministerial Conference,[23] the government of India proposed the creation of a formal, WTO-based multilateral solution to allow an importing country customs administration, with "reasons to doubt" an import value declaration, to obtain from the exporting country customs administration the value declared by the exporter for the goods.[24] Although a number of WTO Members supported the proposal as an immediate means

[21] The Nairobi Convention – the International Convention on Mutual Administrative Assistance for the Prevention, Investigation and Repression of Customs Offences – was concluded under the auspices of the Customs Co-operation Council (now, the World Customs Organization). Article 18 of the Convention allows countries to accept the Convention with reservations against any of its provisions or annexes. The Convention text and commentary can be accessed via the WCO's website, www.wcoomd.org.

[22] As of July 2006, Annex II – related to assistance in the area of valuation fraud – has been ratified by just thirty-five contracting parties, and these are mainly developing countries.

[23] WTO, Ministerial Conference, Second Session, *Ministerial Declaration*, WT/MIN(98)/DEC/1 (May 25, 1998). Paragraph 9 of that Geneva Ministerial Declaration mandated the WTO General Council to prepare recommendations for the WTO's future work, including recommendations – which may be suggested by WTO Members – relating to the implementation of the Uruguay Round Agreements and decisions.

[24] "A multilateral solution that enables customs administrations of importing countries to seek and obtain information on export values contained in the export declaration to the customs administrations of exporting countries, in a time-bound manner, in doubtful cases, is proposed." WTO General Council, *Preparations for the 1999 Ministerial Conference: Proposals Regarding the Implementation of the Agreement on Implementation of Article VII of the GATT 1994 in Terms of Paragraph 9(a)(i) of the Geneva Ministerial Declaration: Communication from India*, WT/GC/W/227 (July 5, 1999). In support of a multilateral-based solution, India noted that the alternative – negotiation of individual bilateral mutual assistance agreements with all trading partners – "is not a practical and enduring solution to the problem."

to ease the implementation burden of developing countries, other Members questioned the utility of the solution in dealing with the problem of fraud, particularly where both the buyer and seller, acting in collusion, both declare a false price to their respective customs administrations. There were also concerns regarding conflict with national laws on protection of data, quality of export declaration data (which is not necessarily controlled or verified by customs in all countries), and the potential burden on customs administrations in the exporting country.[25]

Nevertheless, after subsequent discussions and negotiations of the proposal, both in the WTO Valuation Committee as well as the WTO General Council, in November 2001, WTO Ministers took the following decision:

> [w]hen the customs administration of an importing Member has reasonable grounds to doubt the truth or accuracy of the declared value, it may seek assistance from the customs administration of an exporting Member on the value of the good concerned. In such cases, the exporting Member shall offer cooperation and assistance, consistent with its domestic laws and procedures, including furnishing information on the export value of the good concerned. Any information provided in this context shall be treated in accordance with Article 10 of the Customs Valuation Agreement.
>
> Furthermore, recognizing the legitimate concerns expressed by the customs administrations of several importing Members on the accuracy of the declared value, the Committee on Customs Valuation is directed to identify and assess practical means to address such concerns, including the exchange of information on export values and to report to the General Council by the end of 2002 at the latest.[26]

This **Doha Decision** on the exchange of information is thus based on a "softer" standard than that of the Nairobi Convention: customs in the importing country may request assistance on the basis of "reasonable doubts" about the truth or accuracy of the importer's declaration, as opposed to the Nairobi Convention requirement of a "good reason to believe that a serious Customs offense has been committed." On the other hand, the **Doha Decision** is more limited in scope (applying only to exchange of export value information) and allows the exporting country customs administration to refuse the request where not consistent with its domestic laws and procedures.

[25] See WTO Committee on Customs Valuation, *Minutes of the Meeting of 7, 13, 24, and 29 November 2000*, G/VAL/M/17 (February 14, 2001); WTO, *Report of the Chairman of the Committee on Customs Valuation to the General Council*, G/VAL/36 (December 7, 2000); WTO General Council, *Report of the Chairman of the Committee on Customs Valuation to the Chairman of the General Council*, WT/GC/49 (September 24, 2001).

[26] WTO Ministerial Conference Fourth Session, *Implementation-Related Issues and Concerns: Decision of 14 November 2001*, WT/MIN(01)/17 at para. 8.3 (November 20, 2001).

As noted in the text of the decision, where such information is exchanged, **Article 10** of the Agreement imposes the general obligation of confidentiality on the customs administrations involved: confidential information cannot be disclosed – other than in context of judicial proceedings – without specific permission of the government which supplied the information.[27]

Finally, as is also clear from its terms, the **Doha Decision** is both a WTO Ministerial decision on exchange of information as well as a mandate to the Technical Committee to "identify and assess practical means" to address developing-country Member concerns about valuation fraud, including exchange of export value information.

As of the date of this writing, those discussions on "practical means" to address concerns about valuation fraud are ongoing.[28] However, an important contribution has been made by the Technical Committee. At the request for advice by the WTO Valuation Committee, the Technical Committee issued a comprehensive report on the means that customs administrations can and should take to combat valuation fraud.[29] That report also includes a Guide to the Exchange of Customs Valuation Information, which is comprised of (1) a checklist regarding valuation verification actions to be taken by the customs administration of the importing country before requesting information from the customs administration of the exporting country and (2) a set of recommended procedures, applicable to the customs administrations of both the importing and exporting countries, for the exchange of valuation information.

This Technical Committee report is reproduced in full in Appendix 5.

## 4.4 SPECIAL AND DIFFERENTIAL TREATMENT

Like other WTO agreements, the WTO Customs Valuation Agreement allows developing-country Members certain concessions or "special and differential treatment" which are intended to mitigate the difficulty and cost of

[27] There appears to be some disagreement, however, among WTO Members as to whether confidential information may be disclosed in judicial proceedings in the importing country without specific permission of the exporting country government, where such disclosure could violate laws of the exporting country. See G/VAL/35 (September 30, 2003).

[28] See WTO, *Report of the Committee on Customs Valuation to the General Council on Paragraph 8.3 of the Ministerial Decision on Implementation-Related Issues and Concerns (WT/MIN(01)/17)*, G/VAL/50 (December 11, 2002) (status of Doha mandate as of end of 2002). The Doha mandate regarding exchange of information on export values may be made redundant by the Doha Round trade facilitation negotiations, where proposals for exchange of customs-related information are under consideration. See WTO, Negotiating Group on Trade Facilitation, *Communication from India*, TN/TF/W/123/Rev.1 (October 1, 2007).

[29] WTO Committee on Customs Valuation, *Technical Committee on Customs Valuation Response to the Terms of Reference for the Work of the Technical Committee on Customs Valuation in Connection with the Concerns on the Accuracy of the Declared Value (G/VAL/51)*, G/VAL/54 (May 16, 2003).

implementation. Concessions available to developing-country Members under the WTO Customs Valuation Agreement are:

### 4.4.1 Delay application of the Agreement (Article 20.1 and Annex III, paragraph 1)

Developing-country Members who had not joined the 1979 Tokyo Round Valuation Code (the predecessor to the WTO Customs Valuation Agreement) may, upon notification to the WTO Director General, delay the application of the entire Agreement in their country for "a period not exceeding five years from the date of entry into force of the WTO Agreement for such Members."

> **"Developing" and "least developed countries"**
>
> A definition of "developed" and "developing" countries is not found in the WTO Valuation or other agreements. Rather, WTO Members announce for themselves whether they are "developed" or "developing" countries. Approximately two-thirds of WTO Members are developing countries.
>
> "Least-developed Countries" are a United Nations category that consists of fifty States that are considered highly disadvantaged in their development and have a higher risk of not overcoming their poverty.
>
> To read more about developing countries in the WTO, see the WTO web site pages on trade and development at www.wto.org/english/tratop_e/devel_e/d1who_e.htm

**Paragraph 1 of Annex III** to the Agreement allows developing countries to request extension of the delay, to which other WTO Members must give "sympathetic consideration" where good cause is shown. By the end of 2002, all delays and extensions granted to WTO developing country Members under these provisions had expired.

### 4.4.2 Continue use of price lists/official minimum values (Annex III, paragraph 2)

The primary basis of customs value is transaction value, which is the price *actually* paid or payable for the imported goods. This means that customs value must be based on the prices that traders settle among themselves, whether low or high, unless the transaction value is unacceptable for one of the reasons defined in **Article 1**. In principle, therefore, it would be prohibited for customs to use an "official" price list to value imported goods in place of the importer's transaction value, or refuse to accept the importer's declared price if it falls below an "official" minimum value.

However, there is one exception to this prohibition allowed under **paragraph 2 of Annex III** of the Agreement:

> Developing countries which currently value goods on the basis of officially established minimum values may wish to make a reservation to enable them to retain such values on a limited and transitional basis under such terms and conditions as may be agreed to by the Members.

This concession can be requested by newly acceding countries in the context of the negotiations related to their protocol of accession. As is clear from its terms, this provision would not allow a Member to start to use minimum prices for valuation if they had not done so previously.

As of April 2007, no WTO Member was operating under this reservation.[30]

### 4.4.3 Delay in application of computed value method (Article 20.2 and Annex III, paragraph 3)

Two derogations related to computed value method are available to developing countries. Computed value presents particular implementation difficulties, given that it requires Customs to obtain and validate cost information from a foreign country. For that reason, developing countries may:

1. Delay application of "computed value" method. This concession is allowed those developing countries who were NOT members of the 1979 Tokyo Round Code. It runs for a period of three years, but beginning only after all other provisions of the Agreement take effect (i.e. after the Member's five-year delay on application of the Agreement has expired).
2. Limit importer's right to reverse the order of application of deductive and computed value. Developing countries can make a reservation that customs may refuse an importer's request to use computed value before deductive value method. This is a derogation from Article 4 of the Agreement, which provides the importer with the unilateral right to switch the order.

### 4.4.4 Apply "super deductive" method, regardless of importer's consent (Annex III, paragraph 4)

Developing country Members may value goods under the deductive method even if the goods have undergone further processing in the country of importation, whether or not the importer so requests.

[30] WTO Committee on Customs Valuation, *Agreement on Implementation of Article VII of the GATT 1994: Invocation of Special Provisions Available to Developing Country Members: Note by the Secretariat*, G/VAL/2/Rev.24 (April 27, 2007).

The developing country Members that have requested or are operating under any of these special and differential treatment provisions are identified in a document prepared by the WTO Secretariat, which is regularly updated. The latest version can be accessed via the WTO website (www.wto.org) under the document symbol "G/VAL/2."

## 4.5 ANSWER KEY

### Use of valuation databases

If customs has reasons to doubt the truth or accuracy of the importer's declaration, and the importer fails to respond to requests for information to allay those doubts, customs may, applying the procedure defined in the **Decision Regarding Cases Where Customs Administrations Have Reasons to Doubt the Truth or Accuracy of the Declared Value**, reject the use of the transaction value method. However, under the Agreement, customs must attempt to value the imported goods by applying the remaining methods of valuation in sequential order.

In this case study, it appears that customs – as a rule – directly proceeds to Article 7 (the fall-back method) where the importer fails to respond to its requests for information and supporting documents, without considering application of transaction value of identical or similar goods, or deductive or computed value methods.

Moreover, customs substitution of database average historic price of goods falling under the same tariff category as the import might be considered an "arbitrary" value prohibited under Article 7. A tariff category can include a wider scope of products than would be considered identical or similar under the Agreement. For example, the tariff category "pocket cigarette lighters" would include both imported disposable plastic lighters and imported gold-plated reusable lighters; these would not be considered identical or similar as those terms are defined for Valuation Agreement purposes. Accordingly, an average price, calculated on the basis of goods falling under the same tariff category, might be considered arbitrary.

Even if the database is segmented by goods that are identical or similar within the meaning of the Agreement, substitution of an average in place of the declared price is problematic. Under **Article 2** and **Article 3** of the Agreement, where more than one transaction value of identical goods or similar goods is found, "the lowest such value shall be used to determine the customs value of the imported goods." It is relevant to note here that, when the Agreement was first negotiated during the Tokyo Round, proposals were made to allow use of an average value where two or more transactions of identical or similar goods are found; these proposals were not accepted.[31] If the valuation database is organized into prices of goods that are identical or similar, then a prior transaction value should be selected, rather than an average.

Finally, as indicated in the Technical Committee Guidelines on the Use of Valuation Databases as a Risk Assessment Tool (see section 4.3, above), generally, the difference between a declared price and the valuation database price for the same goods is not, by itself, sufficient justification to doubt the truth or accuracy of the declaration. Generally, other risk factors should also be present, such as country of origin of the goods, compliance history of the parties involved in the transaction, etc., to justify the control decision. This is, however, a guideline and not a WTO Valuation Agreement principle.

[31] See e.g. GATT Multilateral Trade Negotiations Group "Non-Tariff Measures" Sub-Group "Customs Matters," *Customs Valuation: Spain*, MTN/NTM/W/189 (September 18, 1978) (where Spain proposed "[f]or establishing the customs value of imported goods, where there is more than one transaction of identical or similar goods, we propose that the value used be that corresponding to the weighted average").

# 5

# ADMINISTRATION AND DISPUTE SETTLEMENT

## 5.1 WTO AND WCO VALUATION COMMITTEES

> *Article 18*
>
> *Institutions*
>
> 1. There is hereby established a Committee on Customs Valuation (referred to in this Agreement as "the Committee") composed of representatives from each of the Members. The Committee shall elect its own Chairman and shall normally meet once a year, or as is otherwise envisaged by the relevant provisions of this Agreement, for the purpose of affording Members the opportunity to consult on matters relating to the administration of the customs valuation system by any Member as it might affect the operation of this Agreement or the furtherance of its objectives and carrying out such other responsibilities as may be assigned to it by the Members. The WTO Secretariat shall act as the secretariat to the Committee.
>
> 2. There shall be established a Technical Committee on Customs Valuation (referred to in this Agreement as "the Technical Committee") under the auspices of the Customs Co-operation Council (referred to in this Agreement as "the CCC"), which shall carry out the responsibilities described in Annex II to this Agreement and shall operate in accordance with the rules of procedure contained therein.

**Article 18** provides for the creation of two committees to support the administration of the Agreement: the Committee on Customs Valuation, which is comprised of representatives of all WTO Members, and the Technical Committee on Customs Valuation, which works under the auspices of the World Customs Organization.

### 5.1.1 WTO Committee on Customs Valuation

The Committee on Customs Valuation provides WTO Members with a forum to discuss issues arising out of the implementation of the Agreement. It is particularly intended for discussion of questions or concerns that Members may have regarding one another's customs valuation systems or the implementation of the Agreement generally.

For example, during Committee meetings, one WTO Member might ask another about its use of reference prices on particular products, possible misapplication of the valuation methods, or other administrative practices that may be inconsistent with the Agreement that have been encountered by their exporters. The hope is that Members will clarify and resolve implementation issues through dialogue in the Committee meetings, and thereby avoid the formal dispute settlement process.

### A WTO Committee Dialogue

4.2 The delegation of Panama informed Members that … Panama had been encountering serious difficulties in exporting to Colombia as a result of the entry into force of certain customs measures imposed by [Colombia] …

4.3 The [customs valuation measures] … had a negative impact on Panama's activities in the … Colón Free Zone. This was the most important free zone in Panama and was located on the Atlantic side of the Panama Canal, representing a major economic entry point for Panama and contributing 8% to Panama's GDP … The measures adopted by [Colombia] affected many different goods including various types of footwear and socks, textiles, gas and other domestic electronic goods, matches, blankets, and other goods … The [valuation measures] … would need to be assessed in the context of Article VII of GATT 94 and the Customs Valuation Agreement.

[H]is delegation [had] addressed [written] questions to Colombia … to learn about these measures in greater detail.

4.4 The representative of Colombia stated that his delegation had received the questions from Panama but had not concluded the internal deliberations necessary to respond. However, it would do so as soon as possible.

4.5 The representative of Canada said that his delegation looked forward to receiving Colombia's reply to Panama's questions.

4.6 The representative of Panama stated that his delegation looked forward to receiving Colombia's responses and wished to retain the item on the Committee's agenda for its next meeting.

4.7 The representative of China echoed the concerns raised. As his delegation had just received the communication from Panama it was difficult to give detailed comments. However, her initial response was that it seemed worthwhile for the interested parties to discuss the implications of the customs measures concerned and also requested that Colombia circulate to the Committee the resolutions concerned.

4.8 The representative of Colombia said that he had taken careful note of the questions and comments and would transmit them to his capital for full response at the next meeting.

4.9 The representative of Hong Kong, China also asked that his delegation be kept informed of correspondence on this issue.

4.10 The representatives of Malaysia and Thailand supported the statement by Hong Kong, China.

4.11 The Committee agreed to take note of the statements made and to revert to this matter at its next meeting.

WTO Committee on Customs Valuation, *Minutes of the Meeting of 25 April 2006*, G/VAL/M/41 (May 24, 2006).

Over the years, the Committee has adopted important decisions interpreting the terms of the Agreement – such as those on treatment of interest charges and software[1] – as well as decisions on administration of the Agreement and working procedures of the Committee. The text of all of these interpretative and administrative decisions can be found in the Committee on Customs Valuation document G/VAL/5 (October 13, 1995), a copy of which appears in Appendix 3.

Another important function of the Committee is the review of Members' valuation legislation. **Article 22** requires Members to conform their national laws and procedures to the provisions of the Agreement. The Agreement expressly mandates that certain elements be contained in national legislation, namely:

- the importer's right of appeal (Article 11)
- the importer's right to withdraw goods from customs, pending final valuation (Article 13)
- the inclusion or exclusion of costs of international transport in customs value (Article 8).

Otherwise, the framing of national legislation – how a country chooses to implement the terms of the WTO Agreement in national law – is left to the discretion of each Member within their particular constitutional and legal structure.

As previously noted, to allow for the Committee's review, Members are required to submit copies of their valuation laws and regulations to the WTO Secretariat, who then circulates the documents to all Members.[2] In addition, Members must complete a Checklist of Issues, which requires a description of their manner of implementation of certain articles of the Agreement and decisions of the Committee; this "checklist" is intended to serve as the Committee's starting point for examination of the Member's national legislation.[3]

Other important regular tasks of the Committee include:

- submission of an annual report on the work of the Committee and implementation of the Agreement, such as an update on national legislation notified, requests for delay, etc., to the WTO Council for Trade in Goods (required by **Article 23**)
- deciding developing-country requests for delay in the application of the Agreement, or reservations against specific terms. This includes resolving Member's objections to such requests, and setting the terms

[1] See section 2.1, above (discussion of Committee decisions on interest charges and software).

[2] See section 4.2, above (discussion of publication of valuation laws and decisions under Article 12).

[3] See Decisions on Notification and Circulation of National Legislation in Accordance with Article 22 of the Agreement and Checklist of Issues, G/VAL/5 (in Appendix 3); GATT Committee on Customs Valuation, *Minutes of the Meeting Held on 13 January 1981*, VAL/M/1, at 11 (February 27, 1981).

and conditions for approval of reservations (see section 4.4, Special and differential treatment, above)

- monitoring customs valuation-related technical assistance and capacity-building activities that are provided by the WCO or by WTO Member countries
- monitoring the implementation and operation of the Agreement on Preshipment Inspection (PSI) (which does not provide for a committee of its own), including identification of countries where PSI regimes are used.

The Committee normally holds two formal meetings per year in Geneva – in the spring and in the fall – although it can meet more often, when required. Participation is open to all WTO Members. Following the general WTO procedures on decision-making (Article IX of the WTO Agreement), Committee decisions are taken by consensus of Members present.

Countries in accession to the WTO, and other governments that have been granted observer status by the WTO General Council, can attend as observers. The WTO's sister international organizations, such as UNCTAD, the WCO, the World Bank and the IMF, also attend as observers. Under the rules of procedure applied by the Committee, observers may be invited to speak at meetings, but may not present proposals (unless specifically requested) or participate in decision-making.[4]

The Committee on Customs Valuation elects a chairman from a WTO Member country with a term of one year. It is supported by the WTO Secretariat staff, one of whom acts as secretary to the Committee. Minutes of the Committee's meetings can be found on the WTO website under the document code G/VAL/M/*

### 5.1.2 Technical Committee on Customs Valuation

The mission of the Technical Committee, defined in **Annex II**, is to ensure, "at the technical level, uniformity in interpretation and application" of the Agreement.

The Technical Committee's membership is composed of representatives of WTO Member countries, who are typically customs specialists (WCO Members that are not Members of the WTO can participate in Technical Committee meetings as observers). It meets in Brussels at the headquarters of the WCO twice a

[4] The WTO Valuation Committee applies, with some modifications, the same rules for conduct of its meetings as used by the WTO General Council. See Committee of Customs Valuation, *Minutes of the Meeting of 12 May 1995*, G/VAL/M/1 (August 11, 1995); WTO, *Rules of Procedure for Sessions of the Ministerial Conference and Meetings of the General Council*, WT/L/161 (July 25, 1996); WTO, *Rules of Procedure for Meetings of the Committee on Customs Valuation*, G/L/146 (February 24, 1997).

year, and reports to the WTO Committee on Customs Valuation as well as to the Customs Co-operation Council (the official name of the WCO). A report of the Technical Committee's activities is usually given in person by a WCO representative during the WTO Valuation Committee meetings in Geneva.

Like the WTO Valuation Committee, the Technical Committee elects a chairman from among the delegates of its members, with a term of one year. The Technical Committee is supported by the WCO Secretariat, one of whom acts as secretary to the committee.

The Agreement assigns a number of important tasks to the Technical Committee. These include (i) providing advice to Members on specific technical problems that may arise in the day-to-day administration of their customs valuation systems (such as how to value used cars); (ii) facilitating the provision of training or other forms of technical assistance to Members; (iii) providing technical support to the WTO dispute panels under **Article 19**;[5] and (iv) generally supporting the WTO Valuation Committee through studies and reports on valuation practices, when requested.

**TECHNICAL COMMITTEE ON CUSTOMS VALUATION**

*Key deliverables*

The Technical Committee shall:

- draft Explanatory Notes, Case Studies and other instruments to guide the interpretation of the Agreement;
- report to the WTO Committee and the WCO Council on its work;
- report to WTO panels on matters referred to it under Article 19 of the Agreement.

*Means of operation*

The Technical Committee may:

- examine and draft Explanatory Notes, Case Studies and other instruments to guide the interpretation of the Agreement;
- in accordance with WCO Council guidelines establish and direct the work of working bodies as may be necessary for purposes within its competence;
- co-operate, promote joint projects, or share information and experiences with relevant WCO working bodies and international governmental and trade organizations related to the matters within its competence;
- devote part of each alternate meeting to a "theme" seminar with the purpose of providing a more structured form of technical assistance for its developing country Members.

*Resources required*

Meetings of the Technical Committee will normally be held twice a year at WCO Headquarters in Brussels, usually for a period of five days.

[5] See section 5.3, Dispute settlement, below.

The WCO Secretariat is responsible for:

(a) preparation of each meeting, including:

- administrative preparation;
- within eight (8) weeks of the last session, inviting comments of Members of the Technical Committee regarding technical and other matters;
- distributing a draft agenda in the three official languages eight (8) weeks after the last session, that draft agenda to be updated as appropriate;
- drafting comments on working documents, etc.;
- ensuring that all working documents are available to Members of the Technical Committee three (3) weeks prior to meeting dates in the three official languages.

(b) the meeting itself, including:

- presenting reports and proposals;
- facilitating the course of the meeting;
- taking note of discussions;
- preparing a draft report.

(c) follow-up to the meeting, including:

- preparing the final meeting report and distributing it to Members of the Technical Committee;
- publishing instruments adopted by the Technical Committee, after approval by the WCO Council and the WTO Committee, in the form of a loose-leaf compendium.

*Source*: World Customs Organization

The advice that the Technical Committee renders to Members can take the form of an "advisory opinion," which answers a question raised by a Member or Members concerning a specific set of facts. Alternatively, where the advice or information is more general, the Technical Committee may issue:

- A commentary.
  "A treatise consisting of a series of comments on part of the text of the Agreement guidance on application of the Agreement intended to clarify a situation where a literal reading of the text itself can usefully be supplemented by additional guidance."
- An explanatory note.
  "[E]lucidates the Technical Committee's views on a question of a general nature arising from one or more provisions of the Agreement."
- A case study.
  An "exposition of a complex set of facts based on an actual commercial transaction, which can be used to demonstrate the practical application of one or more provisions of the Agreement."

- A study.
  "[S]ets out the results of an examination in some depth of any question related to the Agreement, in particular a question put to the Technical Committee under paragraph 2(b) of Annex II, and which is not more suitably covered by any of the foregoing instruments."[6]

The Technical Committee's advisory opinions and other instruments, a number of which are referenced in this book, are compiled by the WCO Secretariat and published in *WCO Compendium*.

## 5.2 NOTIFICATIONS

To promote greater transparency in individual WTO Members' administration of the Agreement, WTO Members are required by the Agreement and by decisions of the WTO Committee on Customs Valuation to advise other Members by formal notice to the WTO Secretariat of certain, defined issues.

*All* WTO Members are required to advise other Members of any changes they make to their laws, regulations or administrative procedures related to valuation (**Article 22** of the Agreement). Similarly, as noted in the previous section, a WTO Valuation Committee decision requires *all* Members to submit copies of their valuation legislation and to respond in writing to a questionnaire or "checklist of issues" intended to elicit information about valuation practices.

*Some* WTO Members have additional notification obligations under the Agreement. Developing countries who wish to apply for or extend the five-year delay in application of the Agreement, or apply for the three-year delay in application of **Article 6** (computed value method), must so notify the WTO Members.

For further and detailed description of notifications required under WTO Customs Valuation Agreement, as well as assistance in preparing the notifications, please consult the Technical Cooperation Handbook on Notification Requirements (WT/TC/NOTIF/VAL/1, dated September 9, 1996) an excerpt of which is reprinted in Appendix 6.

[6] WCO, *Texts Issued by the Technical Committee*, in *WCO Compendium*. Article 2(b) of Annex II provides that the Technical Committee's responsibilities shall include "to study, as requested, valuation laws, procedures and practices as they relate to this Agreement and to prepare reports on the results of such studies."

## 5.3 DISPUTE SETTLEMENT

> ***Article 18***
>
> *Consultations and dispute settlement*
>
> 1. Except as otherwise provided herein, the Dispute Settlement Understanding is applicable to consultations and the settlement of disputes under this Agreement.
> 2. If any Member considers that any benefit accruing to it, directly or indirectly, under this Agreement is being nullified or impaired, or that the achievement of any objective of this Agreement is being impeded, as a result of the actions of another Member or of other Members, it may, with a view to reaching a mutually satisfactory solution of this matter, request consultations with the Member or Members in question. Each Member shall afford sympathetic consideration to any request from another Member for consultations.
> 3. The Technical Committee shall provide, upon request, advice and assistance to Members engaged in consultations.
> 4. At the request of a party to the dispute, or on its own initiative, a panel established to examine a dispute relating to the provisions of this Agreement may request the Technical Committee to carry out an examination of any questions requiring technical consideration. The panel shall determine the terms of reference of the Technical Committee for the particular dispute and set a time period for receipt of the report of the Technical Committee. The panel shall take into consideration the report of the Technical Committee. In the event that the Technical Committee is unable to reach consensus on a matter referred to it pursuant to this paragraph, the panel should afford the parties to the dispute an opportunity to present their views on the matter to the panel.
> 5. Confidential information provided to the panel shall not be disclosed without formal authorization from the person, body or authority providing such information. Where such information is requested from the panel but release of such information by the panel is not authorized, a non-confidential summary of this information, authorized by the person, body or authority providing the information, shall be provided.

In the October 2006 meeting of the WTO Valuation Committee, the Philippines delegate raised a problem one of her country's major exporters was experiencing with the Thai customs authorities. This Philippine company manufactures and exports cigarettes to a related-company distributor in Thailand. Apparently, beginning in August of that year, Thai authorities began rejecting the prices declared on the cigarettes because they suspected that the parties had set a low price in order to reduce their tax liability. The company claimed, however, that Thai customs was in fact systematically "uplifting" the declared prices on all of its imports by a factor of 13–16 percent, costing the company $37 million per year in incremental tax and duties, in order to protect the interests of the

Thai Tobacco Monopoly, a state enterprise said to control 80 percent of the Thai cigarette market.

The EU and other WTO Members, whose exporters were affected by the Thai customs valuation measures, joined in the discussions in this and subsequent WTO Committee meetings. However, while the discussions clarified the disputed practices, the Members did not reach a resolution satisfactory to the Philippines. Thus, in early 2008, the Philippines decided to trigger the formal WTO dispute process.[7]

Customs valuation disputes between WTO Members, like these, are resolved through the consultation and dispute settlement process that is defined in WTO **Understanding on Rules and Procedures Governing the Settlement of Disputes**. This understanding, which is incorporated by reference in **Article 19.1** of the WTO Valuation Agreement, is the same dispute-resolution mechanism used to settle disputes between the WTO Member countries generally, whether arising under the GATT or one of the other WTO multilateral agreements. Article 19 does include some special procedures that are in addition to those of the Dispute Settlement Understanding; these largely concern the role of the Technical Committee in the dispute process.

The WTO formal dispute process (see Figure 10) begins with a consultations phase, where the governments concerned must attempt to negotiate a resolution of the matter between themselves, with the hope of avoiding formal litigation.[8] The aggrieved country will submit, in writing, a "request for consultations" to the country (or countries) that has taken the offending action. The request identifies the measures at issue, as well as the legal basis of the claim. Other WTO Members, who have a "substantial trade interest" in the dispute, may ask to join the consultations, although their participation is subject to the consent of the responding party. Moreover, **Article 19.2** of the WTO Valuation Agreement allows the parties to call on the WCO Technical Committee for the technical advice and assistance they might require to resolve their dispute.

If these consultations are successful, the parties will normally notify the Dispute Settlement Body (DSB) of a "mutually agreed solution." In fact, about half of all WTO disputes are somehow resolved during this consultation phase.

[7] See WTO Committee on Customs Valuation, *Minutes of the Meeting of 6 October 2006*, G/VAL/M/42 (December 14, 2006); WTO Committee on Customs Valuation, *Minutes of the Meeting of 8 May 2007*, G/VAL/M/43 (May 25, 2007); WTO Committee on Customs Valuation, *Minutes of the Meeting of 18 October 2007*, G/VAL/M/44 (November 8, 2007); Felipe F. Salvosa II, *WTO Asked to Settle RP-Thai Cigarettes Row*, GMANews.TV, February 14, 2008, at www.gmanews.tv/story/80640/BusinessWorld.

[8] The description that follows of the WTO dispute process is based on the WTO Dispute Settlement Gateway "Introduction to Disputes Settlement in the WTO."

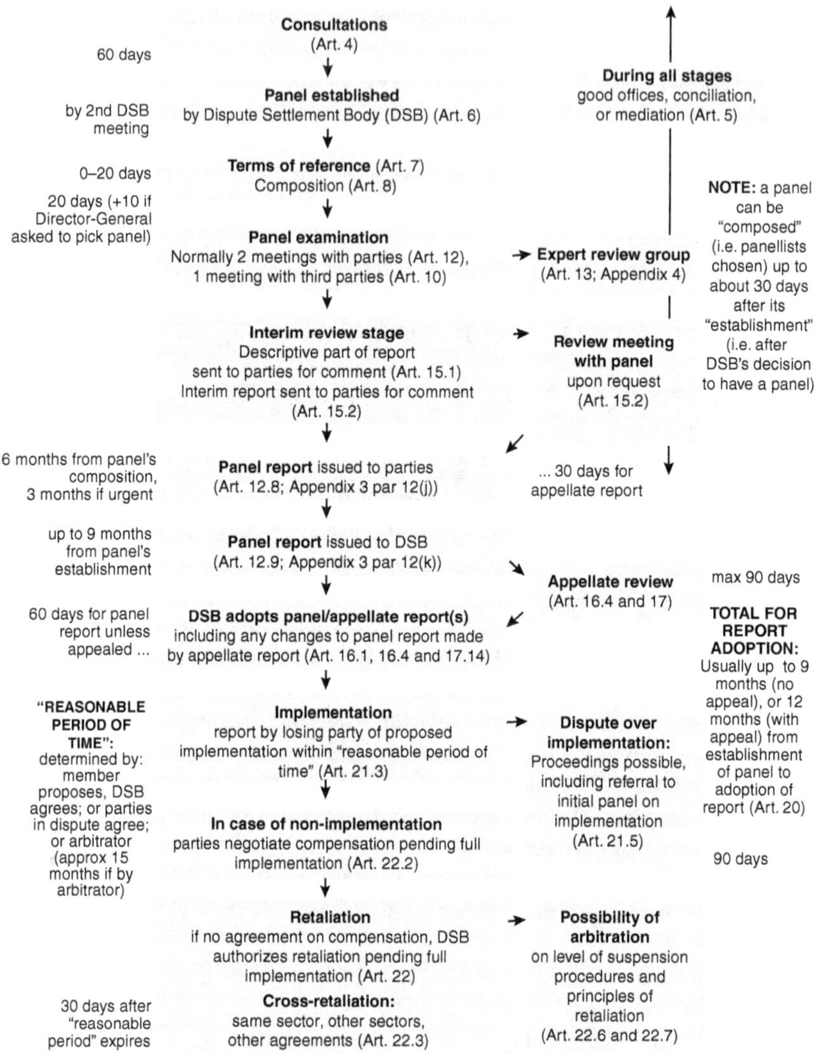


Figure 10 Dispute settlement process

**What is the Dispute Settlement Body?**

"The Dispute Settlement Body (the General Council in another guise), which consists of all WTO members. The Dispute Settlement Body has the sole authority to establish 'panels' of experts to consider the case, and to accept or reject the panels' findings or the results of an appeal. It monitors the implementation of the rulings and recommendations, and has the power to authorize retaliation when a country does not comply with a ruling."

*Source*: WTO Dispute Settlement Gateway.

If consultations are not successful, after sixty days the aggrieved country can request that the DSB establish a panel to decide the case. A panel is an ad hoc adjudicatory body of three (or five, if the parties so agree) independent and "well-qualified individuals," who are citizens of countries other than those involved in the dispute (unless, again, the parties agree otherwise). The parties to the dispute together first attempt to select the panel members by mutual agreement, based on nominations by the WTO Secretariat (often taken from a permanent list of experts maintained by the Secretariat based on Members' inputs). If they cannot agree, at the request of either party, the WTO Director-General will appoint the panel members.

The panel will decide the matter based on the written and oral evidence and arguments submitted by the parties, as well as any reports or testimony of experts. With regard to customs valuation expertise in particular, **Article 19.4** of the Agreement places the Technical Committee at the service of the panel "to carry out an examination of any question requiring technical consideration" and to report the results thereof.

Under the timelines defined in the Dispute Settlement Understanding, the panel's final report is normally issued within six to nine months, although in urgent cases, such as those concerning perishable goods, the deadline is three months. Once issued, the panel report will then be adopted by DSB within sixty days, unless it is rejected by a "negative" consensus of DSB members (i.e. the membership of the WTO) or one (or both) of the parties to the dispute files an appeal.

Appeals are heard by three members of the seven-person Appellate Body. These are "persons of recognized authority, with demonstrated expertise in law, international trade and the subject matter of the [WTO Valuation and other WTO agreements] generally," and not affiliated with any government. Appellate Body members are selected for four-year terms, renewable once. When deciding an appeal, the Appellate Body may not consider new evidence but only points of law or the legal interpretations made by the panel. The appellate decision can uphold, modify or reverse the legal findings and conclusions

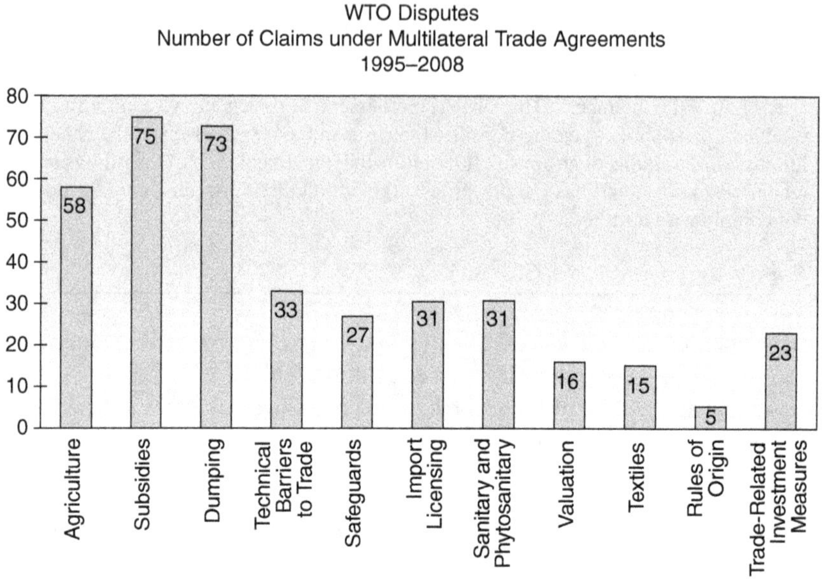


Figure 11 Claims in WTO dispute cases by subject matter 1995–2008

of the panel. Generally, the appeal proceeding must be concluded within sixty days, with an absolute maximum of ninety days. The DSB then must accept or reject the appeals report within thirty days – and rejection is only possible by "negative" consensus.

If the DSB decision is against a WTO Member, that country must comply with the recommendations of the panel report or the appeals report within defined time frames; generally, that will mean the country must withdraw the offending measures. The Dispute Settlement Understanding contains further rules and procedures about implementation of the DSB decision, including provisions for negotiation of compensation if the measures are not withdrawn, and use of trade sanctions as a last resort.

Detailed guides, training materials, and case studies on the WTO dispute settlement process, as well as the documentation of the individual dispute cases, can be found via the WTO Dispute Settlement Gateway on the WTO website (www.wto.org/english/tratop_e/dispu_e/dispu_e.htm).

In the first fifteen years of the WTO, there have been relatively few cases involving customs valuation issues brought to the formal dispute settlement process. Of the total 376 dispute cases initiated by request for consultations between 1995 and May 2008 (see Figure 11), just sixteen of these cases (or about 4 percent) included customs valuation claims. Violations of other multilateral agreements – particularly the Antidumping Agreement, the Agreement on Agriculture, and the Agreement on Subsidies and Countervailing Duties – were much more commonly made in cases brought during this period.[9]

There are some generalizations that can be made about the valuation dispute cases to date. First, nearly all these cases involve the same question or issue: the use of minimum values or reference prices in place of transaction value for selected products (often, sensitive goods, such as textiles or excisable goods). Second, the valuation cases often involve claims under GATT 1994 or one or more of the other multilateral agreements, such as the Anti-Dumping Agreement. And, finally, nearly all the cases involving a valuation claim have been settled or otherwise resolved in the "consultation phase," without the establishment of a panel.

A summary of the WTO dispute settlement cases involving customs valuation issues can be found in Appendix 7.

[9] WTO, *Update of Dispute Settlement Cases*, WT/DS/OV/33 (June 3, 2008).

# 6

# CONCLUSION

The WTO Valuation Agreement is fifteen years old at the time of writing. It is applied by the 153 WTO Members, representing all levels of economic development, to the full variety of their import trade transactions. If one takes into account the predecessor GATT Valuation Code, these valuation rules have been in use in international practice for over thirty years. What then do WTO Members think of the Agreement? What are its major failings, if there are any, and what improvements can be made? What is the future for common customs valuation rules?

## 6.1 A DEVELOPING–DEVELOPED COUNTRY DIVIDE?

Perhaps the main doubt about the WTO customs valuation system, which has been present from the time of the negotiation of the Tokyo Round Code in the late 1970s, is whether it adequately accommodates the needs of the developing and least-developed countries. As described in previous chapters, the main changes that have been made to the Agreement or its predecessor GATT Valuation Code were originated by developing countries, and were driven by a concern that the Agreement did not give these countries sufficient tools to protect themselves against importer fraud, which affects developing countries disproportionately because of their typically higher duty rates and greater dependency on customs for government revenue. Thus, in the Tokyo Round negotiations, developing countries successfully included the *Protocol to the Agreement on Implementation of Article VII*, to allow the use of minimum price systems to continue for a transition period, among other protections. In the Uruguay Round negotiations, Members agreed to the *Decision Regarding Cases Where Customs Administrations Have Reasons to Doubt the Truth or Accuracy of the Declared Value* to clarify the balance of proof between customs and the importer, where fraud is suspected. And in more recent years, developing countries have proposed various changes to the Agreement to deal with fraud, such as binding rules for the exchange of information between national customs authorities to validate an importer's declared value.[1]

[1] See section 4.3.4 above. Other recent "anti-fraud" proposals have included elimination of the current exclusion from customs value of buying commissions and the costs of engineering and design services supplied by the importing country, and authorization to use home-market and exporting market prices as the basis for value. WTO, *Committee on Customs Valuation, Report of the Committee on Customs*

Does the Agreement suffer from a developed-developing country divide? One provocative critique made is that the Agreement was designed by and for the benefit of advanced trading countries to complement their particular trade regimes, and is inappropriate to the situation of some developing countries.[2]

According to this critique, in the "advanced trading countries," tariff rates are low; customs duties make up a small portion of government revenue; a small number of large, sophisticated traders are responsible for a significant percentage of the country's imports;[3] and a high percentage of overall imports are made up of large consignments. In that kind of trade environment, a "transaction value" system – where the price for the goods as declared by the importer is the basis for valuation – is more practicable because importers have less incentive to cheat the government, and there is less impact on the government revenue if fraud goes undetected. Moreover, these advanced trading countries have established institutions, technology and processes to administer and enforce such a system, such as post-entry audit and accounting skills, laws to require and enforce importers to keep records, and automated systems for declaration, risk assessment, and targeting to enable detection of fraud. On the other hand, the argument goes, the trading regime and material conditions are quite different in many developing countries, where much of the importer population is made of small, occasional traders who deal in small consignments, and the customs typically has limited infrastructure and rudimentary administrative capacity.

The view that the Agreement was put together by a handful of advanced trading countries and imposed on the others has been disputed as a "subjective" and incomplete retelling of the Tokyo Round negotiating history.[4] As was recounted in section 1.2.2, the initial negotiating text of what eventually became the GATT Valuation Code was written by European Community representatives, and it incorporated concepts taken from valuation systems of advanced trading countries, such as the United States, Canada and Australia. Arguably, the text had an "advanced trading country" flavor, as provisions such as those on assessment of related-party transactions, valuation of assists, and the treatment of royalties, may be more important to countries who host large multinational importers involved in outsourcing and similar global manufacturing operations. However, it is also true that, in the later stages of the Tokyo Round negotiations, developing countries did become more involved, to the

*Valuation to the Trade Negotiations Committee on the Implementation-Related Issues in Accordance with Paragraph 12 of the Ministerial Declaration*, G/VAL/49 (November 25, 2002).

[2] See J. M. Finger and P. Schuler, *Implementation of Uruguay Round Commitments: The Development Challenge* (October 1999); WTO, Committee on Customs Valuation, *Minutes of the Meeting of 7 May 2002*, G/VAL/M/28 (July 18, 2002).

[3] In the United States, for example, customs receives goods from 810,000 importers, but just 3,000 of those importers account for nearly 75 percent of all goods imported, by value. US Customs and Border Protection, *CDP Trade Strategy: Fiscal Years 2009–2013*, at 6.

[4] See G/VAL/M/28 at 3 (comments of the US and EC representatives).

extent that they forced the acceptance of the *Protocol to the Agreement on Implementation of Article VII*, which incorporates rights of developing countries to delay implementation of part or all of the Agreement, as we have also described. The final text may not have dealt with all or even the central customs problems that were experienced at that time by developing and least-developed countries, but as a set of valuation rules, it did include some important concessions to their particular situation.

Apart from the differing views of the negotiating history, is the WTO Valuation Agreement better suited to the environment of an advanced trading country? Justifiably, governments fear changing systems that have a direct impact on their revenue collection, with unknown results and inadequate tools to protect against fraud and revenue loss. But there are also positive advantages to traders, in both developing and advanced trading countries, that must be taken into account when assessing the WTO Agreement against alternative systems. The WTO system is intended to be fairer and more transparent to traders because it is based on the importer's commercial records rather than, for example, a notional value determined by customs, or a price list decided by government authorities.[5] The terms of the Agreement, and the Ministerial *Decision Regarding Cases Where Customs Administrations Have Reasons to Doubt the Truth or Accuracy of the Declared Value*, circumscribe customs' ability to reject and uplift declared prices. Except in the situations explicitly defined in the Agreement, customs must use the actual deal, including discounts, that the importer negotiated with his supplier as the basis for valuation, rather than a price that a customs officer or government authorities believe the goods are worth. Moreover, the limitations on customs discretion – and therefore opportunities to extort payoffs – would seem to benefit smaller traders, who generally suffer more from corruption than larger companies.[6]

## 6.2 NEED FOR CUSTOMS MODERNIZATION

Nevertheless, there is an essential point underlying this critique of the Agreement that must be acknowledged. Customs experts today recognize that effective customs controls, whether in the area of customs valuation or other customs procedures, require use of risk management techniques, post-entry audit, information

[5] In the article cited at note 2 above, the authors suggest that a price list system of valuation may be more appropriate to some developing countries, provided it is published and periodically reviewed, possibly in co-operation with traders, because it is simpler for customs to administer. As those authors also recognize, practically it is not possible to define (and keep up to date) a price list for products other than a relatively few commodities. Imagine the administrative complexity of maintaining a price list for all goods in trade: the Harmonized System goods classification system has 5,000 or so product lines!

[6] See e.g. C. W. Gray and D. Kaufmann, "Corruption and Development," *Finance & Development*, 35 (1998), at 7.

exchange with traders and other customs administrations – generally, the modernized customs procedures and administrative measures that are described in the Kyoto Convention. This kind of customs modernization, which implies development of human resources, restructuring the customs organization, defining new working relationships with traders, legislative and regulatory changes, implementation of information technology, etc., can involve significant costs for a developing country, which may have other and more pressing priorities. Thus, in the absence of this kind of customs modernization, a country may nominally adopt the WTO valuation rules but, to protect revenue collections, apply practices that are inconsistent with the terms or purposes of the Agreement, such as aggressive use of price lists and valuation databases, frequent rejection of importers' declared values and resort to the fall-back method of valuation, etc.

### IMPLEMENTATION CHALLENGES

*Developing country views*

- Customs lack of access to price data on "identical or similar" goods
  Particularly for the valuation of imports of used goods (appliances, capital equipment, cars, clothes), leased equipment, product samples, new products
- Incomplete or unreliable documents and records submitted/kept by importers
  Particularly in connection with imports by "shuttle," "suitcase" or other informal traders, or imports from neighboring-country free trade zones
- Undervaluation, double-invoicing and other importer frauds
  For example, cash payments to avoid tracing; disclosure of only part of the full payment; transport costs
- Lack of relevant customs technical expertise and information resources
  Particularly in technical valuation rules, accounting and audit, fraud investigation; validation of technical and complex related-party transfer pricing models
- High turnover of (trained) customs personnel
- Inadequate supporting legal framework
  Penalties for valuation violations; importer recordkeeping to support customs audit
- Government-mandated revenue collection targets
- Lack of, or inadequate, information technology
  Particularly, applications and databases required for maintaining effective price references and management of valuation risk
- Lack of appreciation within customs administration or government of the extent of administrative/managerial changes required to support implementation; resistance to change
- Lack of clarity or difficulty in application of certain WTO rules
  Particularly, WTO rules on buying commissions, special discounts given sole agents/distributors, transfer pricing, use of valuation databases, burden of proof where fraud is suspected

*Source*: WTO Valuation Seminars, Developing Country Reports (2003–2007)

Recognizing the challenges that developing countries face, the Agreement does encourage developed countries to assist developing-country Members in implementation on "mutually agreed terms."[7] However, the Agreement is not binding on this point, as no concrete commitments are required from developed countries, and developing countries' obligations under the Agreement are not excused if the assistance is not given. Moreover, at the time of Tokyo Round negotiations in the late 1970s, when this provision on technical assistance was incorporated in the text, countries may not have fully appreciated the broader customs modernization changes that were required to support effective implementation of the new valuation system, and therefore the kind and degree of implementation support that would be needed by developing countries. Many developed-country Members and international organizations have in fact provided technical assistance on customs valuation, but the assistance given, and the countries that have received it, has been determined by the donor country's political, strategic or other national considerations, rather than as part of an overall co-ordinated program.

## 6.3 NEW LEGAL RULES

At least for the foreseeable future, it is unlikely that there will be fundamental changes to the text of the WTO Valuation Agreement, whether to respond to the developing-country implementation critique or otherwise. Generally, WTO Members seem averse to opening up the Agreement to renegotiation in view of the difficulty of reaching consensus among 153 countries, as well as a reluctance to disrupt a system that customs authorities and thousands of traders have applied and relied upon for 15 years or longer. It is instructive to note that, to the extent there have been any substantive legal changes since the time of the Tokyo Round Code, these have been in the form of decisions at Ministerial Meetings or interpretative decisions of the WTO or GATT valuation committees, rather than changes to the text of the Agreement itself.

Even without changes to the Valuation Agreement, the implementation gap between developed and developing countries is closing. In our technical assistance work in developing countries, we have found that customs officials have an increasingly sophisticated understanding of the WTO valuation rules. This may be due to training and technical assistance programs provided by donors over the years, to greater accessibility to information and technical resources

[7] WTO Valuation Agreement, Article 20.3 ("Developed country Members shall furnish, on mutually agreed terms, technical assistance to developing country Members that so request. On this basis developed country Members shall draw up programmes of technical assistance which may include, *inter alia*, training of personnel, assistance in preparing implementation measures, access to sources of information regarding customs valuation methodology, and advice on the application of the provisions of the Agreement.").

via the internet, to exchanges of views among colleagues in regional and international fora, or simply to the practical experience of dealing with the valuation problems under the Agreement on a daily basis. Furthermore, many of these developing countries are engaged in broader customs modernization efforts to upgrade their processes and systems, bringing them closer to the "advanced-country" model described above. Many also have ratified the Kyoto Convention, the "blueprint for modern and efficient Customs procedures in the 21st century" in the words of the WCO.

The costs and know-how that is required for customs modernization remain a barrier for some developing countries. But here a solution may be found through formal WTO action. This action comes not in the area of customs valuation rules, but in a new WTO negotiation, launched in August 2004 in connection with the Doha Round, on a potential agreement on "trade facilitation."

The general subject of these trade facilitation negotiations are rules "to further expedit[e] the movement, release and clearance of goods, including goods in transit."[8] Among other proposals, the new agreement could require all WTO Member countries to implement a risk-management based system of customs controls, including the use of post-clearance audit, and a system for exchange of information between national customs authorities where there are doubts about the truth or accuracy of importer declarations – in other words, the same customs procedures that have been identified as important to full and effective implementation of the Valuation Agreement.

Simply imposing these new rules and obligations on WTO Members will not, of course, resolve the developing countries' implementation challenge. What is novel about the trade facilitation agreement under negotiation is that commitments by developing and least developed countries will be explicitly conditioned on the provision of "adequate and effective technical assistance and capacity building measures" by developed countries and international organizations. Thus, if the technical assistance that developing and least developed countries require is not forthcoming, there will be no obligation on their part to implement the new measures, and they cannot be held accountable by other Members in WTO dispute proceedings. Therefore it will be in the interest of the developed and advanced developing countries, the main proponents of these negotiations, to provide this technical assistance in order to achieve real results from a trade facilitation agreement.

## 6.4 THE FUTURE

What then is the future of the WTO valuation system?

[8] WTO, *Doha Work Programme: Decision Adopted by the General Council on 1 August 2004*, WT/L/579 (August 2, 2004) (Annex D).

In the long term, as the WTO or regional market access negotiations succeed in further reducing import duties, customs valuation issues should become less common and contentious. If customs duties and border taxes are finally eliminated, the need for valuation rules, and the disputes that may arise out of their application, will disappear. However, unless and until the day that free-trade ideal is realized, there will be a need for a common system of valuation rules. The WTO Valuation Agreement will continue to be used, most likely in its present form, as the world trading community's choice of valuation rules that best balances the needs of trade facilitation and the collection of government revenue.

Like any other product of negotiation and compromise, the WTO valuation rules are not perfect. Some provisions of the Agreement are less than clear: the WCO technical committee, for example, has seen the need to issue thirteen advisory opinions on the question of royalties alone! As those WCO interpretative decisions also demonstrate, however, the Agreement does provide a mechanism (namely, the WCO and WTO committees) to allow Members to discuss and resolve these kinds of ambiguities and other questions of valuation technique or policy. A more difficult challenge to the Agreement is that effective implementation of the WTO valuation system does require a certain customs administrative and enforcement capacity, as described above. However, as was also noted, this challenge is being met by the on-going customs modernization efforts by and between WTO Members – an effort that may be accelerated by a new WTO agreement on trade facilitation – and, if successful all countries will have the capacity to apply the Agreement at the same level, and thereby fully realize its intended benefits.

# APPENDICES
# 1
# WTO VALUATION AGREEMENT TEXT

## GENERAL INTRODUCTORY COMMENTARY

1. The primary basis for customs value under this Agreement is "transaction value" as defined in Article 1. Article 1 is to be read together with Article 8 which provides, *inter alia*, for adjustments to the price actually paid or payable in cases where certain specific elements which are considered to form a part of the value for customs purposes are incurred by the buyer but are not included in the price actually paid or payable for the imported goods. Article 8 also provides for the inclusion in the transaction value of certain considerations which may pass from the buyer to the seller in the form of specified goods or services rather than in the form of money. Articles 2 through 7 provide methods of determining the customs value whenever it cannot be determined under the provisions of Article 1.
2. Where the customs value cannot be determined under the provisions of Article 1 there should normally be a process of consultation between the customs administration and importer with a view to arriving at a basis of value under the provisions of Article 2 or 3. It may occur, for example, that the importer has information about the customs value of identical or similar imported goods which is not immediately available to the customs administration in the port of importation. On the other hand, the customs administration may have information about the customs value of identical or similar imported goods which is not readily available to the importer. A process of consultation between the two parties will enable information to be exchanged, subject to the requirements of commercial confidentiality, with a view to determining a proper basis of value for customs purposes.
3. Articles 5 and 6 provide two bases for determining the customs value where it cannot be determined on the basis of the transaction value of the imported goods or of identical or similar imported goods. Under paragraph 1 of Article 5 the customs value is determined on the basis of the price at which the goods are sold in the condition as imported to an unrelated buyer in the country of importation. The importer also has the right to have goods which are further processed after importation valued under the provisions of Article 5 if the importer so requests. Under Article 6 the customs value is determined on the basis of the computed value. Both these methods present certain difficulties and because of this the importer is given the right, under the provisions of Article 4, to choose the order of application of the two methods.
4. Article 7 sets out how to determine the customs value in cases where it cannot be determined under the provisions of any of the preceding Articles.

*Members*,

*Having regard* to the Multilateral Trade Negotiations;

*Desiring* to further the objectives of GATT 1994 and to secure additional benefits for the international trade of developing countries;

*Recognizing* the importance of the provisions of Article VII of GATT 1994 and desiring to elaborate rules for their application in order to provide greater uniformity and certainty in their implementation;

*Recognizing* the need for a fair, uniform and neutral system for the valuation of goods for customs purposes that precludes the use of arbitrary or fictitious customs values;

*Recognizing* that the basis for valuation of goods for customs purposes should, to the greatest extent possible, be the transaction value of the goods being valued;

*Recognizing* that customs value should be based on simple and equitable criteria consistent with commercial practices and that valuation procedures should be of general application without distinction between sources of supply;

*Recognizing* that valuation procedures should not be used to combat dumping;

Hereby *agree* as follows:

## PART I RULES ON CUSTOMS VALUATION

### *Article 1*

1. The customs value of imported goods shall be the transaction value, that is the price actually paid or payable for the goods when sold for export to the country of importation adjusted in accordance with the provisions of Article 8, provided:

   (a) that there are no restrictions as to the disposition or use of the goods by the buyer other than restrictions which:
      (i) are imposed or required by law or by the public authorities in the country of importation;
      (ii) limit the geographical area in which the goods may be resold; or
      (iii) do not substantially affect the value of the goods;

   (b) that the sale or price is not subject to some condition or consideration for which a value cannot be determined with respect to the goods being valued;

   (c) that no part of the proceeds of any subsequent resale, disposal or use of the goods by the buyer will accrue directly or indirectly to the seller, unless an appropriate adjustment can be made in accordance with the provisions of Article 8; and

   (d) that the buyer and seller are not related, or where the buyer and seller are related, that the transaction value is acceptable for customs purposes under the provisions of paragraph 2.

2. (a) In determining whether the transaction value is acceptable for the purposes of paragraph 1, the fact that the buyer and the seller are related within the meaning of Article 15 shall not in itself be grounds for regarding the transaction value as unacceptable. In such case the circumstances surrounding the sale shall be examined and the transaction value shall be accepted provided that the relationship did not influence the price.

If, in the light of information provided by the importer or otherwise, the customs administration has grounds for considering that the relationship influenced the price, it shall communicate its grounds to the importer and the importer shall be given a reasonable opportunity to respond. If the importer so requests, the communication of the grounds shall be in writing.

(b) In a sale between related persons, the transaction value shall be accepted and the goods valued in accordance with the provisions of paragraph 1 whenever the importer demonstrates that such value closely approximates to one of the following occurring at or about the same time:
   (i) the transaction value in sales to unrelated buyers of identical or similar goods for export to the same country of importation;
   (ii) the customs value of identical or similar goods as determined under the provisions of Article 5;
   (iii) the customs value of identical or similar goods as determined under the provisions of Article 6;

   In applying the foregoing tests, due account shall be taken of demonstrated differences in commercial levels, quantity levels, the elements enumerated in Article 8 and costs incurred by the seller in sales in which the seller and the buyer are not related that are not incurred by the seller in sales in which the seller and the buyer are related.

(c) The tests set forth in paragraph 2(b) are to be used at the initiative of the importer and only for comparison purposes. Substitute values may not be established under the provisions of paragraph 2(b).

*Article 2*

1. (a) If the customs value of the imported goods cannot be determined under the provisions of Article 1, the customs value shall be the transaction value of identical goods sold for export to the same country of importation and exported at or about the same time as the goods being valued.

(b) In applying this Article, the transaction value of identical goods in a sale at the same commercial level and in substantially the same quantity as the goods being valued shall be used to determine the customs value. Where no such sale is found, the transaction value of identical goods sold at a different commercial level and/or in different quantities, adjusted to take account of differences attributable to commercial level and/or to quantity, shall be used, provided that such adjustments can be made on the basis of demonstrated evidence which clearly establishes the reasonableness and accuracy of the adjustment, whether the adjustment leads to an increase or a decrease in the value.

2. Where the costs and charges referred to in paragraph 2 of Article 8 are included in the transaction value, an adjustment shall be made to take account of significant differences in such costs and charges between the imported goods and the identical goods in question arising from differences in distances and modes of transport.

3. If, in applying this Article, more than one transaction value of identical goods is found, the lowest such value shall be used to determine the customs value of the imported goods.

*Article 3*

1. (a) If the customs value of the imported goods cannot be determined under the provisions of Articles 1 and 2, the customs value shall be the transaction value of similar goods sold for export to the same country of importation and exported at or about the same time as the goods being valued.
   (b) In applying this Article, the transaction value of similar goods in a sale at the same commercial level and in substantially the same quantity as the goods being valued shall be used to determine the customs value. Where no such sale is found, the transaction value of similar goods sold at a different commercial level and/or in different quantities, adjusted to take account of differences attributable to commercial level and/or to quantity, shall be used, provided that such adjustments can be made on the basis of demonstrated evidence which clearly establishes the reasonableness and accuracy of the adjustment, whether the adjustment leads to an increase or a decrease in the value.

2. Where the costs and charges referred to in paragraph 2 of Article 8 are included in the transaction value, an adjustment shall be made to take account of significant differences in such costs and charges between the imported goods and the similar goods in question arising from differences in distances and modes of transport.
3. If, in applying this Article, more than one transaction value of similar goods is found, the lowest such value shall be used to determine the customs value of the imported goods.

*Article 4*

If the customs value of the imported goods cannot be determined under the provisions of Articles 1, 2 and 3, the customs value shall be determined under the provisions of Article 5 or, when the customs value cannot be determined under that Article, under the provisions of Article 6 except that, at the request of the importer, the order of application of Articles 5 and 6 shall be reversed.

*Article 5*

1. (a) If the imported goods or identical or similar imported goods are sold in the country of importation in the condition as imported, the customs value of the imported goods under the provisions of this Article shall be based on the unit price at which the imported goods or identical or similar imported goods are so sold in the greatest aggregate quantity, at or about the time of the importation of the goods being valued, to persons who are not related to the persons from whom they buy such goods, subject to deductions for the following:
      (i) either the commissions usually paid or agreed to be paid or the additions usually made for profit and general expenses in connection with sales in such country of imported goods of the same class or kind;

(ii) the usual costs of transport and insurance and associated costs incurred within the country of importation;
(iii) where appropriate, the costs and charges referred to in paragraph 2 of Article 8; and
(iv) the customs duties and other national taxes payable in the country of importation by reason of the importation or sale of the goods.

(b) If neither the imported goods nor identical nor similar imported goods are sold at or about the time of importation of the goods being valued, the customs value shall, subject otherwise to the provisions of paragraph 1(a), be based on the unit price at which the imported goods or identical or similar imported goods are sold in the country of importation in the condition as imported at the earliest date after the importation of the goods being valued but before the expiration of 90 days after such importation.

2. If neither the imported goods nor identical nor similar imported goods are sold in the country of importation in the condition as imported, then, if the importer so requests, the customs value shall be based on the unit price at which the imported goods, after further processing, are sold in the greatest aggregate quantity to persons in the country of importation who are not related to the persons from whom they buy such goods, due allowance being made for the value added by such processing and the deductions provided for in paragraph 1(a).

*Article 6*

1. The customs value of imported goods under the provisions of this Article shall be based on a computed value. Computed value shall consist of the sum of:

(a) the cost or value of materials and fabrication or other processing employed in producing the imported goods;
(b) an amount for profit and general expenses equal to that usually reflected in sales of goods of the same class or kind as the goods being valued which are made by producers in the country of exportation for export to the country of importation;
(c) the cost or value of all other expenses necessary to reflect the valuation option chosen by the Member under paragraph 2 of Article 8.

2. No Member may require or compel any person not resident in its own territory to produce for examination, or to allow access to, any account or other record for the purposes of determining a computed value. However, information supplied by the producer of the goods for the purposes of determining the customs value under the provisions of this Article may be verified in another country by the authorities of the country of importation with the agreement of the producer and provided they give sufficient advance notice to the government of the country in question and the latter does not object to the investigation.

*Article 7*

1. If the customs value of the imported goods cannot be determined under the provisions of Articles 1 through 6, inclusive, the customs value shall be determined using reasonable means consistent with the principles and general provisions of

this Agreement and of Article VII of GATT 1994 and on the basis of data available in the country of importation.

2. No customs value shall be determined under the provisions of this Article on the basis of:

(a) the selling price in the country of importation of goods produced in such country;
(b) a system which provides for the acceptance for customs purposes of the higher of two alternative values;
(c) the price of goods on the domestic market of the country of exportation;
(d) the cost of production other than computed values which have been determined for identical or similar goods in accordance with the provisions of Article 6;
(e) the price of the goods for export to a country other than the country of importation;
(f) minimum customs values; or
(g) arbitrary or fictitious values.

3. If the importer so requests, the importer shall be informed in writing of the customs value determined under the provisions of this Article and the method used to determine such value.

*Article 8*

1. In determining the customs value under the provisions of Article 1, there shall be added to the price actually paid or payable for the imported goods:

(a) the following, to the extent that they are incurred by the buyer but are not included in the price actually paid or payable for the goods:
    (i) commissions and brokerage, except buying commissions;
    (ii) the cost of containers which are treated as being one for customs purposes with the goods in question;
    (iii) the cost of packing whether for labor or materials;
(b) the value, apportioned as appropriate, of the following goods and services where supplied directly or indirectly by the buyer free of charge or at reduced cost for use in connection with the production and sale for export of the imported goods, to the extent that such value has not been included in the price actually paid or payable:
    (i) materials, components, parts and similar items incorporated in the imported goods;
    (ii) tools, dies, moulds and similar items used in the production of the imported goods;
    (iii) materials consumed in the production of the imported goods;
    (iv) engineering, development, artwork, design work, and plans and sketches undertaken elsewhere than in the country of importation and necessary for the production of the imported goods;
(c) royalties and licence fees related to the goods being valued that the buyer must pay, either directly or indirectly, as a condition of sale of the goods being valued, to the extent that such royalties and fees are not included in the price actually paid or payable;

(d) the value of any part of the proceeds of any subsequent resale, disposal or use of the imported goods that accrues directly or indirectly to the seller.

2. In framing its legislation, each Member shall provide for the inclusion in or the exclusion from the customs value, in whole or in part, of the following:

(a) the cost of transport of the imported goods to the port or place of importation;
(b) loading, unloading and handling charges associated with the transport of the imported goods to the port or place of importation; and
(c) the cost of insurance.

3. Additions to the price actually paid or payable shall be made under this Article only on the basis of objective and quantifiable data.
4. No additions shall be made to the price actually paid or payable in determining the customs value except as provided in this Article.

*Article 9*

1. Where the conversion of currency is necessary for the determination of the customs value, the rate of exchange to be used shall be that duly published by the competent authorities of the country of importation concerned and shall reflect as effectively as possible, in respect of the period covered by each such document of publication, the current value of such currency in commercial transactions in terms of the currency of the country of importation.
2. The conversion rate to be used shall be that in effect at the time of exportation or the time of importation, as provided by each Member.

*Article 10*

All information which is by nature confidential or which is provided on a confidential basis for the purposes of customs valuation shall be treated as strictly confidential by the authorities concerned who shall not disclose it without the specific permission of the person or government providing such information, except to the extent that it may be required to be disclosed in the context of judicial proceedings.

*Article 11*

1. The legislation of each Member shall provide in regard to a determination of customs value for the right of appeal, without penalty, by the importer or any other person liable for the payment of the duty.
2. An initial right of appeal without penalty may be to an authority within the customs administration or to an independent body, but the legislation of each Member shall provide for the right of appeal without penalty to a judicial authority.
3. Notice of the decision on appeal shall be given to the appellant and the reasons for such decision shall be provided in writing. The appellant shall also be informed of any rights of further appeal.

*Article 12*

Laws, regulations, judicial decisions and administrative rulings of general application giving effect to this Agreement shall be published in conformity with Article X of GATT 1994 by the country of importation concerned.

*Article 13*

If, in the course of determining the customs value of imported goods, it becomes necessary to delay the final determination of such customs value, the importer of the goods shall nevertheless be able to withdraw them from customs if, where so required, the importer provides sufficient guarantee in the form of a surety, a deposit or some other appropriate instrument, covering the ultimate payment of customs duties for which the goods may be liable. The legislation of each Member shall make provisions for such circumstances.

*Article 14*

The notes at Annex I to this Agreement form an integral part of this Agreement and the Articles of this Agreement are to be read and applied in conjunction with their respective notes. Annexes II and III also form an integral part of this Agreement.

*Article 15*

1. In this Agreement:

   (a) "customs value of imported goods" means the value of goods for the purposes of levying ad valorem duties of customs on imported goods;
   (b) "country of importation" means country or customs territory of importation; and
   (c) "produced" includes grown, manufactured and mined.

2. In this Agreement:

   (a) "identical goods" means goods which are the same in all respects, including physical characteristics, quality and reputation. Minor differences in appearance would not preclude goods otherwise conforming to the definition from being regarded as identical;
   (b) "similar goods" means goods which, although not alike in all respects, have like characteristics and like component materials which enable them to perform the same functions and to be commercially interchangeable. The quality of the goods, their reputation and the existence of a trademark are among the factors to be considered in determining whether goods are similar;
   (c) the terms "identical goods" and "similar goods" do not include, as the case may be, goods which incorporate or reflect engineering, development, artwork, design work, and plans and sketches for which no adjustment has been made under paragraph 1(b)(iv) of Article 8 because such elements were undertaken in the country of importation;
   (d) goods shall not be regarded as "identical goods" or "similar goods" unless they were produced in the same country as the goods being valued;
   (e) goods produced by a different person shall be taken into account only when there are no identical goods or similar goods, as the case may be, produced by the same person as the goods being valued.

3. In this Agreement "goods of the same class or kind" means goods which fall within a group or range of goods produced by a particular industry or industry sector, and includes identical or similar goods.

4. For the purposes of this Agreement, persons shall be deemed to be related only if:

(a) they are officers or directors of one another's businesses;
(b) they are legally recognized partners in business;
(c) they are employer and employee;
(d) any person directly or indirectly owns, controls or holds 5 per cent or more of the outstanding voting stock or shares of both of them;
(e) one of them directly or indirectly controls the other;
(f) both of them are directly or indirectly controlled by a third person;
(g) together they directly or indirectly control a third person; or
(h) they are members of the same family.

5. Persons who are associated in business with one another in that one is the sole agent, sole distributor or sole concessionaire, however described, of the other shall be deemed to be related for the purposes of this Agreement if they fall within the criteria of paragraph 4.

*Article 16*

Upon written request, the importer shall have the right to an explanation in writing from the customs administration of the country of importation as to how the customs value of the importer's goods was determined.

*Article 17*

Nothing in this Agreement shall be construed as restricting or calling into question the rights of customs administrations to satisfy themselves as to the truth or accuracy of any statement, document or declaration presented for customs valuation purposes.

## PART II ADMINISTRATION, CONSULTATIONS AND DISPUTE SETTLEMENT

*Article 18*
*Institutions*

1. There is hereby established a Committee on Customs Valuation (referred to in this Agreement as "the Committee") composed of representatives from each of the Members. The Committee shall elect its own Chairman and shall normally meet once a year, or as is otherwise envisaged by the relevant provisions of this Agreement, for the purpose of affording Members the opportunity to consult on matters relating to the administration of the customs valuation system by any Member as it might affect the operation of this Agreement or the furtherance of its objectives and carrying out such other responsibilities as may be assigned to it by the Members. The WTO Secretariat shall act as the secretariat to the Committee.
2. There shall be established a Technical Committee on Customs Valuation (referred to in this Agreement as "the Technical Committee") under the auspices of the Customs Co-operation Council (referred to in this Agreement as "the CCC"), which shall carry out the responsibilities described in Annex II to this Agreement and shall operate in accordance with the rules of procedure contained therein.

*Article 19*

*Consultations and dispute settlement*

1. Except as otherwise provided herein, the Dispute Settlement Understanding is applicable to consultations and the settlement of disputes under this Agreement.
2. If any Member considers that any benefit accruing to it, directly or indirectly, under this Agreement is being nullified or impaired, or that the achievement of any objective of this Agreement is being impeded, as a result of the actions of another Member or of other Members, it may, with a view to reaching a mutually satisfactory solution of this matter, request consultations with the Member or Members in question. Each Member shall afford sympathetic consideration to any request from another Member for consultations.
3. The Technical Committee shall provide, upon request, advice and assistance to Members engaged in consultations.
4. At the request of a party to the dispute, or on its own initiative, a panel established to examine a dispute relating to the provisions of this Agreement may request the Technical Committee to carry out an examination of any questions requiring technical consideration. The panel shall determine the terms of reference of the Technical Committee for the particular dispute and set a time period for receipt of the report of the Technical Committee. The panel shall take into consideration the report of the Technical Committee. In the event that the Technical Committee is unable to reach consensus on a matter referred to it pursuant to this paragraph, the panel should afford the parties to the dispute an opportunity to present their views on the matter to the panel.
5. Confidential information provided to the panel shall not be disclosed without formal authorization from the person, body or authority providing such information. Where such information is requested from the panel but release of such information by the panel is not authorized, a non-confidential summary of this information, authorized by the person, body or authority providing the information, shall be provided.

## PART III SPECIAL AND DIFFERENTIAL TREATMENT

*Article 20*

1. Developing country Members not party to the Agreement on Implementation of Article VII of the General Agreement on Tariffs and Trade done on 12 April 1979 may delay application of the provisions of this Agreement for a period not exceeding five years from the date of entry into force of the WTO Agreement for such Members. Developing country Members who choose to delay application of this Agreement shall notify the Director-General of the WTO accordingly.
2. In addition to paragraph 1, developing country Members not party to the Agreement on Implementation of Article VII of the General Agreement on Tariffs and Trade done on 12 April 1979 may delay application of paragraph 2(b)(iii) of Article 1 and Article 6 for a period not exceeding three years following their application of all other provisions of this Agreement. Developing country Members that choose to delay application of the provisions specified in this paragraph shall notify the Director-General of the WTO accordingly.

3. Developed country Members shall furnish, on mutually agreed terms, technical assistance to developing country Members that so request. On this basis developed country Members shall draw up programmes of technical assistance which may include, *inter alia*, training of personnel, assistance in preparing implementation measures, access to sources of information regarding customs valuation methodology, and advice on the application of the provisions of this Agreement.

## PART IV FINAL PROVISIONS

*Article 21*

*Reservations*

Reservations may not be entered in respect of any of the provisions of this Agreement without the consent of the other Members.

*Article 22*

*National legislation*

1. Each Member shall ensure, not later than the date of application of the provisions of this Agreement for it, the conformity of its laws, regulations and administrative procedures with the provisions of this Agreement.
2. Each Member shall inform the Committee of any changes in its laws and regulations relevant to this Agreement and in the administration of such laws and regulations.

*Article 23*

*Review*

The Committee shall review annually the implementation and operation of this Agreement taking into account the objectives thereof. The Committee shall annually inform the Council for Trade in Goods of developments during the period covered by such reviews.

*Article 24*

*Secretariat*

This Agreement shall be serviced by the WTO Secretariat except in regard to those responsibilities specifically assigned to the Technical Committee, which will be serviced by the CCC Secretariat.

## ANNEX I INTERPRETATIVE NOTES

### GENERAL NOTE

*Sequential application of valuation methods*

1. Articles 1 through 7 define how the customs value of imported goods is to be determined under the provisions of this Agreement. The methods of valuation are set out in a sequential order of application. The primary method for customs valuation

is defined in Article 1 and imported goods are to be valued in accordance with the provisions of this Article whenever the conditions prescribed therein are fulfilled.
2. Where the customs value cannot be determined under the provisions of Article 1, it is to be determined by proceeding sequentially through the succeeding Articles to the first such Article under which the customs value can be determined. Except as provided in Article 4, it is only when the customs value cannot be determined under the provisions of a particular Article that the provisions of the next Article in the sequence can be used.
3. If the importer does not request that the order of Articles 5 and 6 be reversed, the normal order of the sequence is to be followed. If the importer does so request but it then proves impossible to determine the customs value under the provisions of Article 6, the customs value is to be determined under the provisions of Article 5, if it can be so determined.
4. Where the customs value cannot be determined under the provisions of Articles 1 through 6 it is to be determined under the provisions of Article 7.

*Use of generally accepted accounting principles*

1. "Generally accepted accounting principles" refers to the recognized consensus or substantial authoritative support within a country at a particular time as to which economic resources and obligations should be recorded as assets and liabilities, which changes in assets and liabilities should be recorded, how the assets and liabilities and changes in them should be measured, what information should be disclosed and how it should be disclosed, and which financial statements should be prepared. These standards may be broad guidelines of general application as well as detailed practices and procedures.
2. For the purposes of this Agreement, the customs administration of each Member shall utilize information prepared in a manner consistent with generally accepted accounting principles in the country which is appropriate for the Article in question. For example, the determination of usual profit and general expenses under the provisions of Article 5 would be carried out utilizing information prepared in a manner consistent with generally accepted accounting principles of the country of importation. On the other hand, the determination of usual profit and general expenses under the provisions of Article 6 would be carried out utilizing information prepared in a manner consistent with generally accepted accounting principles of the country of production. As a further example, the determination of an element provided for in paragraph 1(b)(ii) of Article 8 undertaken in the country of importation would be carried out utilizing information in a manner consistent with the generally accepted accounting principles of that country.

## Note to Article 1

*Price actually paid or payable*

1. The price actually paid or payable is the total payment made or to be made by the buyer to or for the benefit of the seller for the imported goods. The payment

need not necessarily take the form of a transfer of money. Payment may be made by way of letters of credit or negotiable instruments. Payment may be made directly or indirectly. An example of an indirect payment would be the settlement by the buyer, whether in whole or in part, of a debt owed by the seller.

2. Activities undertaken by the buyer on the buyer's own account, other than those for which an adjustment is provided in Article 8, are not considered to be an indirect payment to the seller, even though they might be regarded as of benefit to the seller. The costs of such activities shall not, therefore, be added to the price actually paid or payable in determining the customs value.

3. The customs value shall not include the following charges or costs, provided that they are distinguished from the price actually paid or payable for the imported goods:

(a) charges for construction, erection, assembly, maintenance or technical assistance, undertaken after importation on imported goods such as industrial plant, machinery or equipment;
(b) the cost of transport after importation;
(c) duties and taxes of the country of importation.

4. The price actually paid or payable refers to the price for the imported goods. Thus the flow of dividends or other payments from the buyer to the seller that do not relate to the imported goods are not part of the customs value.

*Paragraph 1(a)(iii)*

Among restrictions which would not render a price actually paid or payable unacceptable are restrictions which do not substantially affect the value of the goods. An example of such restrictions would be the case where a seller requires a buyer of automobiles not to sell or exhibit them prior to a fixed date which represents the beginning of a model year.

*Paragraph 1(b)*

1. If the sale or price is subject to some condition or consideration for which a value cannot be determined with respect to the goods being valued, the transaction value shall not be acceptable for customs purposes. Some examples of this include:

(a) the seller establishes the price of the imported goods on condition that the buyer will also buy other goods in specified quantities;
(b) the price of the imported goods is dependent upon the price or prices at which the buyer of the imported goods sells other goods to the seller of the imported goods;
(c) the price is established on the basis of a form of payment extraneous to the imported goods, such as where the imported goods are semi-finished goods which have been provided by the seller on condition that the seller will receive a specified quantity of the finished goods.

2. However, conditions or considerations relating to the production or marketing of the imported goods shall not result in rejection of the transaction value. For example, the fact that the buyer furnishes the seller with engineering and plans undertaken in the country of importation shall not result in rejection of the transaction value for the purposes of Article 1. Likewise, if the buyer undertakes on the buyer's own account, even though by agreement with the seller, activities relating to the marketing of the imported goods, the value of these activities is not part of the customs value nor shall such activities result in rejection of the transaction value.

*Paragraph 2*

1. Paragraphs 2(a) and 2(b) provide different means of establishing the acceptability of a transaction value.
2. Paragraph 2(a) provides that where the buyer and the seller are related, the circumstances surrounding the sale shall be examined and the transaction value shall be accepted as the customs value provided that the relationship did not influence the price. It is not intended that there should be an examination of the circumstances in all cases where the buyer and the seller are related. Such examination will only be required where there are doubts about the acceptability of the price. Where the customs administration have no doubts about the acceptability of the price, it should be accepted without requesting further information from the importer. For example, the customs administration may have previously examined the relationship, or it may already have detailed information concerning the buyer and the seller, and may already be satisfied from such examination or information that the relationship did not influence the price.
3. Where the customs administration is unable to accept the transaction value without further inquiry, it should give the importer an opportunity to supply such further detailed information as may be necessary to enable it to examine the circumstances surrounding the sale. In this context, the customs administration should be prepared to examine relevant aspects of the transaction, including the way in which the buyer and seller organize their commercial relations and the way in which the price in question was arrived at, in order to determine whether the relationship influenced the price. Where it can be shown that the buyer and seller, although related under the provisions of Article 15, buy from and sell to each other as if they were not related, this would demonstrate that the price had not been influenced by the relationship. As an example of this, if the price had been settled in a manner consistent with the normal pricing practices of the industry in question or with the way the seller settles prices for sales to buyers who are not related to the seller, this would demonstrate that the price had not been influenced by the relationship. As a further example, where it is shown that the price is adequate to ensure recovery of all costs plus a profit which is representative of the firm's overall profit realized over a representative period of time (e.g. on an annual basis) in sales of goods of the same class or kind, this would demonstrate that the price had not been influenced.
4. Paragraph 2(b) provides an opportunity for the importer to demonstrate that the transaction value closely approximates to a "test" value previously accepted by the customs administration and is therefore acceptable under the provisions of

Article 1. Where a test under paragraph 2(b) is met, it is not necessary to examine the question of influence under paragraph 2(a). If the customs administration has already sufficient information to be satisfied, without further detailed inquiries, that one of the tests provided in paragraph 2(b) has been met, there is no reason for it to require the importer to demonstrate that the test can be met. In paragraph 2(b) the term "unrelated buyers" means buyers who are not related to the seller in any particular case.

*Paragraph 2(b)*

A number of factors must be taken into consideration in determining whether one value "closely approximates" to another value. These factors include the nature of the imported goods, the nature of the industry itself, the season in which the goods are imported, and, whether the difference in values is commercially significant. Since these factors may vary from case to case, it would be impossible to apply a uniform standard such as a fixed percentage, in each case. For example, a small difference in value in a case involving one type of goods could be unacceptable while a large difference in a case involving another type of goods might be acceptable in determining whether the transaction value closely approximates to the "test" values set forth in paragraph 2(b) of Article 1.

## Note to Article 2

1. In applying Article 2, the customs administration shall, wherever possible, use a sale of identical goods at the same commercial level and in substantially the same quantities as the goods being valued. Where no such sale is found, a sale of identical goods that takes place under any one of the following three conditions may be used:

(a) a sale at the same commercial level but in different quantities;
(b) a sale at a different commercial level but in substantially the same quantities; or
(c) a sale at a different commercial level and in different quantities.

2. Having found a sale under any one of these three conditions adjustments will then be made, as the case may be, for:

(a) quantity factors only;
(b) commercial level factors only; or
(c) both commercial level and quantity factors.

3. The expression "and/or" allows the flexibility to use the sales and make the necessary adjustments in any one of the three conditions described above.
4. For the purposes of Article 2, the transaction value of identical imported goods means a customs value, adjusted as provided for in paragraphs 1(b) and 2, which has already been accepted under Article 1.

5. A condition for adjustment because of different commercial levels or different quantities is that such adjustment, whether it leads to an increase or a decrease in the value, be made only on the basis of demonstrated evidence that clearly establishes the reasonableness and accuracy of the adjustments, e.g. valid price lists containing prices referring to different levels or different quantities. As an example of this, if the imported goods being valued consist of a shipment of 10 units and the only identical imported goods for which a transaction value exists involved a sale of 500 units, and it is recognized that the seller grants quantity discounts, the required adjustment may be accomplished by resorting to the seller's price list and using that price applicable to a sale of 10 units. This does not require that a sale had to have been made in quantities of 10 as long as the price list has been established as being bona fide through sales at other quantities. In the absence of such an objective measure, however, the determination of a customs value under the provisions of Article 2 is not appropriate.

## NOTE TO ARTICLE 3

1. In applying Article 3, the customs administration shall, wherever possible, use a sale of similar goods at the same commercial level and in substantially the same quantities as the goods being valued. Where no such sale is found, a sale of similar goods that takes place under any one of the following three conditions may be used:

(a) a sale at the same commercial level but in different quantities;
(b) a sale at a different commercial level but in substantially the same quantities; or
(c) a sale at a different commercial level and in different quantities.

2. Having found a sale under any one of these three conditions adjustments will then be made, as the case may be, for:

(a) quantity factors only;
(b) commercial level factors only; or
(c) both commercial level and quantity factors.

3. The expression "and/or" allows the flexibility to use the sales and make the necessary adjustments in any one of the three conditions described above.
4. For the purpose of Article 3, the transaction value of similar imported goods means a customs value, adjusted as provided for in paragraphs 1(b) and 2, which has already been accepted under Article 1.
5. A condition for adjustment because of different commercial levels or different quantities is that such adjustment, whether it leads to an increase or a decrease in the value, be made only on the basis of demonstrated evidence that clearly establishes the reasonableness and accuracy of the adjustment, e.g. valid price lists containing prices referring to different levels or different quantities. As an example of this, if the imported goods being valued consist of a shipment of 10 units and the only similar imported goods for which a transaction value exists involved a sale of 500 units, and it is recognized that the seller grants quantity discounts, the required

adjustment may be accomplished by resorting to the seller's price list and using that price applicable to a sale of 10 units. This does not require that a sale had to have been made in quantities of 10 as long as the price list has been established as being bona fide through sales at other quantities. In the absence of such an objective measure, however, the determination of a customs value under the provisions of Article 3 is not appropriate.

### Note to Article 5

1. The term "unit price at which … goods are sold in the greatest aggregate quantity" means the price at which the greatest number of units is sold in sales to persons who are not related to the persons from whom they buy such goods at the first commercial level after importation at which such sales take place.
2. As an example of this, goods are sold from a price list which grants favourable unit prices for purchases made in larger quantities.

| *Sale quantity* | *Unit price* | *Number of sales* | *Total quantity sold at each price* |
|---|---|---|---|
| 1–10 units | 100 | 10 sales of 5 units<br>5 sales of 3 units | 65 |
| 11–25 units | 95 | 5 sales of 11 units | 55 |
| over 25 units | 90 | 1 sale of 30 units<br>1 sale of 50 units | 80 |

The greatest number of units sold at a price is 80; therefore, the unit price in the greatest aggregate quantity is 90.
3. As another example of this, two sales occur. In the first sale 500 units are sold at a price of 95 currency units each. In the second sale 400 units are sold at a price of 90 currency units each. In this example, the greatest number of units sold at a particular price is 500; therefore, the unit price in the greatest aggregate quantity is 95.
4. A third example would be the following situation where various quantities are sold at various prices.

*(a) Sales*

| *Sale quantity* | *Unit price* |
|---|---|
| 40 units | 100 |
| 30 units | 90 |
| 15 units | 100 |
| 50 units | 95 |
| 25 units | 105 |
| 35 units | 90 |
| 5 units | 100 |

*(b) Totals*

| *Total quantity sold* | *Unit price* |
| --- | --- |
| 65 | 90 |
| 50 | 95 |
| 60 | 100 |
| 25 | 105 |

In this example, the greatest number of units sold at a particular price is 65; therefore, the unit price in the greatest aggregate quantity is 90.

5. Any sale in the importing country, as described in paragraph 1 above, to a person who supplies directly or indirectly free of charge or at reduced cost for use in connection with the production and sale for export of the imported goods any of the elements specified in paragraph 1(b) of Article 8, should not be taken into account in establishing the unit price for the purposes of Article 5.

6. It should be noted that "profit and general expenses" referred to in paragraph 1 of Article 5 should be taken as a whole. The figure for the purposes of this deduction should be determined on the basis of information supplied by or on behalf of the importer unless the importer's figures are inconsistent with those obtained in sales in the country of importation of imported goods of the same class or kind. Where the importer's figures are inconsistent with such figures, the amount for profit and general expenses may be based upon relevant information other than that supplied by or on behalf of the importer.

7. The "general expenses" include the direct and indirect costs of marketing the goods in question.

8. Local taxes payable by reason of the sale of the goods for which a deduction is not made under the provisions of paragraph 1(a)(iv) of Article 5 shall be deducted under the provisions of paragraph 1(a)(i) of Article 5.

9. In determining either the commissions or the usual profits and general expenses under the provisions of paragraph 1 of Article 5, the question whether certain goods are "of the same class or kind" as other goods must be determined on a case-by-case basis by reference to the circumstances involved. Sales in the country of importation of the narrowest group or range of imported goods of the same class or kind, which includes the goods being valued, for which the necessary information can be provided, should be examined. For the purposes of Article 5, "goods of the same class or kind" includes goods imported from the same country as the goods being valued as well as goods imported from other countries.

10. For the purposes of paragraph 1(b) of Article 5, the "earliest date" shall be the date by which sales of the imported goods or of identical or similar imported goods are made in sufficient quantity to establish the unit price.

11. Where the method in paragraph 2 of Article 5 is used, deductions made for the value added by further processing shall be based on objective and quantifiable data relating to the cost of such work. Accepted industry formulas, recipes, methods of construction, and other industry practices would form the basis of the calculations.

12. It is recognized that the method of valuation provided for in paragraph 2 of Article 5 would normally not be applicable when, as a result of the further processing, the imported goods lose their identity. However, there can be instances where, although the identity of the imported goods is lost, the value added by the processing can be determined accurately without unreasonable difficulty. On the other hand, there can also be instances where the imported goods maintain their identity but form such a minor element in the goods sold in the country of importation that the use of this valuation method would be unjustified. In view of the above, each situation of this type must be considered on a case-by-case basis.

## Note to Article 6

1. As a general rule, customs value is determined under this Agreement on the basis of information readily available in the country of importation. In order to determine a computed value, however, it may be necessary to examine the costs of producing the goods being valued and other information which has to be obtained from outside the country of importation. Furthermore, in most cases the producer of the goods will be outside the jurisdiction of the authorities of the country of importation. The use of the computed value method will generally be limited to those cases where the buyer and seller are related, and the producer is prepared to supply to the authorities of the country of importation the necessary costings and to provide facilities for any subsequent verification which may be necessary.
2. The "cost or value" referred to in paragraph 1(a) of Article 6 is to be determined on the basis of information relating to the production of the goods being valued supplied by or on behalf of the producer. It is to be based upon the commercial accounts of the producer, provided that such accounts are consistent with the generally accepted accounting principles applied in the country where the goods are produced.
3. The "cost or value" shall include the cost of elements specified in paragraphs 1(a)(ii) and (iii) of Article 8. It shall also include the value, apportioned as appropriate under the provisions of the relevant note to Article 8, of any element specified in paragraph 1(b) of Article 8 which has been supplied directly or indirectly by the buyer for use in connection with the production of the imported goods. The value of the elements specified in paragraph 1(b)(iv) of Article 8 which are undertaken in the country of importation shall be included only to the extent that such elements are charged to the producer. It is to be understood that no cost or value of the elements referred to in this paragraph shall be counted twice in determining the computed value.
4. The "amount for profit and general expenses" referred to in paragraph 1(b) of Article 6 is to be determined on the basis of information supplied by or on behalf of the producer unless the producer's figures are inconsistent with those usually reflected in sales of goods of the same class or kind as the goods being valued which are made by producers in the country of exportation for export to the country of importation.

5. It should be noted in this context that the "amount for profit and general expenses" has to be taken as a whole. It follows that if, in any particular case, the producer's profit figure is low and the producer's general expenses are high, the producer's profit and general expenses taken together may nevertheless be consistent with that usually reflected in sales of goods of the same class or kind. Such a situation might occur, for example, if a product were being launched in the country of importation and the producer accepted a nil or low profit to offset high general expenses associated with the launch. Where the producer can demonstrate a low profit on sales of the imported goods because of particular commercial circumstances, the producer's actual profit figures should be taken into account provided that the producer has valid commercial reasons to justify them and the producer's pricing policy reflects usual pricing policies in the branch of industry concerned. Such a situation might occur, for example, where producers have been forced to lower prices temporarily because of an unforeseeable drop in demand, or where they sell goods to complement a range of goods being produced in the country of importation and accept a low profit to maintain competitivity. Where the producer's own figures for profit and general expenses are not consistent with those usually reflected in sales of goods of the same class or kind as the goods being valued which are made by producers in the country of exportation for export to the country of importation, the amount for profit and general expenses may be based upon relevant information other than that supplied by or on behalf of the producer of the goods.

6. Where information other than that supplied by or on behalf of the producer is used for the purposes of determining a computed value, the authorities of the importing country shall inform the importer, if the latter so requests, of the source of such information, the data used and the calculations based upon such data, subject to the provisions of Article 10.

7. The "general expenses" referred to in paragraph 1(b) of Article 6 covers the direct and indirect costs of producing and selling the goods for export which are not included under paragraph 1(a) of Article 6.

8. Whether certain goods are "of the same class or kind" as other goods must be determined on a case-by-case basis with reference to the circumstances involved. In determining the usual profits and general expenses under the provisions of Article 6, sales for export to the country of importation of the narrowest group or range of goods, which includes the goods being valued, for which the necessary information can be provided, should be examined. For the purposes of Article 6, "goods of the same class or kind" must be from the same country as the goods being valued.

## Note to Article 7

1. Customs values determined under the provisions of Article 7 should, to the greatest extent possible, be based on previously determined customs values.

2. The methods of valuation to be employed under Article 7 should be those laid down in Articles 1 through 6 but a reasonable flexibility in the application of such methods would be in conformity with the aims and provisions of Article 7.

3. Some examples of reasonable flexibility are as follows:

(a) *Identical goods* – the requirement that the identical goods should be exported at or about the same time as the goods being valued could be flexibly interpreted; identical imported goods produced in a country other than the country of exportation of the goods being valued could be the basis for customs valuation; customs values of identical imported goods already determined under the provisions of Articles 5 and 6 could be used.

(b) *Similar goods* – the requirement that the similar goods should be exported at or about the same time as the goods being valued could be flexibly interpreted; similar imported goods produced in a country other than the country of exportation of the goods being valued could be the basis for customs valuation; customs values of similar imported goods already determined under the provisions of Articles 5 and 6 could be used.

(c) *Deductive method* – the requirement that the goods shall have been sold in the "condition as imported" in paragraph 1(a) of Article 5 could be flexibly interpreted; the "90 days" requirement could be administered flexibly.

## NOTE TO ARTICLE 8

*Paragraph 1(a)(i)*

The term "buying commissions" means fees paid by an importer to the importer's agent for the service of representing the importer abroad in the purchase of the goods being valued.

*Paragraph 1(b)(ii)*

1. There are two factors involved in the apportionment of the elements specified in paragraph 1(b)(ii) of Article 8 to the imported goods – the value of the element itself and the way in which that value is to be apportioned to the imported goods. The apportionment of these elements should be made in a reasonable manner appropriate to the circumstances and in accordance with generally accepted accounting principles.

2. Concerning the value of the element, if the importer acquires the element from a seller not related to the importer at a given cost, the value of the element is that cost. If the element was produced by the importer or by a person related to the importer, its value would be the cost of producing it. If the element had been previously used by the importer, regardless of whether it had been acquired or produced by such importer, the original cost of acquisition or production would have to be adjusted downward to reflect its use in order to arrive at the value of the element.

3. Once a value has been determined for the element, it is necessary to apportion that value to the imported goods. Various possibilities exist. For example, the value might be apportioned to the first shipment if the importer wishes to pay duty on the entire value at one time. As another example, the importer may request that the value be apportioned over the number of units produced up to the time of the first shipment. As a further example, the importer may request that the value be apportioned over the entire anticipated production where contracts or firm commitments exist for that production. The method of apportionment used will depend upon the documentation provided by the importer.
4. As an illustration of the above, an importer provides the producer with a mould to be used in the production of the imported goods and contracts with the producer to buy 10,000 units. By the time of arrival of the first shipment of 1,000 units, the producer has already produced 4,000 units. The importer may request the customs administration to apportion the value of the mould over 1,000 units, 4,000 units or 10,000 units.

*Paragraph 1(b)(iv)*

1. Additions for the elements specified in paragraph 1(b)(iv) of Article 8 should be based on objective and quantifiable data. In order to minimize the burden for both the importer and customs administration in determining the values to be added, data readily available in the buyer's commercial record system should be used in so far as possible.
2. For those elements supplied by the buyer which were purchased or leased by the buyer, the addition would be the cost of the purchase or the lease. No addition shall be made for those elements available in the public domain, other than the cost of obtaining copies of them.
3. The ease with which it may be possible to calculate the values to be added will depend on a particular firm's structure and management practice, as well as its accounting methods.
4. For example, it is possible that a firm which imports a variety of products from several countries maintains the records of its design centre outside the country of importation in such a way as to show accurately the costs attributable to a given product. In such cases, a direct adjustment may appropriately be made under the provisions of Article 8.
5. In another case, a firm may carry the cost of the design centre outside the country of importation as a general overhead expense without allocation to specific products. In this instance, an appropriate adjustment could be made under the provisions of Article 8 with respect to the imported goods by apportioning total design centre costs over total production benefiting from the design centre and adding such apportioned cost on a unit basis to imports.
6. Variations in the above circumstances will, of course, require different factors to be considered in determining the proper method of allocation.
7. In cases where the production of the element in question involves a number of countries and over a period of time, the adjustment should be limited to the value actually added to that element outside the country of importation.

*Paragraph 1(c)*

1. The royalties and licence fees referred to in paragraph 1(c) of Article 8 may include, among other things, payments in respect to patents, trade marks and copyrights. However, the charges for the right to reproduce the imported goods in the country of importation shall not be added to the price actually paid or payable for the imported goods in determining the customs value.
2. Payments made by the buyer for the right to distribute or resell the imported goods shall not be added to the price actually paid or payable for the imported goods if such payments are not a condition of the sale for export to the country of importation of the imported goods.

*Paragraph 3*

Where objective and quantifiable data do not exist with regard to the additions required to be made under the provisions of Article 8, the transaction value cannot be determined under the provisions of Article 1. As an illustration of this, a royalty is paid on the basis of the price in a sale in the importing country of a litre of a particular product that was imported by the kilogram and made up into a solution after importation. If the royalty is based partially on the imported goods and partially on other factors which have nothing to do with the imported goods (such as when the imported goods are mixed with domestic ingredients and are no longer separately identifiable, or when the royalty cannot be distinguished from special financial arrangements between the buyer and the seller), it would be inappropriate to attempt to make an addition for the royalty. However, if the amount of this royalty is based only on the imported goods and can be readily quantified, an addition to the price actually paid or payable can be made.

## Note to Article 9

For the purposes of Article 9, "time of importation" may include the time of entry for customs purposes.

## Note to Article 11

1. Article 11 provides the importer with the right to appeal against a valuation determination made by the customs administration for the goods being valued. Appeal may first be to a higher level in the customs administration, but the importer shall have the right in the final instance to appeal to the judiciary.
2. "Without penalty" means that the importer shall not be subject to a fine or threat of fine merely because the importer chose to exercise the right of appeal. Payment of normal court costs and lawyers' fees shall not be considered to be a fine.
3. However, nothing in Article 11 shall prevent a Member from requiring full payment of assessed customs duties prior to an appeal.

### Note to Article 15

*Paragraph 4*

For the purposes of Article 15, the term "persons" includes a legal person, where appropriate.

*Paragraph 4(e)*

For the purposes of this Agreement, one person shall be deemed to control another when the former is legally or operationally in a position to exercise restraint or direction over the latter.

## ANNEX II TECHNICAL COMMITTEE ON CUSTOMS VALUATION

1. In accordance with Article 18 of this Agreement, the Technical Committee shall be established under the auspices of the CCC with a view to ensuring, at the technical level, uniformity in interpretation and application of this Agreement.
2. The responsibilities of the Technical Committee shall include the following:

   (a) to examine specific technical problems arising in the day-to-day administration of the customs valuation system of Members and to give advisory opinions on appropriate solutions based upon the facts presented;
   (b) to study, as requested, valuation laws, procedures and practices as they relate to this Agreement and to prepare reports on the results of such studies;
   (c) to prepare and circulate annual reports on the technical aspects of the operation and status of this Agreement;
   (d) to furnish such information and advice on any matters concerning the valuation of imported goods for customs purposes as may be requested by any Member or the Committee. Such information and advice may take the form of advisory opinions, commentaries or explanatory notes;
   (e) to facilitate, as requested, technical assistance to Members with a view to furthering the international acceptance of this Agreement;
   (f) to carry out an examination of a matter referred to it by a panel under Article 19 of this Agreement; and
   (g) to exercise such other responsibilities as the Committee may assign to it.

### General

3. The Technical Committee shall attempt to conclude its work on specific matters, especially those referred to it by Members, the Committee or a panel,

in a reasonably short period of time. As provided in paragraph 4 of Article 19, a panel shall set a specific time period for receipt of a report of the Technical Committee and the Technical Committee shall provide its report within that period.
4. The Technical Committee shall be assisted as appropriate in its activities by the CCC Secretariat.

### Representation

5. Each Member shall have the right to be represented on the Technical Committee. Each Member may nominate one delegate and one or more alternates to be its representatives on the Technical Committee. Such a Member so represented on the Technical Committee is referred to in this Annex as a "member of the Technical Committee". Representatives of members of the Technical Committee may be assisted by advisers. The WTO Secretariat may also attend such meetings with observer status.
6. Members of the CCC which are not Members of the WTO may be represented at meetings of the Technical Committee by one delegate and one or more alternates. Such representatives shall attend meetings of the Technical Committee as observers.
7. Subject to the approval of the Chairman of the Technical Committee, the Secretary-General of the CCC (referred to in this Annex as "the Secretary-General") may invite representatives of governments which are neither Members of the WTO nor members of the CCC and representatives of international governmental and trade organizations to attend meetings of the Technical Committee as observers.
8. Nominations of delegates, alternates and advisers to meetings of the Technical Committee shall be made to the Secretary-General.

### Technical Committee meetings

9. The Technical Committee shall meet as necessary but at least two times a year. The date of each meeting shall be fixed by the Technical Committee at its preceding session. The date of the meeting may be varied either at the request of any member of the Technical Committee concurred in by a simple majority of the members of the Technical Committee or, in cases requiring urgent attention, at the request of the Chairman. Notwithstanding the provisions in sentence 1 of this paragraph, the Technical Committee shall meet as necessary to consider matters referred to it by a panel under the provisions of Article 19 of this Agreement.
10. The meetings of the Technical Committee shall be held at the headquarters of the CCC unless otherwise decided.
11. The Secretary-General shall inform all members of the Technical Committee and those included under paragraphs 6 and 7 at least 30 days in advance, except in urgent cases, of the opening date of each session of the Technical Committee.

### Agenda

12. A provisional agenda for each session shall be drawn up by the Secretary-General and circulated to the members of the Technical Committee and to those included under paragraphs 6 and 7 at least 30 days in advance of the session, except in urgent cases. This agenda shall comprise all items whose inclusion has been approved by the Technical Committee during its preceding session, all items included by the Chairman on the Chairman's own initiative, and all items whose inclusion has been requested by the Secretary-General, by the Committee or by any member of the Technical Committee.
13. The Technical Committee shall determine its agenda at the opening of each session. During the session the agenda may be altered at any time by the Technical Committee.

### Officers and conduct of business

14. The Technical Committee shall elect from among the delegates of its members a Chairman and one or more Vice-Chairmen. The Chairman and Vice-Chairmen shall each hold office for a period of one year. The retiring Chairman and Vice-Chairmen are eligible for re-election. The mandate of a Chairman or Vice-Chairman who no longer represents a member of the Technical Committee shall terminate automatically.
15. If the Chairman is absent from any meeting or part thereof, a Vice-Chairman shall preside. In that event, the latter shall have the same powers and duties as the Chairman.
16. The Chairman of the meeting shall participate in the proceedings of the Technical Committee as such and not as the representative of a member of the Technical Committee.
17. In addition to exercising the other powers conferred upon the Chairman by these rules, the Chairman shall declare the opening and closing of each meeting, direct the discussion, accord the right to speak, and, pursuant to these rules, have control of the proceedings. The Chairman may also call a speaker to order if the speaker's remarks are not relevant.
18. During discussion of any matter a delegation may raise a point of order. In this event, the Chairman shall immediately state a ruling. If this ruling is challenged, the Chairman shall submit it to the meeting for decision and it shall stand unless overruled.
19. The Secretary-General, or officers of the CCC Secretariat designated by the Secretary-General, shall perform the secretarial work of meetings of the Technical Committee.

### Quorum and voting

20. Representatives of a simple majority of the members of the Technical Committee shall constitute a quorum.

21. Each member of the Technical Committee shall have one vote. A decision of the Technical Committee shall be taken by a majority comprising at least two thirds of the members present. Regardless of the outcome of the vote on a particular matter, the Technical Committee shall be free to make a full report to the Committee and to the CCC on that matter indicating the different views expressed in the relevant discussions. Notwithstanding the above provisions of this paragraph, on matters referred to it by a panel, the Technical Committee shall take decisions by consensus. Where no agreement is reached in the Technical Committee on the question referred to it by a panel, the Technical Committee shall provide a report detailing the facts of the matter and indicating the views of the members.

### Languages and records

22. The official languages of the Technical Committee shall be English, French and Spanish. Speeches or statements made in any of these three languages shall be immediately translated into the other official languages unless all delegations agree to dispense with translation. Speeches or statements made in any other language shall be translated into English, French and Spanish, subject to the same conditions, but in that event the delegation concerned shall provide the translation into English, French or Spanish. Only English, French and Spanish shall be used for the official documents of the Technical Committee. Memoranda and correspondence for the consideration of the Technical Committee must be presented in one of the official languages.
23. The Technical Committee shall draw up a report of all its sessions and, if the Chairman considers it necessary, minutes or summary records of its meetings. The Chairman or a designee of the Chairman shall report on the work of the Technical Committee at each meeting of the Committee and at each meeting of the CCC.

## ANNEX III

1. The five-year delay in the application of the provisions of the Agreement by developing country Members provided for in paragraph 1 of Article 20 may, in practice, be insufficient for certain developing country Members. In such cases a developing country Member may request before the end of the period referred to in paragraph 1 of Article 20 an extension of such period, it being understood that the Members will give sympathetic consideration to such a request in cases where the developing country Member in question can show good cause.
2. Developing countries which currently value goods on the basis of officially established minimum values may wish to make a reservation to enable them to retain such values on a limited and transitional basis under such terms and conditions as may be agreed to by the Members.
3. Developing countries which consider that the reversal of the sequential order at the request of the importer provided for in Article 4 of the Agreement may give

rise to real difficulties for them may wish to make a reservation to Article 4 in the following terms:

> "The Government of ... reserves the right to provide that the relevant provision of Article 4 of the Agreement shall apply only when the customs authorities agree to the request to reverse the order of Articles 5 and 6."

If developing countries make such a reservation, the Members shall consent to it under Article 21 of the Agreement.

4. Developing countries may wish to make a reservation with respect to paragraph 2 of Article 5 of the Agreement in the following terms:

> "The Government of ... reserves the right to provide that paragraph 2 of Article 5 of the Agreement shall be applied in accordance with the provisions of the relevant note thereto whether or not the importer so requests."

If developing countries make such a reservation, the Members shall consent to it under Article 21 of the Agreement.

5. Certain developing countries may have problems in the implementation of Article 1 of the Agreement insofar as it relates to importations into their countries by sole agents, sole distributors and sole concessionaires. If such problems arise in practice in developing country Members applying the Agreement, a study of this question shall be made, at the request of such Members, with a view to finding appropriate solutions.

6. Article 17 recognizes that in applying the Agreement, customs administrations may need to make enquiries concerning the truth or accuracy of any statement, document or declaration presented to them for customs valuation purposes. The Article thus acknowledges that enquiries may be made which are, for example, aimed at verifying that the elements of value declared or presented to customs in connection with a determination of customs value are complete and correct. Members, subject to their national laws and procedures, have the right to expect the full cooperation of importers in these enquiries.

7. The price actually paid or payable includes all payments actually made or to be made as a condition of sale of the imported goods, by the buyer to the seller, or by the buyer to a third party to satisfy an obligation of the seller.

# 2

# WTO URUGUAY ROUND MINISTERIAL DECISIONS

WORLD TRADE ORGANIZATION
**G/VAL/1**
27 April 1995
**Committee on Customs Valuation**

## MARRAKESH MINISTERIAL DECISIONS AND TEXTS RELATING TO CUSTOMS VALUATION

In accordance with the recommendation made by Ministers at Marrakesh, the following Decision and texts are being put forward to the Committee for adoption.

### I. Decision regarding cases where customs administrations have reasons to doubt the truth or accuracy of the declared value

*The Committee on Customs Valuation,*

*Reaffirming* that the transaction value is the primary basis of valuation under the Agreement on Implementation of Article VII of GATT 1994 (hereinafter referred to as the "Agreement");

*Recognizing* that the customs administration may have to address cases where it has reason to doubt the truth or accuracy of the particulars or of documents produced by traders in support of a declared value;

*Emphasizing* that in so doing the customs administration should not prejudice the legitimate commercial interests of traders;

*Taking into account* Article 17 of the Agreement, paragraph 6 of Annex III to the Agreement, and the relevant decisions of the Technical Committee on Customs Valuation;

*Decides* as follows:

1. When a declaration has been presented and where the customs administration has reason to doubt the truth or accuracy of the particulars or of documents produced in support of this declaration, the customs administration may ask the importer to provide further explanation, including documents or other evidence, that the declared value represents the total amount actually paid or payable for the imported goods, adjusted in accordance with the provisions of Article 8. If, after receiving further information, or in the absence of a response, the customs

administration still has reasonable doubts about the truth or accuracy of the declared value, it may, bearing in mind the provisions of Article 11, be deemed that the customs value of the imported goods cannot be determined under the provisions of Article 1. Before taking a final decision, the customs administration shall communicate to the importer, in writing if requested, its grounds for doubting the truth or accuracy of the particulars or documents produced and the importer shall be given a reasonable opportunity to respond. When a final decision is made, the customs administration shall communicate to the importer in writing its decision and the grounds therefor.

2. It is entirely appropriate in applying the Agreement for one Member to assist another Member on mutually agreed terms.

## II. Decision on texts relating to minimum values and imports by sole agents, sole distributors and sole concessionaires

*The Committee on Customs Valuation,*

*Decides* to adopt the following texts:

I

Where a developing country makes a reservation to retain officially established minimum values within the terms of paragraph 2 of Annex III and shows good cause, the Committee shall give the request for the reservation sympathetic consideration.

Where a reservation is consented to, the terms and conditions referred to in paragraph 2 of Annex III shall take full account of the development, financial and trade needs of the developing country concerned.

II

1. A number of developing countries have a concern that problems may exist in the valuation of imports by sole agents, sole distributors and sole concessionaires. Under paragraph 1 of Article 20, developing country Members have a period of delay of up to five years prior to the application of the Agreement. In this context, developing country Members availing themselves of this provision could use the period to conduct appropriate studies and to take such other actions as are necessary to facilitate application.

2. In consideration of this, the Committee recommends that the Customs Co-operation Council assist developing country Members, in accordance with the provisions of Annex II, to formulate and conduct studies in areas identified as being of potential concern, including those relating to importations by sole agents, sole distributors and sole concessionaires.

# 3

# WTO/GATT VALUATION COMMITTEE DECISIONS

WORLD TRADE ORGANIZATION
**G/VAL/5**
13 October 1995
**Committee on Customs Valuation**

## DECISIONS CONCERNING THE INTERPRETATION AND ADMINISTRATION OF THE AGREEMENT ON IMPLEMENTATION OF ARTICLE VII OF THE GATT 1994 (CUSTOMS VALUATION)

The following Decisions concerning the interpretation and administration of the Agreement were adopted by the WTO Committee on Customs Valuation at its meeting of 12 May 1995. These decisions, contained in sections A and B of document G/VAL/W/1, were originally adopted by the Tokyo Round Committee on Customs Valuation. The decisions contained in Section A were adopted by the WTO Committee without any amendments, while the text of the decisions in Section B was adapted to the WTO situation. The Committee decided not to take any action on the Procedures for the derestriction of documents set out in section B.3 of document G/VAL/W/1, until the General Council would take a decision on this question.

### A. DECISIONS CONCERNING THE INTERPRETATION OF THE AGREEMENT

#### *A.1 Meaning of the word "undertaken" in Article 8.1(b) (iv) of the English text of the Agreement*

***Adopted by the Tokyo Round Committee on 3 March 1983 (VAL/M/6, paragraph 18)***

The Committee agreed that in the context of Article 8.1(b) (iv) of the Agreement, the English word "undertaken" was to be understood as meaning "carried out". It noted that the French and Spanish texts of the Agreement were not affected.

### A.2 Linguistic consistency of the item "development" in Article 8.1(b)(iv) of the Agreement (VAL/M/13)

The Chairman made the following statement at the Tokyo Round Committee meeting of 9–10 May 1985:

"Consultations have taken place and in the light of these I suggest that the matter be settled by including the following statement in the minutes of the meeting, on the understanding that this would be without prejudice to rights and obligations under the Agreement and that members of the Committee can revert to the matter should the need arise.

"The Parties to the Agreement considered that the terms "development" in English, "travaux d'étude" in French and "creación y perfeccionamiento" in Spanish in Article 8.1(b) are understood to exclude "research" in English, "recherche" in French and "investigación" in Spanish, as stated in paragraph 6 of VAL/W/24/Rev.1. However, one signatory, Argentina, considered that, as used in Article 8.1(b), the Spanish expression "creación y perfeccionamiento" could not be interpreted as allowing any part of the value to be excluded from the "creación y perfeccionamiento"."

### A.3 Decision on the treatment of interest charges in the customs value of imported goods (VAL/6/Rev.1)

***Adopted by the Tokyo Round Committee on 26 April 1984 (VAL/M/9, paragraph 38) and rectified (French and Spanish texts only) by the Committee on 24 September 1984 (VAL/M/10, paragraph 17)***

The Parties to the Agreement on Implementation of Article VII of the GATT agree as follows:

Charges for interest under a financing arrangement entered into by the buyer and relating to the purchase of imported goods shall not be regarded as part of the customs value provided that:

(a) the charges are distinguished from the price actually paid or payable for the goods;
(b) the financing arrangement was made in writing;
(c) where required, the buyer can demonstrate that
   - such goods are actually sold at the price declared as the price actually paid or payable, and
   - the claimed rate of interest does not exceed the level for such transactions prevailing in the country where, and at the time when the finance was provided.

This Decision shall apply regardless of whether the finance is provided by the seller, a bank or another natural or legal person. It shall also apply, if appropriate, where goods are valued under a method other than the transaction value.

Each Party shall notify the Committee of the date from which it will apply the Decision.

### A.4 *Decision on the valuation of carrier media bearing software for data processing equipment (VAL/8)*

***Adopted by the Tokyo Round Committee on 24 September 1984 (VAL/M/10, paragraph 7)***

The Committee on Customs Valuation DECIDES as follows:

1. It is reaffirmed that transaction value is the primary basis of valuation under the Agreement on Implementation of Article VII of the General Agreement on Tariffs and Trade (the Agreement) and that its application with regard to data or instructions (software) recorded on carrier media for data processing equipment is fully consistent with the Agreement.

2. Given the unique situation[1] with regard to data or instructions (software) recorded on carrier media for data processing equipment, and that some Parties have sought a different approach, it would also be consistent with the Agreement for those Parties which wish to do so to adopt the following practice:

In determining the customs value of imported carrier media bearing data or instructions, only the cost or value of the carrier medium itself shall be taken into account. The customs value shall not, therefore, include the cost or value of the data or instructions, provided that this is distinguished from the cost or the value of the carrier medium.

For the purpose of this Decision, the expression "carrier medium" shall not be taken to include integrated circuits, semiconductors and similar devices or articles incorporating such circuits or devices; the expression "data or instructions" shall not be taken to include sound, cinematic or video recordings.

3. Those Parties adopting the practice referred to in paragraph 2 of this Decision shall notify the Committee of the date of its application.

4. Those Parties adopting the practice in paragraph 2 of this Decision will do so on a most-favoured-nation (m.f.n.) basis, without prejudice to the continued use by any Party of the transaction value practice.

### A.5 *Rectification of the French text of paragraph 1 of the Note to Article 2 and the Note to Article 3*

***Refer to the Tokyo Round Committee meeting of 20 March 1990 (VAL/M/26, paragraph 24)***

No objections were raised to the proposed rectification of the French text of paragraph 1 of both the Note to Article 2 and the Note to Article 3 which suggested replacing "la vente" in the first sentence by "celui" and to change the second sentence to read "En l'absence d'une telle vente .... differente" (VAL/W/49/Add.4).

[1] See paragraph 5 of VAL/M/10.

## B. Decisions concerning the administration of the Agreement and working procedures of the Committee (The Decisions have been adapted to the WTO situation)

### B.1 *Reservations under the Agreement on Customs Valuation*

***Adopted by the Tokyo Round Committee on 13 January 1981 (VAL/M/1, paragraph 36 and Annex 2)***

1. A reservation made under Article 21 of the Agreement by a Member accepting the WTO Agreement before 1 January 1995 shall be deemed to be accepted by the other Members unless the Committee is notified (through the Secretariat) by a particular Member to the contrary before 1 February 1995. Upon request of a Member or Members notified to the Secretariat before 1 February 1995, the time-limit shall be extended for another thirty days.
2. Members that accept the WTO Agreement on or after 1 January 1995 shall be deemed to accept all reservations previously accepted by the Members. Reservations made by Members which accept the WTO Agreement on or after 1 January 1995 shall be deemed to be accepted by the other Members unless the Committee is notified (through the Secretariat) to the contrary by a particular Member before expiry of thirty days following the date on which the WTO Agreement enters into force for the Members making the reservation. Upon request of a Member or Members notified to the Secretariat before the expiry of the period referred to in the preceding sentence, the time-limit shall be extended for a further thirty days.
3. For reservations made under paragraph 2 of Annex III, the Member having made the reservation shall communicate to the Committee (through the Secretariat) in due course a proposal containing the terms and conditions under which it wants to retain the minimum customs values (or similar schemes). This proposal would be discussed by the Committee with the aim of reaching an agreement on the terms and conditions of such reservation. Agreement should be reached as quickly as possible and at any rate not later than the date at which the Member having availed itself of the possibility of Article 20.1 starts implementing the provisions of the Agreement.
4. A reservation shall not come into force if:

- in the case of a reservation made under Article 21 of the Agreement another Member objects to the reservation within the time-limits as specified in paragraphs 1 and 2 or,
- in the case of a reservation made under paragraph 2 of Annex III, no agreement has been reached on the content (terms and conditions) of the reservation by the time that the Agreement is implemented by the Member in question.

Cases where a minority view about the acceptability or non-acceptability of a reservation exists would be examined in the Committee, at the request of the Member wishing to enter the reservation, with a view to seeking a mutually acceptable solution.

5. Reservations made by a developing country Member in conformity with paragraphs 3 or 4 of Annex III to the Agreement shall be deemed to be consented to by the other Members.

*B.2* *Notification and circulation of national legislation in accordance with Article 22 of the Agreement*

***Adopted by the Tokyo Round Committee on 13 January 1981 (VAL/M/1, paragraph 37)***

(i) Members will submit the complete texts of their national legislation (laws, regulations, etc.) on customs valuation in one of the three official WTO languages as soon as possible to the Secretariat which will circulate them as Committee documents to the other Members in the language submitted. If a general interest is expressed in the Committee that the text of a particular Member be available also in other official WTO languages, this text will be translated and circulated as a Committee document. In those cases where the national legislation is not in an official WTO language, the original texts shall also be submitted to the Secretariat where they will be open for inspection.

(ii) It is understood that the texts of the national legislation of developing country Members availing themselves of the provisions of Article 20, paragraphs 1 and 2 of the Agreement will be supplied to the Committee before the developing country Members begin the application of the provisions of the Agreement.

(iii) At its meeting of 12 May 1995 the WTO Committee decided that in cases of Members who were Tokyo Round signatories and whose legislation had already been examined, a communication from those Members could be sent to the WTO Secretariat indicating that legislation notified under the Tokyo Round Customs Valuation Agreement remained valid under the WTO Customs Valuation Agreement with a specific reference to the document containing the legislation. The Secretariat would then proceed to circulate this notification in a WTO document (G/VAL/M/1, paragraph 29–35).

*B.3* *Checklist of issues*

***Adopted by the Tokyo Round Committee on 5 May 1981 (VAL/M/2, paragraph 52)***

(i) "The Committee decided that Members should respond in writing to the points contained in the checklist."[2]

(ii) At its meeting of 12 May 1995 the WTO Committee decided that in cases of Members who were Tokyo Round signatories and whose legislation

[2] The checklist is reproduced in the Annex to this document.

had already been examined, a communication from those Members could be sent to the Secretariat indicating that their responses to the checklist of issues remained valid under the WTO Customs Valuation Agreement (G/VAL/M/1, paragraph 36–39).

*B.4 Information on technical assistance*

***Agreed by the Tokyo Round Committee on 9–10 May 1985 (VAL/M/13, paragraph 8)***

"... In regard to the point raised at the Committee's last meeting about whether there was need to ensure greater transparency of technical assistance activities so as to give interested developing country Members further information and also to help Members in their planning (VAL/M/1, paragraph 18), the Committee agreed that the information documents prepared for the Technical Committee on such activities were also made available as a WTO document ..."

## ANNEX CHECKLIST OF ISSUES

1. Questions concerning Article 1:

 (a) Sales between related persons:
  (i) Are sales between related persons subject to special provisions?
  (ii) Is the fact of intercompany prices prima facie considered as grounds for regarding the respective prices as being influenced?
  (iii) What is the provision for giving the communication of the aforementioned grounds in writing if the importer so requests? (Article 1.2(a))
  (iv) How has Article 1.2(b) been implemented?
 (b) Price of lost or damaged goods:
 Are there any special provisions or practical arrangements concerning the valuation of lost or damaged goods?

2. How has the provision of Article 4 to allow the importer an option to reverse the order of application of Articles 5 and 6 been implemented?
3. How has Article 5.2 been implemented?
4. How has Article 6.2 been implemented?
5. Questions concerning Article 7:

 (a) What provisions have been made for making value determinations pursuant to Article 7?
 (b) What is the provision for informing the importer of the customs value determined under Article 7?
 (c) Are the prohibitions found in Article 7.2 delineated?

6. How have the options found in Article 8.2 been handled? In the case of f.o.b. application, are ex-factory prices also accepted?

7. Where is the rate of exchange published, as required by Article 9.1?
8. What steps have been taken to ensure confidentiality, as required by Article 10?
9. Questions concerning Article 11:

    (a) What rights of appeal are open to the importer or any other person?
    (b) How is he to be informed of his right to further appeal?

10. Provide information on the publication, as required by Article 12, of:
    (a) (i) the relevant national laws;
        (ii) the regulations concerning the application of the Agreement;
        (iii) the judicial decision and administrative rulings of general application relating to the Agreement;
        (iv) general or specific laws being referred to in the rules of implementation or application.
    (b) Is the publication of further rules anticipated? Which topics would they cover?

11. Questions concerning Article 13:

    (a) How is the obligation of Article 13 (last sentence) being dealt with in the respective legislation?
    (b) Have additional explanations been laid down?

12. Questions concerning Article 16:

    (a) Does the respective national legislation contain a provision requiring customs authorities to give an explanation in writing as to how the customs value was determined?
    (b) Are there any further regulations concerning an above-mentioned request?

13. How have the Interpretative Notes of the Agreement been included?

14. How have the provisions of the Decision on the Treatment of Interest Charges in the Customs Value of Imported Goods been implemented?

15. For those countries applying paragraph 2 of the Decision on the Valuation of Carrier Media Bearing Software for Data Processing Equipment, how have the provisions of this paragraph been implemented?

– For all questions listed above, an indication of the references is requested.

# 4

# WORLD CUSTOMS ORGANIZATION VALUATION DATABASE GUIDELINES

WORLD TRADE ORGANIZATION
**G/VAL/54/Suppl.1**
13 October 2004
**Committee on Customs Valuation**
Original: English/French/Spanish

## TECHNICAL COMMITTEE ON CUSTOMS VALUATION – RESPONSE TO THE TERMS OF REFERENCE FOR THE WORK OF THE TECHNICAL COMMITTEE ON CUSTOMS VALUATION IN CONNECTION WITH CONCERNS ON THE ACCURACY OF THE DECLARED VALUE (G/VAL/51)

**SUPPLEMENT**

The attached communication, dated 7 October 2004, together with the letter of transmission of the Chairperson of the TCCV below, is being circulated to Members.

Brussels, 27 August 2004

In accordance with the mandate of the Technical Committee on Customs Valuation (TCCV) under paragraph 8.3 of the Doha Decision and further to the response to that mandate which the TCCV communicated to the WTO Committee on Customs Valuation in May 2003, I have the honour to transmit herewith the text of the Guidelines on the Development and Use of a National Valuation Database as a Risk Assessment Tool, as adopted by the TCCV at its 18th session and by the WCO Council during its sessions of June 2004.

Chairperson
Technical Committee on Customs Valuation

**WCO** **OMD**

# GUIDELINES ON THE DEVELOPMENT AND USE OF A NATIONAL VALUATION DATABASE AS A RISK ASSESSMENT TOOL

## Table of Contents



## Preamble:

1. These Guidelines address various issues pertaining to the development and use of a national valuation database. A national valuation database is a risk assessment tool which may be used by a Customs Administration along with other risk tools to assess potential risk regarding the truth or accuracy of the declared Customs value for imported goods. The information in the database should be recent data reflecting the Customs value and other pertinent information for previously imported goods. The values may not be used to determine the Customs value for imported goods, as a substitute value for imported goods, or as a mechanism to establish minimum values. In addition, recognizing that differences in prices, including substantial declines, are a part of international trade, a difference between the declared value and the database value(s) is not by itself a reliable indicator of potential risk with respect to the truth or accuracy of the declared value, subject to the provisions of Decision 6.1.

2. A Customs Administration that uses a valuation database should establish a monitoring mechanism to ensure that the database is being used as a risk assessment tool and that the information stored in the database is updated on a regular basis.

## Introduction:

3. The Agreement on Implementation of Article VII of the GATT 1994, more commonly known as the WTO Agreement on Customs Valuation (the Agreement), introduces a fair, uniform and neutral system for the Customs valuation of imported goods, which is consistent with commercial practices and precludes the use of arbitrary or fictitious Customs values.

4. The basis for the valuation of goods under this system is, to the greatest extent possible, the transaction value of the imported goods which is the price actually paid or payable for the goods when sold for export to the country of importation, adjusted in accordance with the provisions of Article 8 of the Agreement.
5. Where the Customs value cannot be determined using the transaction value method, the Agreement provides for five other methods, to be used in turn.
6. Customs has the right to satisfy itself as to the truth or accuracy of the value declared. The application of an appropriate risk assessment and management procedure enables Customs to exercise this right in a pragmatic manner. Such procedures may use, *inter alia*, a valuation database.
7. The data contained in a valuation database should be treated in accordance with the applicable confidentiality provisions.
8. Within the context of Customs controls, Chapter 6 of the Guidelines on the General Annex to the Revised Kyoto Convention *(Customs controls)* includes the following definitions of the concepts of risk assessment and risk management:

Risk assessment: "The systematic determination of risk management priorities by evaluating and comparing the level of risk against predetermined standards, target risk levels or other criteria."
Risk management: "The systematic application of management procedures and practices which provide Customs with the necessary information to address movements or consignments which present a risk."

9. In the context of Customs valuation, application of the above concepts requires that risk assessment mechanisms must be selective and targeted. It is not appropriate to apply simple statistical or price indicators to all imports on a comprehensive basis, as a means to measure potential risk with regard to the truth or accuracy of Customs value. The development and use of a valuation database must take account of the above-mentioned risk assessment and management procedures.

### Use of a database:

10. A valuation database may be used by a Customs Administration only as a risk assessment tool. It has to be designed specially to assess potential risk regarding the truth or accuracy of the declared value for imported goods.
11. Database management systems will usually enable a Customs Administration to compare the declared value to previously accepted Customs value(s). Recognizing that price variations are a normal part of international trade, the results of any such comparison do not in themselves represent a comprehensive or sufficient indicator of potential risk. Therefore, while an abnormally large difference between the declared value and the databases value(s) for that product could constitute a potential risk factor, any such difference must be considered along with other potential risk factors, such as the lack of supporting documentation, prior problems with the importer, etc., in determining what further action, if any, is appropriate with regard to the declared value.

12. Where the application of appropriate database technology indicates the existence of potential risk in well-defined circumstances, Customs may apply a number of measures. For example, Customs may place the operations of a particular importer under scrutiny and take appropriate monitoring action. In other cases where there are concrete indications that the declared values represent a risk with respect to their truth or accuracy, and after taking into account all the relevant risk factors the Customs Administration has doubts about the truth or accuracy of the declared value, it could follow the procedures set forth in Decision 6.1 of the WTO Committee on Customs Valuation. Such procedures start by asking the importer to provide further evidence to support the declared value. Another example of a measure that can be taken by Customs Administration in cases of potential risk is a post-importation audit of the importer.
13. The Customs Administration cannot reject the declared value based solely on a difference between the declared value and the database value(s). Rather, the value(s) stored in the database should, alongside other indicators applied by Customs, serve only as an indicator of potential risk and represents no more than initial indicative information helping to reinforce or dispel Customs' doubts about the truth or accuracy of the declared value.
14. The database can also be used as a risk assessment tool to perform cross-checks in order to target specific import declarations for examination.
15. Normally, a valuation database should form part of a more extensive database embracing risk assessment linked to other aspects of the import/export operation, such as origin, tariff code number, importer's profile, exporter's profile, etc.
16. Each Customs Administration should determine, with reference to its own needs, which authorized staff will have access to the national valuation database.
17. The use of databases in the risk assessment context may occur at any stage: prior to the lodging of the import declaration, at the time when the declaration is lodged (verification of the data entered in the declaration), throughout the clearance process and/or after the goods have been released.

### Caveat regarding the use of a database:

18. A Customs Administration may not:

- Use a database to determine the Customs value of imported goods, as a substitute value for imported goods or as a mechanism to establish minimum values;
- Reject the declared value solely on the basis of a difference between the declared value and the database values;
- Disregard the requirements of Article 13 of the WTO Valuation Agreement (concerning release of imported goods upon sufficient guarantee) in order to employ a valuation database; or
- Use a valuation database as a substitute for other techniques, such as post-importation audit, to assess the truth or accuracy of the declared value.

### Data to be included in a database:

19. Within the framework of a risk assessment policy for valuation, the data to be included in a valuation database may vary, depending on the state of development of the risk management policy of the Member concerned and should be based on relevant elements from the WCO Customs Data Model.

20. The usefulness of a valuation database as a risk assessment tool depends on the reliability and relevance of the data for the purposes of determining the truth or accuracy of the declared value. Therefore, the data should include the Customs value for previous importations determined in accordance with the Agreement. The data may also include the applicable method of valuation (for example, transaction value, computed value, etc.) and elements included in the Customs value (for example, assists, royalties, selling commissions, etc.). Other data from the import declaration, such as whether the parties are related, may also be included.

21. The data to be included in the database is generally the data found in the import declarations and supporting documents of previous importations. The database may also include other pertinent and reliable data for risk assessment purposes.

22. In an automated database, virtually all of this data could constitute key-words providing search access. For example, doing a search on "country of origin" should, at least, make it possible to find information about all importations of goods from the country concerned during a specified period; at best, it should provide a range of information about the type of goods exported from that country, etc.

### Validity of the data:

23. In order to properly perform its function as a risk assessment tool, data in the database should be recent and up-to-date. What is considered recent and up-to-date may depend on the commodity involved, the frequency of price fluctuations, and other pertinent factors.

### Possibility of cross-checking:

24. The database can also be used as a means of performing cross-checks in order to target those importations which are likely to contain a potential risk and, from that starting-point, select the import declarations concerned for examination.

25. Thus, for example, if it has been established in the past – under the provisions of paragraphs 1 (d) and 2 of Article 1 of the Agreement, and paragraph 4 of Article 15 thereof – that a buyer/importer is related to his supplier/seller, that this relationship has influenced the price, and that this has caused the declared value to be rejected, there could be a function in the system which selects all future declarations concerning transactions between that buyer/importer and that supplier/seller, so that Customs will be in a position to check whether the relationship still exists and, if so, whether it is still producing the same effects.

26. Similarly, if it has been established in the past – under the provisions of paragraph 1 (a) of Article 8 – that commissions (other than buying commissions) have been paid in connection with a transaction between a buyer/importer and a supplier/seller, and the declared value was adjusted as a result, the system should be able to select all future declarations for transactions between that buyer/importer and that supplier/seller, so that Customs can check whether this type of payment is still being made and, where appropriate, adjust the declared value accordingly.
27. The same would apply to several other provisions of the Agreement (conditions of application of Article 1, goods and services supplied by the buyer, royalties, proceeds of resale, etc.).

## Monitoring Mechanism:

A Customs Administration that uses a valuation database should establish a monitoring mechanism to ensure that it is being used only for the purpose of risk assessment described in these Guidelines and to ensure that the information in the database is updated on a regular and continual basis.

# 5

# WORLD CUSTOMS ORGANIZATION: MEASURES TO COMBAT VALUATION FRAUD

WORLD TRADE ORGANIZATION
**G/VAL/54**
16 May 2003
**Committee on Customs Valuation**
Original: English/French/Spanish

**TECHNICAL COMMITTEE ON CUSTOMS VALUATION RESPONSE TO THE TERMS OF REFERENCE FOR THE WORK OF THE TECHNICAL COMMITTEE ON CUSTOMS VALUATION IN CONNECTION WITH CONCERNS ON THE ACCURACY OF THE DECLARED VALUE (G/VAL/51)**

The attached document contains the response of the Technical Committee on Customs Valuation to the terms of reference sent by the Committee on Customs Valuation in connection with its work on paragraph 8.3 of the Ministerial Declaration (WT/MIN(01)/17).

WORLD CUSTOMS ORGANIZATION
ORGANISATION MONDIALE DES DOUANES
ORGANIZACIÓN MUNDIAL DE ADUANAS

TECHNICAL COMMITTEE ON CUSTOMS VALUATION

-

16th Session

-

VT0330E1

Brussels, 2 May 2003.

# TECHNICAL COMMITTEE ON CUSTOMS VALUATION RESPONSE TO THE TERMS OF REFERENCE FOR THE WORK OF THE TECHNICAL COMMITTEE ON CUSTOMS VALUATION IN CONNECTION WITH CONCERNS ON THE ACCURACY OF THE DECLARED VALUE

1. The Technical Committee has examined all of the points in the Terms of Reference set out in WTO Doc. G/VAL/51 arising out of the mandate of Doha Decision, paragraph 8.3, which underlines the importance of strengthening co-operation between the Customs administrations of Members in the prevention of Customs fraud.
2. The Technical Committee recognised that Member administrations should have the necessary legal and administrative framework for the effective implementation of the WTO Valuation Agreement. This framework consists of (1) a supporting legislative framework that facilitates truthful and accurate value declarations, (2) a comprehensive sanctions regime to address non-compliance and support voluntary compliance, (3) a legal framework that provides for the right of appeal to the importer, (4) policies and procedures governing valuation and compliance, (5) administrative and technical capacity, (6) strategies for dealing with particular sectors (e.g. the informal sector) of trade and (7) partnership with trade. These items are discussed in more detail in paragraphs 20 to 27, below.
3. With this important foundation in mind, the Technical Committee provides the following response to the Committee on Customs Valuation as requested by the Terms of Reference.

1) **Examine the technical aspects of the practical means considered in the Committee or others related to them to address concerns about the accuracy of declared value, including the exchange of information on export values, to cover, inter alia, the following points:**

- *The elements contained in the format provided in the Annex of G/VAL/W/102, possibly taking note of the current work in the TCCV (such as the Draft Guide to the Exchange of Customs Valuation Information, under consideration by the TCCV)*

4. The Technical Committee reviewed the elements in the format contained in the Annex to Doc. G/VAL/W/102. With regard to Part A : Details to be furnished by the Requesting Administration (Items 1–18), the Technical Committee was of the view that no rigid rule was needed regarding the details to be provided. The key point was for the requesting administration to provide the minimum data elements needed to identify the export transaction.
5. Specific clarification was sought from India regarding Point 4 of Part B (Information Sought by the Requesting Administration, other, please specify). The Technical Committee noted the explanation provided by India that this point was designed to cover residual information or assistance that the Customs administration in the country of importation might seek depending on the circumstances, e.g. information necessary for the verification of the authenticity of an invoice which was suspected of not being genuine.

6. Clarification was also sought from India regarding Point 2 of Part C, which states that the information provided by the requested administration may be disclosed in judicial proceedings. India, supported by several delegations, was of the opinion that this point served as a reminder of Article 10 of the Valuation Agreement, which authorises disclosure of confidential information to the extent that it may be required to be disclosed in the context of judicial proceedings, even without the specific permission of the person or government providing such information. Those delegations also pointed out that Doha Decision (paragraph 8.3) specifically referred to Article 10, and that the information exchanged would be of no use if it could not be used in judicial proceedings. Several other delegations were of the opinion that Article 10 did not cover information provided to the authorities in the country of exportation by the exporter. In addition, those delegations considered that the authorities in the country of exportation should consent before their confidential information is used in judicial proceedings in the country of importation. Nevertheless, the Technical Committee agreed that confidentiality of information must be considered in accordance with the applicable confidentiality provisions.

7. Subject to the observations set out in paragraphs 4 to 6 above, the Technical Committee has completed its consideration of the elements contained in the Annex to Doc. G/VAL/W/102.

8. The Technical Committee has finished its examination of the Guide to the Exchange of Customs Valuation Information. The Guide was developed to facilitate the exchange of valuation information among Customs administrations. It consists of (1) a checklist regarding valuation verification actions to be taken by the Customs administration in the importing country before requesting information from the Customs administration in the exporting country and (2) a set of recommended procedures, applicable to the Customs administrations of both the importing and exporting countries, for the exchange of valuation information. Certain elements contained in the Guide, namely, the details to identify the goods to be provided by the importing country in the request for information, are similar to the elements contained in Part A of the Annex to Doc. G/VAL/W/102. A copy of the Guide, as developed by the Technical Committee, is attached and forms part of the response.

- *The bilateral approach through exchange of information arrangements*

9. The bilateral approach was identified as the desirable means for the exchange of information in many cases. The bilateral approach is useful for both valuation and other Customs issues. It provides the flexibility to address the particular needs of the parties concerned, such as with regard to specific expectations, confidentiality, safeguards, etc. Many Members have entered into various Customs Mutual Assistance Agreements on a bilateral basis with positive results. In many cases, these agreements are used to provide assistance to develop or verify suspicions of fraud. The WCO has developed a Model Bilateral Agreement, which can be used as the basis for the negotiation of a bilateral agreement between two parties relative to mutual administrative assistance and information exchange on all Customs issues. In particular, paragraph 2 of Article 3 of the Model Bilateral Agreement covers the provision of information to ensure the correct determination of Customs value.

10. There may be practical obstacles to the bilateral approach to information exchange, namely, (1) it can be a difficult and complex process to conclude bilateral agreements, particularly with all trading partners, (2) different levels of administrative capacity and trade between parties might impede the negotiation and the administration of a bilateral agreement on an equal footing, and (3) confidentiality of information must be highly respected but it may limit the ability of Customs administrations to exchange information as they wish.
11. In view of the above, several Members supported the position that the bilateral approach should not be the only or the ideal solution and preferred the multilateral approach to the exchange of information in many cases.

- *Techniques or processes used by Customs administrations in the final determination and/or verification in respect of the value of goods*

12. The Technical Committee has identified a number of techniques and processes for the determination and verification of the value of the goods. The techniques and processes begin prior to the importation of the goods and continue until all post importation checks have been completed. These techniques and processes include, but are not limited to, the following:

- Use of a special value declaration form.
- Verification at the border, which involves an examination of the value declaration, supporting documents or records, or, where necessary, of the goods themselves, in order to ensure the truth and accuracy of the Customs value.
- Valuation risk management: the goal of valuation risk management is to concentrate valuation fraud controls on targeting areas of highest risk, so that resources can be allocated in an efficient way. It involves the process of identifying risk areas in terms of valuation fraud and valuation fraud trends and methodologies so as to exercise appropriate general and specific controls to ensure compliance. Customs administrations need to develop special information strategies to enhance their capacity to compile, analyse and use a range of relevant information sources. One of the valuation risk-assessment tools can be the use of a national valuation database (see response to Point 2 of the Terms of Reference).
- Dialogue with the importer: Maintaining an active dialogue with the importer regarding questions and concerns about issues relating to the declared value can often eliminate doubts about the accuracy of the declared value and dispel suspicions of fraud.
- Application of approach set forth in Decision 6.1 and Technical Committee Case Study 13.1 in cases where Customs administrations have reasons to doubt the truth or accuracy of the declared value.
- Post-clearance audit techniques for valuation control purposes : this process enables Customs officers to verify, after the clearance of the goods, the truth and accuracy of the declarations through the examination of the books, records, and other relevant commercial data held by the importer.
- Investigation and intelligence techniques for fraud investigation, which require close co-ordination between the valuation/clearance functions and the investigation and intelligence functions.

13. The Customs Valuation Control Handbook developed by the Technical Committee provides guidance to Member Customs administrations on how to maintain appropriate control mechanisms and procedures to ensure correct valuation management.
14. The Control Handbook sets out means for the control of the declaration of value and the verification of the Customs value of goods for each of the valuation methods provided for in the Valuation Agreement to ensure that : (1) the conditions for the use of the transaction value method are fulfilled; (2) the declared value includes the total payment made (to be made) by the buyer for the imported goods; (3) the declared value includes all additions necessary under Article 8 of the Agreement; (4) an alternative method of valuation, where indicated, is being used correctly. These means include the use of valuation rulings, procedures for checking the value declaration and supporting documents, techniques for making further enquiries concerning the truth or accuracy of a declaration, such as how to carry out an audit at an importer's premises.
15. The Control Handbook also discusses means of verification of more complex elements such as related party transactions, buying commissions, assists, royalties and licence fees. The Handbook contains a list of revenue risk areas and a model of computerisation for valuation control. It also highlights the different alternatives regarding the organisation of valuation control.

- *The method of communication and ideal time frame for the exchange of information*

16. The Technical Committee agreed that requests for information should be made in writing or electronically. The requested Customs administration may require written confirmation of electronic requests. Where circumstances so require, requests may be made verbally. Such requests should be confirmed as soon as possible either in writing or by electronic means.
17. An ideal time frame for the exchange of information can not be fixed because the response time varies depending largely on the nature of the information requested, resource availability, as well as the degree of technological development for the collection and transmission of the information. Therefore, while it is important to respond to a request expeditiously, flexibility is needed depending on the situation.
18. It is important that the replies to requests for information be communicated as quickly as possible and preferably within a mutually agreed time frame.

- *The usefulness of contact points for the exchange of information on export values*

19. Contact points are essential for the fast, simple and effective exchange of information. To assist requesting administration officials in transmitting a request for information, the appropriate office, preferably at the headquarters level, which is responsible for the exchange of valuation information, should be identified in each Customs administration. The WCO will centralise the information on the contact points of Member administrations.

### Further relevant considerations

20. As stated in the introduction in paragraph 2 of this response, the Technical Committee recognised that there are several necessary components of a Customs legal and administrative framework, namely:

- *A supporting legislative framework that facilitates truthful and accurate value declarations*

21. Such a legislative compliance framework should (1) require importers to provide accurate and truthful Customs value declarations; (2) shift the onus for such declarations onto the importer, including importer self assessment obligations; and, (3) require the importer to maintain books, records and supporting documents and allow Customs to access them.

- *A comprehensive sanctions regime to address non-compliance and support voluntary compliance*

22. This should include (1) legislative penalty and enforcement provisions that deal with non-Ecompliance based on the severity of non-compliance; (2) provisions to waive or reduce penalties where the importer brings mistakes or violations to the attention of Customs and voluntarily corrects them; and (3) provisions that discourage undervaluation, such as giving the government the right to purchase goods at the declared value or providing benefits to compliant importers (e.g. reduced inspections).

- *A legal framework that provides the right of appeal to the importer*

23. In line with Article 11 of the Valuation Agreement, an appeals mechanism which provides the right of appeal to the importer, including the final right of appeal to a judicial authority, will help to ensure transparency and fairness regarding the determination of the Customs value and fosters uniform and consistent valuation practices within the Customs administration.

- *Policies and procedures for value and compliance*

24. In line with Article 12 of the Valuation Agreement, this should include the development and publication of valuation policies and procedures and the engagement of the trade for greater transparency and fairness. This will promote greater understanding of the valuation provisions, contribute to improve compliance and encourage truthful and accurate declarations. These policies and procedures should also extend to compliance provisions.

- *Administrative and technical capacity*

25. All Member Customs administrations must make their best efforts to establish appropriate work programmes to develop their administrative and technical capacity with a view to using the effective and efficient procedures and tools that address concerns about the truth and accuracy of the declared value (see response to point 4 of the Terms of Reference).

- *Strategies dealing with particular sectors of trade*

26. Appropriate strategies need to be developed to manage cases which might present difficulties to Customs administrations, such as "informal sector" trade, sole agency transactions and transfer pricing within multinational companies.

- *Partnership with Trade*

27. Mutual confidence between the Trade and Customs should be fostered. Training programmes should be established to ensure that both the Trade and Customs develop a comprehensive understanding of the Valuation Agreement and its applicability to the diversity of trade flows.

**2) Intensify its efforts towards finalising the guidelines on the development and use of a valuation database as a risk assessment tool. The Committee also urges the TCCV to explore co-operation and co-ordination with similar work being carried out by other international organisations.**

28. The Technical Committee continues to pursue completion of the guidelines on the development and use of a valuation database as a risk assessment tool and is currently reviewing a draft document. In preparing the draft, the WCO Secretariat contacted UNCTAD in order to benefit from UNCTAD's experience with regard to ASYCUDA. In addition, numerous Member administrations have submitted information on their experience with valuation databases. A symposium was also held on 24 and 25 April, 2003 at the WCO in which Members provided information on the use of databases as a risk assessment tool.

29. The Technical Committee will submit the final guidelines to the Committee on Customs Valuation when they are completed.

**3) Taking into account relevant work of other bodies, indicate appropriate Customs tools, mechanisms and practices in cases involving fraud and suspected fraud, in Customs valuation; indicate the feasibility of making a distinction between such cases in the context of exchange of information on Customs value.**

## Customs tools, mechanisms and practices in cases involving fraud or suspected fraud

30. Many of the tools discussed previously in this response become very useful in addressing cases involving fraud and suspected fraud. Customs administrations should have in place a number of tools, mechanisms and practices, which have an essential role to play in preventing or minimising the opportunities for, and incidence of, attempted fraud. These should include : (1) an adequate general legal framework, including the provision of general administrative powers, (2) adequate and well functioning Customs procedures and controls, (3) knowledge of international trade and commercial practices, (4) import verification, risk analysis and control capacity, (5) post import controls, (6) post import audit capacity and

powers to conduct such audits, (7) internal information systems to profile and track importers and to keep adequate records, (8) internal information systems which takes into account the relevant links between the import obligations of economic operators and any further obligations of a fiscal nature, (9) means to examine the accounting or financial (including bank) records of an importer, (10) a legally based system for the imposition of sanctions and penalties relating to Customs fraud, (11) a surety system to release goods and protect revenue, (12) automation and selectivity systems to identify cases of suspected fraud, and (13) bilateral and/or multilateral mutual administrative assistance agreements to help gather evidence that establishes fraud.

31. Customs administrations should have full access to, and should have developed operational capacity in the use of, all of the various tools developed by the WCO and its respective committees with respect to valuation fraud and suspected fraud. Many of these tools are currently in development but should all be available by the end of 2003. These tools include:

- A post importation audit course.
- A risk assessment course on valuation fraud.
- A model operation to combat commercial fraud using false or double invoices.
- A publication on the essential elements for the control of fraud under the WTO Valuation Agreement.
- A manual on measures to combat commercial fraud.
- A commercial fraud manual for senior Customs officials.
- A handbook for commercial fraud investigators.

## Distinction between fraud and suspected fraud

32. Each administration may have a definition of fraud in its domestic legislation. One international definition is found in Article 1(c) of the International Convention on Mutual Administrative Assistance for the Prevention, Investigation and Repression of Customs Offences (commonly referred to as the "Nairobi Convention"). In the Nairobi Convention, fraud is defined as "a Customs offence by which a person deceives the Customs and thus evades, wholly or partly, the payment of import or export duties and taxes or the application of prohibitions or restrictions laid down by Customs law or obtains any advantage contrary to Customs law". Further, a "customs offence" is defined in Article 1(b) as any breach, or attempted breach, of Customs law.

33. With regard to the distinction between fraud and suspected fraud, such a distinction depends on the burden of proof needed to establish fraud and the evidence that is available to meet that burden. National laws need to be in place which specify the burden of proof needed to establish valuation fraud. When there is sufficient evidence to meet the burden of proof, the suspicion of fraud is confirmed and fraud is established. Nothing in the Valuation Agreement prevents an administration from enacting tough enforcement provisions in cases of valuation fraud.

**4. Provide data and information on the principles and practices governing co-operation and assistance between Customs administrations, including practical technical assistance and capacity building initiatives that might be appropriate to address concerns regarding the accuracy of the declared value.**

### Principles and practices governing co-operation and assistance between Customs administrations

34. Co-operation and assistance between Customs administrations can take many forms, embracing activities such as seminars and joint training operations to the setting up of specific co-operation mechanisms which are designed to address specific problems of common interest. As regards breaches of Customs legislation and the fight against fraud, the preferred way to provide co-operation and assistance between individual administrations now consists of : (1) Customs co-operation agreements and (2) mutual administrative assistance agreements. These agreements provide a concrete basis for reliable, committed and well structured assistance, which addresses a range of Customs issues including problems relating to the correct determination of the Customs value. These agreements can ensure that the real needs of the parties are addressed, while at the same time ensuring that all necessary safeguards relating to the rights of all parties concerned are taken into account.

35. In the area of Customs valuation, the major attribute of co-operation between Customs administrations is the ability to share lessons learned from practical application of the Valuation Agreement as well as the exchange of best practices for administration of the Agreement.

36. To assist the Technical Committee in responding to the request for the "provision of data and information on the ... practices governing co-operation and assistance between Customs administrations" the WCO Secretariat circulated a questionnaire on current practices with regard to the exchange of value information. Responses were received from more than 50 Members and Observers and indicated that the exchange of value information between Customs administrations is a common practice and appears to be working reasonably well for most respondents.

### Practical technical assistance and capacity building initiatives that might be appropriate to address concerns regarding the accuracy of the declared value

37. The provision of technical assistance and capacity building initiatives will have a substantial effect on the ability to deal with the challenges of implementing valuation rules in a manner that ensures that declarations of the Customs value and

the resulting controls are a sufficient basis for revenue protection. The Technical Committee subscribes fully to the emphasis on capacity building which is a major part of initiatives at international level at the present time. It is important to tailor technical assistance and capacity building efforts to the specific needs of the recipient administration.

### Existing forms of technical assistance

38. The Customs community has already developed focused technical assistance and capacity building initiatives to establish:

- Comprehensive understanding of the Valuation Agreement.
- Adequate and transparent national laws, regulations and policies.
- A modern post importation audit system.
- A modern risk management programme.
- A modern surety system.
- Computer systems.
- Procedures relating to administrative/judicial appeals.
- Procedures to investigate cases of suspected fraud.
- Adequate training of Customs personnel regarding the above functions.
- Procedures to promote voluntary compliance.
- Bilateral or multilateral mutual administrative assistance agreements.

39. In addition, the following resources are available to assist administrations in the interpretation and application of the Valuation Agreement:

- The Valuation Control Handbook.
- The Basic Valuation Training Module.

40. Further, the Technical Committee has established an alternative means of assisting administrations in the exchange of practical experience on implementation and application of the Valuation Agreement. This assistance is the Theme Meetings that are held at alternative meetings of the Technical Committee. Each Theme Meeting is devoted to a topic or series of topics determined by delegates. The themes for the three Technical Committee Theme Meetings to date have covered:

- Application of Risk Assessment in Managing Valuation Risk (May 2000).
- Valuation Management in a Post Import Audit Environment (May 2001).
- Administrative Considerations in the Implementation and Application of the Valuation Agreement (April 2002).

41. These meetings bring together guest speakers from Member administrations as well as from the private sector. They are highly regarded by Members as providing a more hands-on transfer of knowledge and lessons learned through application of the Valuation Agreement.

42. The delivery of national and regional valuation technical assistance programmes by the WCO Secretariat and other donor organisations (including Member administrations) to least developed and developing country Members, as well as the WCO Fellowship Programme, have been effective. Other international organisations, in partnership with the WCO, have been able to provide further impetus in this area, for example, the WCO/USAID (US Agency for International Development) programme. In addition, the Technical Committee noted that Member administrations provide technical assistance both bilaterally and regionally.

43. The Technical Committee emphasised that all capacity building initiatives must be conducted in such a way that the results of a preliminary diagnostic study will form the basis of an individually tailored programme for that Customs administration.

### New capacity building initiatives

44. The WCO Secretariat is currently developing a WCO Customs Capacity Building Framework. This framework is intended to assist its Members to be better equipped to become an effective and efficient modern Customs administration in today's international trading environment and to also mobilise support from the donor community and governments.

45. The Customs Capacity Building Framework will consist of seven separate but inter-related parts, including valuation, designed to:

- Promote the importance of effective Customs administrations to national governments, international organisations and donor agencies.
- Promote a standardised diagnostic and project design and implementation guide for WCO officials, Customs specialists from Member administrations and private sector consultants engaged in capacity building projects in Customs administrations of developing countries.
- Promote the WCO's conventions, instruments and best practice approaches.
- Provide an information and marketing tool for the WCO and senior officials from Member administrations (to better equip senior Customs officials with the information necessary to participate fully in discussions/negotiations with donor agencies and other government officials).
- Assist donor organisations such as the World Bank/IMF to understand and accurately diagnose Customs capacity building needs and design programmes that achieve substantial results.

46. The Technical Committee also noted that the WCO's Compendium of Capacity Building Tools was now available to all Members. The Compendium was developed to identify and describe the wide-range of capacity building products currently available through the WCO Secretariat.

### POTENTIAL ADDITIONAL CAPACITY BUILDING INITIATIVES THAT MIGHT BE APPROPRIATE TO ADDRESS CONCERNS REGARDING THE ACCURACY OF THE DECLARED VALUE

47. A suggested capacity building effort is the "twinning" of administrations to work and mentor on specific cases. Further, engaging importers and Chambers of Commerce in the effort is also critical.

48. Finally, the trade has a major role and responsibility to provide correct, accurate and unambiguous information to both the importing and exporting Customs administrations. In order to enable the trade to better meet its responsibilities, consideration should be given to the following measures:

- Work with appropriate international organisations to identify and investigate measures to establish (or validate) the correctness of commercial invoices presented to Customs and devise a data set of recommended content for such invoices. The purpose would be to receive from importers a more complete description of the imported goods that could lead more directly to the identification (as necessary) of previously verified transactions. Such information could be used in an increased application of Articles 2 and 3 of the Valuation Agreement when Article 1 is deemed inappropriate as well as for test value requests.
- Examine the functional use of the "declaration of value" and make appropriate recommendations regarding possible strengthening of the obligations of importers in providing reliable data.
- Study the role and impact (including economic) of the informal trade sector on Customs valuation in Customs administrations experiencing such trade. Identify the problems encountered by the administrations in this area and develop an international or national strategic solution.
- Develop and deliver education programmes in partnership with the private sector, including local Chambers of Commerce, for local Customs administration's personnel on business practices techniques and trade trends while respecting business and Customs confidentiality standards.

## CONCLUSION

49. The Technical Committee is pleased to have been able to respond to the Terms of Reference from the Committee and stands prepared to carry out further work in this connection at the request of the Committee.

## ANNEX GUIDE TO THE EXCHANGE OF CUSTOMS VALUATION INFORMATION

### PREAMBLE

This Guide is designed to facilitate the exchange of valuation information among Customs administrations. It consists of (1) a checklist regarding valuation verification actions to be taken by the Customs administration of the importing country before requesting information from the Customs administration of the exporting country and (2) a set of recommended procedures, applicable to the Customs administrations of both the importing and exporting countries, for the exchange of valuation information.

In accordance with the terms of the WTO Valuation Agreement, the basis for the valuation of goods for Customs purposes should, to the greatest extent possible, be the transaction value of goods. If (taking into account Decision 6.1 of the Committee on Customs Valuation and Case Study 13.1 of the Technical Committee on Customs Valuation on the Application of Decision 6.1) the Customs administration of the importing country has reasonable grounds to doubt the truth or accuracy of the declared value, the administration may conclude that the Customs value of the imported goods cannot be determined under the provisions of Article 1.

The exchange of valuation information between Customs administrations may be used when there are reasonable grounds to doubt the truth or accuracy of the declared value and fraud is suspected. The information should not be used as a basis for the determination of Customs value.

Exchange of information is only part of the solution to effective valuation control and should form part of a more comprehensive approach. Successful valuation control depends on a long-term strategy of reform and modernisation of Customs administrations. In particular, Customs administrations should rely on a control mechanism, using intelligence-based risk assessment and post-clearance auditing systems, which are fundamental to improving Customs valuation control regimes. Focused capacity building and technical assistance efforts are also called for.

In requesting valuation information, the requesting administration needs to bear in mind the associated resource and cost implications for the requested administration. The proportionality between the fiscal interest involved in a request and the efforts to be made in providing the information should be considered and frivolous requests should be avoided.

Any information provided under the procedures of this Guide should be treated in accordance with the applicable confidentiality provisions.

# CHECKLIST REGARDING VALUATION VERIFICATION ACTIONS TO BE TAKEN BY THE CUSTOMS ADMINISTRATION OF AN IMPORTING COUNTRY BEFORE REQUESTING INFORMATION FROM THE CUSTOMS ADMINISTRATION OF THE EXPORTING COUNTRY

1. Before requesting information from the Customs administration of the exporting country, the requesting administration should ensure that, to the extent possible, all appropriate verification procedures in the importing country have been undertaken. The following listing, although not exhaustive, provides requesting administrations with a checklist that confirms the substance of the request being made.

## CHECKS IN REGARD TO THE VALUE DECLARATION OR CUSTOMS ENTRY

(a) That all appropriate documentation has been made available to the Customs administration and has been inspected. This may include:
   (i) Customs entries;
   (ii) bills of lading;
   (iii) commercial invoices;
   (iv) contracts of sale;
   (v) valuation declarations;
   (vi) payment and bank records;
   (vii) other legal documents, such as licence and warranty agreements;
   (viii) relevant correspondence.

(b) That internal (Customs) research and analysis has been conducted. This may include:

   (i) Records of previous importations by the same importer have been checked:

   - Customs entries;
   - declared values;
   - duties paid;
   - method of valuation;
   - other historical records.

   (ii) Risk assessment and risk analysis procedures have been fully undertaken; this may include the use of appropriate database resources.

## CHECKS RELATING TO THE STATUS OF THE IMPORTER

This may include:

(a) Customs offence records have been examined;
(b) compliance with the tax authorities has been checked;
(c) the WCO CEN database has been checked.

### Contacts with the importer

(a) The importer has been advised in writing of the administration's reasons for doubt.
(b) The importer has been requested to supply additional information and advised of the level of proof to be supplied, including copies of all correspondence between the exporter and the importer.
(c) The importer has been interviewed, as appropriate.

### Checks to be conducted during post importation audit (where appropriate).

(a) Verification of financial records pertaining to the transaction.
(b) Verification of trader's systems.
(c) Examination of commercial records, including contracts.
(d) The importer has been interviewed.

2. If, after following the relevant checklist items, to the extent possible, there are still reasonable grounds to doubt the truth or accuracy of the declared value and fraud is suspected, assistance from the Customs administration of the exporting country may be sought, in accordance with the following recommended procedures.

## RECOMMENDED PROCEDURES FOR THE EXCHANGE OF VALUATION INFORMATION

1. Valuation-related information to be requested from the Customs administration in the country of exportation should be limited to information which is necessary for verifying the truth or accuracy of the Customs value declared by the importer and fraud is suspected. The requested information may include the value of the goods stated in the export declaration/entry presented to the Customs administration of the exporting country.
2. The use of bilateral or multilateral mutual administrative assistance agreements to delineate the appropriate terms for the exchange of valuation information among Customs administrations is recommended.
3. Communication in regard to the exchange of valuation information should take place between appropriate offices designated for this purpose. The designated offices should be notified to the Secretary General of the WCO by the Customs administrations concerned. The Secretary General will make the

information concerning designated offices available to Members on the WCO Members Web site.

4. Requests for information should be made in writing or electronically. The requested Customs administration may require written confirmation of electronic requests. Where the circumstances so require, requests may be made verbally. Such requests shall be confirmed as soon as possible either in writing or, if acceptable to the requested and requesting administrations, by electronic means.

5. Requests for information should specify:

(a) the purpose of the request and the type of information requested;
(b) the measures taken by the requesting Customs administration in accordance with the "Checklist";
(c) the information necessary to identify the goods and their export declaration/entry, which may include:
   (i) details regarding the goods (name, quantity, tariff code number, shipping marks, number of packages, invoice number, etc.);
   (ii) name and address of the importer/buyer/consignee;
   (iii) name and address of the exporter/seller/consignor;
   (iv) means of transportation and transport document number;
   (v) date and place of departure/exportation;
   (vi) date and place of arrival/importation;
(d) any other information deemed useful by the requesting administration.

6. The requested Customs administration should notify the requesting Customs administration of the receipt of the request as soon as administratively possible.

7. The requested information should be provided as quickly as possible, preferably on the basis of a mutually agreed time frame, in accordance with national legal and administrative provisions in the country of exportation and within the limits of the Customs administration's competence and available resources. The response to the request for information should provide the requested information as fully and accurately as possible. The response could also include, as appropriate, the following information:

(a) whether the export consignment has been identified;
(b) whether the export entry documents have been verified;
(c) whether the Customs administration's records have been consulted;
(d) whether relevant information has been sought from other government agencies concerned;
(e) whether the exporter/seller/consignor has been consulted.

8. Where the requested Customs administration cannot provide the information expeditiously, it shall notify the requesting Customs administration of the reasons for its inability or delay in providing the information.

# 6

# WTO HANDBOOK ON VALUATION NOTIFICATION REQUIREMENTS

WORLD TRADE ORGANIZATION
**WT/TC/NOTIF/VAL/1**
9 September 1996
Original: English

## TECHNICAL COOPERATION HANDBOOK ON NOTIFICATION REQUIREMENTS

### Agreement on the Implementation of Article VII of the GATT 1994

1. This section of the Handbook on Notification Requirements covers the notification obligations under the Agreement on the Implementation of Article VII of the GATT 1994. It consists of the following five parts:

Part I: Overview of notification requirements
Part II: Listing of the notification obligations
Part III: Document(s) concerning guidelines and formats
Part IV: "Mock" examples of notifications
Part V: Text of the Agreement

2. For acceding countries, the deadlines for the submission of their notifications will be governed by their respective Protocols of Accession.

> **Note**: The Handbook on Notification Requirements does not constitute a legal interpretation of the notification obligations under the respective Agreement(s). It has been prepared by the Secretariat to assist Members in complying with their notification obligations.

VAL – I

# AGREEMENT ON THE IMPLEMENTATION OF ARTICLE VII OF THE GATT 1994 OVERVIEW OF NOTIFICATION REQUIREMENTS

## (A) NOTIFICATION REQUIREMENTS REGARDING LEGISLATION

### *(I) Members, non-signatories to the Tokyo Round Agreement on Customs Valuation*

#### (i) Notification and circulation of national legislation

The notification of full and complete legislation is covered by a decision taken by the WTO Committee on Customs Valuation at its first meeting on 12 May 1995 where it agreed that Members, non-signatories to the Tokyo Round Agreement, should adopt the procedures established by the Tokyo Round Committee on Customs Valuation on "Notification and Circulation of National Legislation" (G/VAL//5 para.B.2(i) and (ii)):

- Members will submit the complete texts of their national legislation (laws, regulations, etc.) on customs valuation in one of the three official WTO languages as soon as possible to the Secretariat which will circulate them as Committee documents to the other Members in the language submitted. If a general interest is expressed in the Committee that the text of a particular Member be available also in other official WTO languages, this text will be translated and circulated as a Committee document. In those cases where the national legislation is not in an official WTO language, the original texts shall also be submitted to the Secretariat where they will be open for inspection.
- It is understood that the texts of the national legislation of developing country Members availing themselves of the provisions of Article 20, paragraphs 1 and 2 of the Agreement will be supplied to the Committee before the developing country Members begin the application of the provisions of the Agreement.

#### (ii) Changes to legislation, regulations and their administration

The notification requirement in paragraph 2 of Article 22 relates to any changes or amendments introduced to a Member's customs valuation laws and regulations and states that "Each Member shall inform the Committee of any changes in its laws and regulations relevant to this Agreement and in the administration of such laws and regulations."

#### (iii) Checklist of issues

The WTO Committee on Customs Valuation agreed, at its meeting of 12 May 1995, to continue with the system of checklist of issues which was elaborated by the Tokyo Round Committee on Customs Valuation to serve as a basis of an initial examination of national legislations. The WTO Committee also agreed that Members, non-signatories to the Tokyo Round Agreement, should submit responses to the checklist of issues at the time of or as soon as possible after the Member concerned had started applying the Customs Valuation Agreement.

### *(II) Members – Signatories to the Tokyo Round Customs Valuation Agreement*

In the case of a Member, a signatory to the Tokyo Round Customs Valuation Agreement, and whose legislation has been examined, the WTO Committee on Customs Valuation agreed, at its meeting of 12 May 1995, that such a Member should send a communication to the Secretariat indicating that the legislation and responses to the checklist of issues notified under the Tokyo Round Agreement on Customs Valuation remain valid. It was also agreed, at the Committee's meeting on 25 April 1996, that such a Member should submit its response to the checklist of issues only in the case where its response to the checklist of issues notified under the Tokyo Round Customs Valuation Agreement is no longer valid under the WTO Customs Valuation Agreement. Any amendment to a Member's customs valuation laws and regulations should also be notified to the Committee in accordance with paragraph 2 of Article 22.

## (B) NOTIFICATION OF SPECIAL AND DIFFERENTIAL PROVISIONS INVOKED BY DEVELOPING COUNTRY MEMBERS

### *(I) Members, Non-Signatories to the Tokyo Round Agreement on Customs Valuation*

Paragraph 1 of Article 20 enables a developing country Member, not a signatory to the Tokyo Round Customs Valuation Agreement, to delay the application of the WTO Customs Valuation Agreement for a period not exceeding five years from the date of entry into force of the WTO Agreement for it. The provision further states that "Developing country Members who choose to delay application of this Agreement shall notify the Director-General of the WTO accordingly." This notification should preferably be made at the time of acceptance of the WTO Agreement for the developing country Member concerned.

Paragraph 2 of Article 20 enables a developing country Member, not a signatory to the Tokyo Round Agreement, to delay the application of certain provisions of the WTO Customs Valuation Agreement for an additional period of three-years following its application of all other provisions of the Agreement. Developing country Members wishing to invoke this provision are required to "notify the Director-General of the WTO accordingly". This notification should preferably be made at the latest before the developing country Member concerned begins to apply the Customs Valuation Agreement.

Paragraph 1 of Annex III enables a developing country Member having invoked the five-year delay-period provided for under paragraph 1 of Article 20 of the Customs Valuation Agreement to request an extension of such a period. Such a request should be communicated to the Committee before the delay-period provided for under paragraph 1 of Article 20 expires.

Paragraph 2 of Annex III enables developing countries "which currently value goods on the basis of officially established minimum values" to make a reservation to "enable them to retain such values on a limited and transitional basis under such terms and conditions as may be agreed to by the Members". In this regard, The WTO Committee on Customs Valuation agreed at its meeting of 12 May 1995 to adopt the procedures established by the Tokyo Round Committee on Customs Valuation on these reservations.

For reservations made under paragraph 2 of Annex III, the Member having made the reservation shall communicate to the Committee (through the Secretariat) in due course a proposal containing the terms and conditions under which it wants to retain the minimum customs values (or similar schemes). This proposal would be discussed by the Committee with the aim of reaching an agreement on the terms and conditions of such reservation. Agreement should be reached as quickly as possible and at any rate not later than the date at which the Member having availed itself of the possibility of Article 20.1 starts implementing the provisions of the Agreement.

A developing country Member wishing to make such a reservation should do so at the time of its acceptance of the WTO Agreement. It should, then, communicate to the Committee a proposal of the terms and conditions under which it would like to retain this system. This proposal should be submitted sufficiently in advance of the date of application of the Customs Valuation Agreement for the developing country Member concerned so as to provide enough time to the Committee to reach agreement on such terms and conditions.

Paragraph 3 of Annex III enables a developing country Member to reserve the right for its customs administration to refuse the request from an importer to reverse the order of Articles 5 and 6. Notification of this reservation should preferably be made at the time of acceptance of the WTO Agreement or before the developing country Member concerned begins to apply the Customs Valuation Agreement.

Paragraph 4 of Annex III enables a developing country Member to reserve the right for its customs administration to apply paragraph 2 of Article 5 of the Agreement whether or not the importer so requests. Notification of this reservation should preferably be made at the time of acceptance of the WTO Agreement or before the developing country Member concerned begins to apply the Customs Valuation Agreement.

### *(II) Members – Signatories to the Tokyo Round Customs Valuation Agreement*

In the case of Members, signatories to the Tokyo Round Customs Valuation Agreement, notifications of invocations of delayed application and/or reservations made under the Tokyo Round Customs Valuation Agreement continue to remain valid under the WTO Agreement on Customs Valuation in view of the Decision on "Continued Application under the WTO Customs Valuation Agreement on Customs Valuation Agreement of Invocations of Provisions for Developing Countries for Delayed Application and Reservations under the Customs Valuation Agreement 1979" which was taken by the General Council on 31 January 1995 (WT/L/38).

VAL-II

## AGREEMENT ON IMPLEMENTATION OF ARTICLE VII OF THE GATT 1994 (CUSTOMS VALUATION) NOTIFICATION OBLIGATIONS

| Item | Notification requirement | Type of measure | Periodicity | Format | Members notifying | To Whom |
|---|---|---|---|---|---|---|
| 1. | Agreement on Implementation of Article VII of the GATT 1994, Art. 20.1 | Deferred application of CV Agreement | Once upon entry into force of the WTO Agreement for the Member concerned | NO | WTO Members – ad hoc (developing country Members not parties to the Tokyo Round Code) | WTO Director-General |
| 2. | Agreement on Implementation of Article VII of the GATT 1994, Art. 20.2 | Deferred application of CV Agreement, Art. 1.2(b)(iii) and Art. 6 | Once upon entry into force of the WTO Agreement for the Member concerned or before application of the other provisions of the CV Agreement | NO | WTO Members – ad hoc (developing country Members not parties to the Tokyo Round Code) | WTO Director-General |
| 3. | Agreement on Implementation of Article VII of the GATT 1994, Art. 22.2 | Changes in its laws/ regulations and administrative arrangements (Concerning the languages of notification with respect to Article 22: Document to be issued by Committee on Customs Valuation). | Ad hoc | NO | WTO Members – ad hoc | Committee on Customs Valuation |

| Item | Notification requirement | Type of measure | Periodicity | Format | Members notifying | To Whom |
|---|---|---|---|---|---|---|
| 4. | Agreement on Implementation of Article VII of the GATT 1994, Annex III, paragraph 1 | Extension of deferred application of CV Agreement | Before the end of the period referred to in Art. 20.1 of CV Agreement | NO | WTO Members (developing country Members not parties to the Tokyo Round Code who have invoked Art. 20.1 and those who are parties to the Tokyo Round Code and whose five-year delay period has not yet come to a term) | Committee on Customs Valuation |
| 5. | Agreement on Implementation of Article VII of the GATT 1994, Annex III, paragraph 2 | Reservations in respect of minimum values | Once upon entry into force of the WTO Agreement for the Member concerned | NO | WTO Members – ad hoc (developing country Members not parties to the Tokyo Round Code) | Committee on Customs Valuation |
| 6. | Agreement on Implementation of Article VII of the GATT 1994, Annex III, paragraph 3 | Reservations in respect of Art. 4 (sequential order of valuation methods) | Once upon entry into force of the WTO Agreement for the Member concerned | NO | WTO Members – ad hoc (developing country Members) | Committee on Customs Valuation |
| 7. | Agreement on Implementation of Article VII of GATT 1994, Annex III, paragraph 4 | Reservations in respect of Art. 5.2 (price of imported goods after further processing) | Once upon entry into force of the WTO Agreement for the Member concerned | NO | WTO Members – ad hoc (developing country Members) | Committee on Customs Valuation |

| | | | | | | |
|---|---|---|---|---|---|---|
| 8. | Agreement on Implementation of Article VII of GATT 1994, Article 22<br>Decision on notification and circulation of national legislation (taken by the WTO Committee on 12 May 1995) | Notification of national legislation<br>Communication notifying validity of legislation under the Tokyo Round Agreement – if that is the case | Once (as soon as possible following entry into force of the CV Agreement)<br>Once (before application of the CV Agreement)<br>Once (as soon as possible) | NO<br>NO<br>NO | WTO Members (excluding developing country Members who deferred application of the Customs Valuation Agreement as well as parties to the Tokyo Round Code)<br>developing country Members who deferred application of the Customs Valuation Agreement<br>WTO Members who were parties to the Tokyo Round Code | Committee on Customs Valuation<br>Committee on Customs Valuation<br>Committee on Customs Valuation |
| 9. | Agreement on Implementation of Article VII of GATT 1994<br>Decision on checklist of issues (taken by the WTO Committee on 12 May 1995 and 25 April 1996) | Responses to the checklist of issues | Once (at the time or as soon as possible after the Member concerned has started applying the Agreement) | G/VAL/ W/5 (Annex) | WTO Members (excluding developing country Members who deferred application of the Customs Valuation Agreement as well as parties to the Tokyo Round Code) | Committee on Customs Valuation |

| Item | Notification requirement | Type of measure | Periodicity | Format | Members notifying | To Whom |
|---|---|---|---|---|---|---|
| 10. | Agreement on Implementation of Article VII of GATT 1994<br>Decision on the treatment of interest charges in the customs value of imported goods (G/VAL/5 para.A.3 adopted by the WTO Committee on 12 May 1995) | Date from which the Member will apply the Decision | Once | NO | WTO Members – ad hoc | Committee on Customs Valuation |
| 11. | Agreement on Implementation of Article VII of GATT 1994<br>Decision on the valuation of carrier media bearing software for data processing equipment (G/VAL/5 para.A.4 – adopted by the WTO Committee on 12 May 1996) | Date of application of the practice referred to in paragraph 2 of the Decision | Ad hoc | NO | WTO Members – ad hoc | Committee on Customs Valuation |

# 7

# WTO DISPUTE SETTLEMENT CASE SUMMARIES – CUSTOMS VALUATION

## WTO DISPUTE SETTLEMENT CASES CUSTOMS VALUATION[1] 1995–2009

[1] WTO disputes in which the Request for Consultations notified to the WTO Dispute Settlement Body includes a legal claim under GATT Article VII or the WTO Customs Valuation Agreement. As of May 2009.

| Respondent | Complainant | Valuation Claim(s) | Result/Status | Case No. | Initiated |
|---|---|---|---|---|---|
| Thailand | Philippines | **Use of "arbitrarily pre-determine[d] values"** to calculate the amount of the guarantee that importers are required to deposit in order to withdraw imported cigarettes from customs custody, as well as to determine the final valuation amount.<br>**Failure to provide importer with explanation and to publish the bases and methods for determining value** of imported cigarettes.<br>**Disclosure of confidential information**. | Panel established at request of Philippines (November 2008). | DS371 | February 7, 2008 |
| Thailand | European Communities | **Use of "arbitrary values"** for customs valuation of imported alcoholic beverages and other products from the European Communities.<br>The arbitrary value ("assessed value") is claimed to be calculated by deducting (1) a standard margin of profit and general expenses and (2) the customs duty and internal taxes paid from (3) the wholesale price of those goods in the Thai market, regardless of the transaction price provided by the importer. It is further claimed that broad standard margins of profit and general expenses have been fixed by the customs authorities on the basis of sources that have never been explained or disclosed. | Under consultations. | DS370 | January 25, 2008 |

| | | | | | |
|---|---|---|---|---|---|
| Colombia | Panama | **Use of indicative unit prices** or estimated prices for customs valuation of certain goods that originate in and/or are imported from all countries except those with which Colombia has signed free trade agreements. | A panel decision, issued April 27, 2009 (WT/DS366/R), finds in favor of Panama. The Panel holds that Colombia's use of indicative prices for customs valuation purposes are inconsistent "as such" with the obligation under the Agreement to apply, in a sequential manner, the methods of valuation provided in Articles 1, 2, 3, 5 and 6 of the Agreement.<br>The Panel further held that Colombia's use of indicative prices, by mandating the use of the higher of two values or a minimum price as the customs value of subject goods, was inconsistent "as such" with Article 7.2(b) and (f) of the Agreement and that, therefore, such a methodology does not constitute a "reasonable means [of customs valuation] consistent with the principles and general provisions" of the Agreement permissible under Article 7.1. | DS366 | July 12, 2007 |

| Respondent | Complainant | Valuation Claim(s) | Result/Status | Case No. | Initiated |
|---|---|---|---|---|---|
| Colombia | Panama | **Use of indicative unit prices** or estimated prices for customs valuation of certain goods that originate in and/or are imported from Panama and specified other countries or customs territories. | Mutually-agreed solution notified. Colombia repealed the measures at issue, and the parties concluded a "Customs Cooperation and Exchange Agreement." (December 1, 2006) | DS348 | July 20, 2006 |
| Mexico | Guatemala | **Use of officially-established minimum prices** for customs valuation of selected products. | Mutually-agreed solution notified (terms not described). (August 29, 2005) | DS298 | July 22, 2003 |
| Argentina | Brazil | Customs value of imported poultry determined on the basis of **minimum customs value**. | The valuation issue was not further litigated. The dispute presented and decided by a WTO Panel involved claims under the Anti-Dumping Agreement only. (WT/DS241/R (April 22, 2003)) | DS241 | November 7, 2001 |
| Belgium | United States | **Use of reference prices** for customs valuation of imported rice, and lack of transparency in customs valuation determinations. | Mutually-agreed solution notified. Belgium "redetermined the duties in dispute on the basis of new evidence produced" which, the parties agreed, thereby resolved the matter. (January 2, 2002) | DS210 | October 12, 2000 |
| Romania | United States | **Use of officially established minimum prices** for customs valuation of selected products. | Mutually-agreed solution notified (October 2, 2001). Romania agrees: | DS198 | May 20, 2000 |

| | | | | | |
|---|---|---|---|---|---|
| | | | (i) not to use minimum reference prices to determine customs value,<br>(ii) to implement a "special legal act" reiterating the exclusive use of the valuation methodology of WTO Agreement valuation and the Decision Regarding Cases where Customs Administrations Have Reasons to Doubt the Truth and Accuracy of the Declared Value, and<br>(iii) to use its valuation database system only as a tool in the risk assessment process and not for the purpose of the determination of the acceptability of a declared value.<br>The United States undertakes to provide Romania with materials on risk assessment and to identify ways and means to provide technical assistance related to risk assessment. | | |
| Brazil | United States | **Use of minimum prices** for valuation of selected products. | Pending, but no request made for establishment of a panel, and no notification of a mutually-agreed solution received. | DS197 | May 30, 2000 |

| Respondent | Complainant | Valuation Claim(s) | Result/Status | Case No. | Initiated |
|---|---|---|---|---|---|
| Brazil | European Communities | **Use of minimum prices** for valuation of selected products, and the measures imposing the minimum prices are not published. | Pending, but no request made for establishment of a panel, and no notification of a mutually agreed solution received. | DS183 | October 14, 1999 |
| European Communities | India | Infringement of Articles 1 through 7, 11 and Annex I of the WTO Agreement as a result of the restrictions introduced by the European Commission through the Cumulative Recovery System (CRS), for determining certain import duties on rice. | Pending, but no request made for establishment of a panel, and no notification of a mutually agreed solution received. | DS134 | May 27, 1998 |
| Argentina | United States | Complaint against Argentina's application of either a "**minimum specific duty**" or *ad valorem* duty rate, whichever was higher, against imports of certain textiles, apparel and footwear. The "specific minimum duty" is determined by multiplying the *ad valorem* rate – which was the WTO bound rate – against the "average" import price for goods of the same tariff category. Among other claims, the US argued that Argentina's use of the "average import price" instead of actual transaction values in setting its specific duties was contrary to GATT Article VII prohibitions against altering valuation methods "so as to impair the value of any of […] concessions" and the use of "arbitrary or fictitious values." | A WTO panel determined that the minimum specific duties imposed by Argentina were inconsistent with Article II of GATT; no finding was made on the customs valuation claim (WT/DS56/R November 25, 1997). The panel report upheld by the Appellate Body. (WT/DS56/AB/R (March 27, 1998)). | DS56 | October 4, 1996 |

| | | | | | |
|---|---|---|---|---|---|
| European Communities | Uruguay | Same grounds as DS17 | Settled and/or Inactive. | DS25 | December 12, 1995 |
| European Communities | Thailand | EC regulation violates GATT Articles and WTO Valuation Agreement by defining a unique method for calculating the amount of duty owed on imports of rice; *viz.* the "intervention buying-in price" valid for those products on importation, increased by a certain percentage according to the specific kind of rice imported, and minus the import price. | Settled and/or Inactive. | DS17 | October 3, 1995 |
| European Communities | US | EC's **use of a "reference price system"** to determine duties applicable to imports of certain grains. | Settled. No decision taken on the valuation claim. U.S. withdrew request for a panel in view of fact that the EC adopted regulations implementing an agreement between the parties on the matter. | DS13 | November 21, 1996 |
| European Communities | Canada | EC's use of **reference prices** rather than transaction values to determine duties on imports of wheat. | Settled and/or Inactive. A panel was established in 1995, but no further action taken. | DS9 | June 30, 1995 |

# 8

# WTO WEBSITE AND OFFICIAL DOCUMENTS

## WTO WEBSITE NAVIGATION[1]

The WTO website (www.wto.org) is organized around "gateways" leading to various subjects.

Each gateway provides links to all material on its subject. References in this text show you where to find the material. This is in the form of a path through gateways, starting with one of the navigation links in the top right of the homepage or any other page on the site.

For example, to find material on customs valuation, you go through this series of gateways and links: www.wto.org > trade topics > goods > customs valuation.

[1] Adapted from the "On the Web Site" introduction in WTO, *Understanding the WTO*, at 3 (2007).

You can follow this path, either by clicking directly on the links, or via drop-down menus that will appear in most browsers when you place your cursor over the "trade topics" link at the top of any web page on the site.

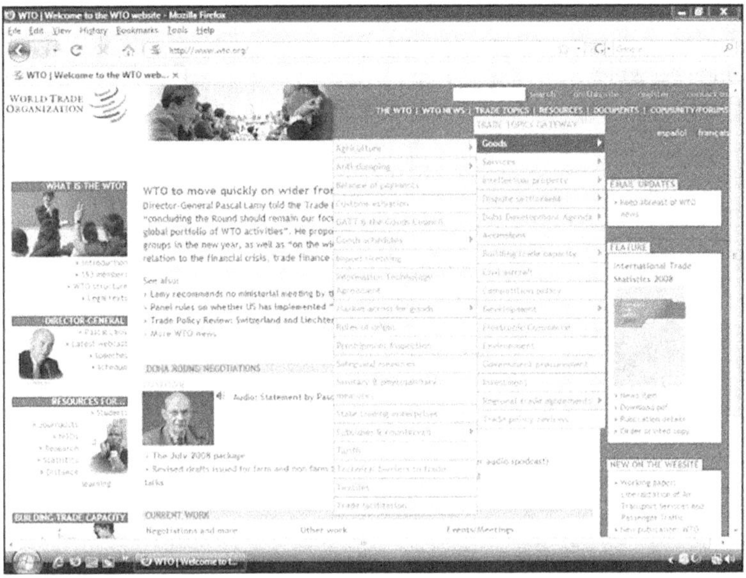


By clicking on the "customs valuation" link, you arrive at the Customs Valuation Gateway.

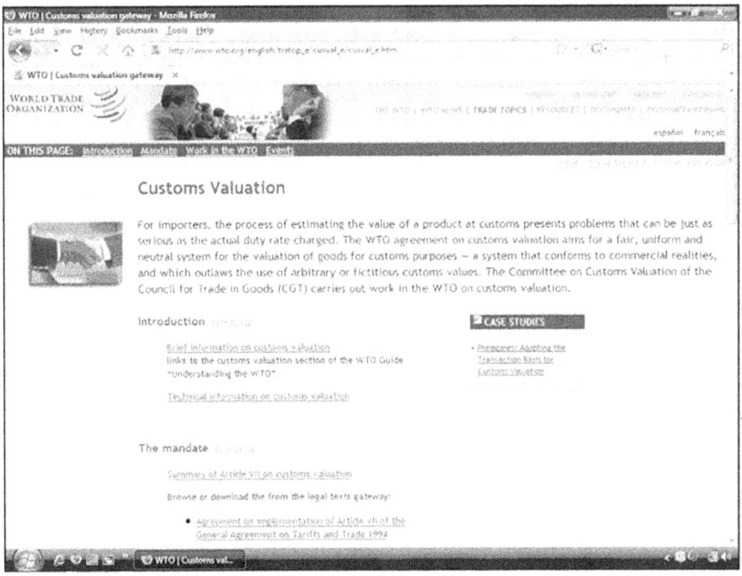

The Customs Valuation Gateway contains pre-configured searches that you can use to find valuation-related documents. These pre-configured searches are links found in the boxes on the Valuation Gateway marked "Search Documents Online." Clicking on the links automatically retrieves lists of relevant documents from Documents Online. You can then select and download the document(s) which interest you.

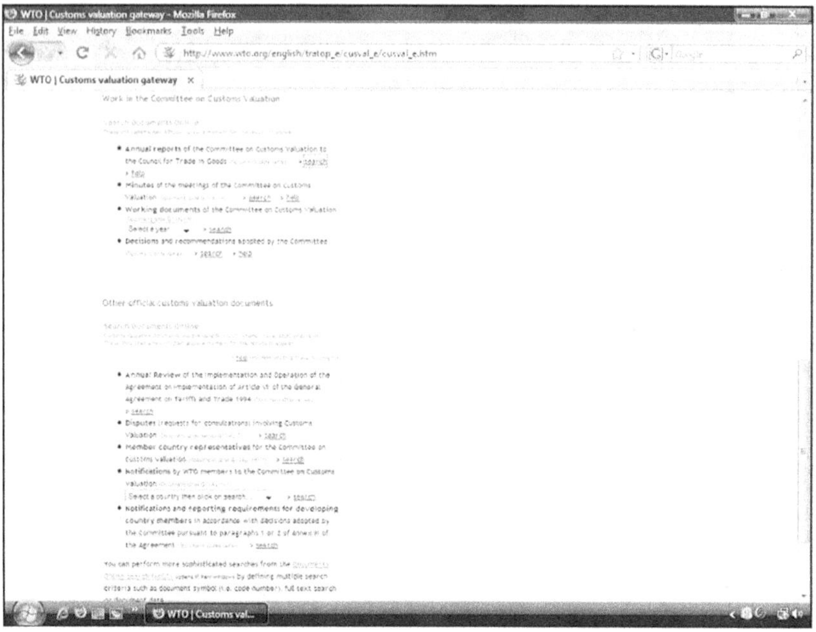


## WTO CUSTOMS VALUATION DOCUMENT SYMBOLS[2]

All official WTO documents are assigned a unique reference symbol.

This symbol is the counterpart of the call number or shelf number that is used commonly in libraries to identify books and other loan items. Based on the WTO Document Nomenclature (or classification scheme), the symbol can be more or less complex according to the series in which the document is being issued, its subject or its type.

Here are some examples of WTO document symbols used for customs valuation documents:

**G/VAL/54/Suppl.1**
**G/VAL/N/1/ROM/2**
**G/VAL/M/30/Add.1**

[2] Adapted from *Frequently Asked Questions about WTO Official Documentation and its Dissemination on the Internet via Documents On Line* (June 2004), which can be found via the "Help" link on the WTO Documents Gateway web page.

Each symbol is made up of a combination of letters, numbers and suffixes. Letters are used to identify collections, series, types and the status of documents while numbers are used to indicate sequential order. Three letter ISO standard codes are also used to identify Members (e.g. POL for Poland, ZWE for Zimbabwe, etc.). All documents are numbered in chronological order of issue and some documents may have more than one symbol.

Example:
**G/VAL/M/30/Add.1**
Explanation:

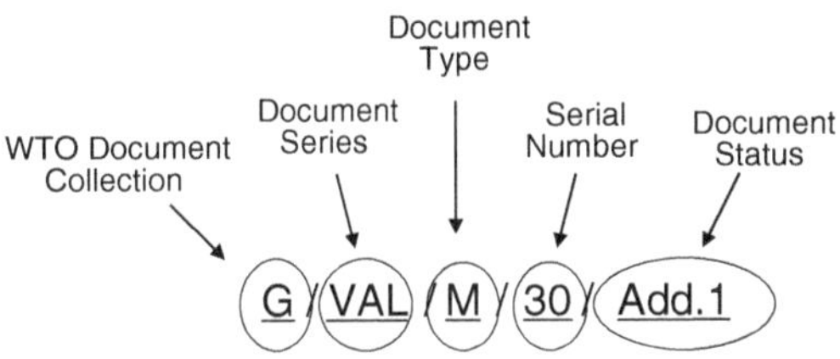


A5
**G = WTO Document Collection**.
WTO documents are currently organized into seven collections, one for each sector of activity and one for administrative matters pertaining to the Secretariat. The letters identifying these collections all appear as the first characters in the document symbol:

| | |
|---|---|
| G | Trade in Goods (1994) |
| IP | Intellectual Property (1995) |
| JOBS | Informal restricted documents (1999) |
| S | Trade in Services (1994) |
| TN | Trade Negotiations (2002) |
| WT | World Trade Overseeing Bodies (1995) |
| OFFICE | Secretariat administrative (1995) |

Most WTO documents relating to customs valuation will be within the Trade in Goods collection ("G").

**VAL = Document Series**
Each document collection is made up of certain classes of documents which share a common framework. The different classes of documents are called series.
The document series referenced in this book include the following:

WTO document series:

| | |
|---|---|
| G/VAL | Customs Valuation |
| TN/TF/... | Trade Facilitation |
| WT/DS/... | Dispute Settlement |

GATT / Uruguay Round document series:

| | |
|---|---|
| MTN.GNG/... | Negotiating Group on Goods (Uruguay Round) |
| NTM/... | Non Tariff Measures and Quantitative Restrictions (GATT) |

Tokyo Round Agreements document series:

VAL/... Customs Valuation

**M = Document Type**
Standard abbreviations are used in the document symbol to denote documents that share certain attributes, for example, a common structure or a specific type of data content:

| | |
|---|---|
| GEN | General |
| INF | Information |
| M | Minutes |
| N | Notification |
| Q | Questions and Replies |
| R | Report in some document series, R is also used to denote Minutes of meetings |
| W | Working Paper |

**30 = Serial Number**
A sequential number. In this example, the serial number signifies that this document is the 30th set of customs valuation meeting minutes that have been issued.
**Add.1 = Document Status**
The following suffixes are used in the symbol to denote the status of a document:

| | |
|---|---|
| Add. | Addendum |
| Corr. | Corrigendum |
| Rev. | Revision |
| Suppl. | Supplement |

# INDEX

For EU product safety concerns, contact us at Calle de José Abascal, 56–1°,
28003 Madrid, Spain or eugpsr@cambridge.org.

www.ingramcontent.com/pod-product-compliance
Lightning Source LLC
LaVergne TN
LVHW011523200926
848484LV00001B/137

* 9 7 8 1 1 0 7 0 0 0 8 4 1 *